ALANIS OBOMSAWIN

ALANIS OBOMSAWIN

The Vision of a Native Filmmaker

RANDOLPH LEWIS

University of Nebraska Press
Lincoln & London

⊗

Library of Congress Cataloging-
in-Publication Data
Lewis, Randolph, 1966–
Alanis Obomsawin : the vision of a
native filmmaker / Randolph Lewis.
p. cm.—(American Indian lives)
Includes bibliographical references and index.
ISBN-13: 978-0-8032-2963-1 (cloth : alk. paper)
ISBN-10: 0-8032-2963-1 (cloth : alk. paper)
ISBN-13: 978-0-8032-8045-8 (pbk. : alk. paper)
ISBN-10: 0-8032-8045-9 (pbk. : alk. paper)
1. Obomsawin, Alanis—Criticism
and interpretation.
I. Title.   II. Series.
PN1998.3.O24 2006
791.4302'33092–dc22
2005026933

Once we abandoned ourselves for television, the box that separates the dreamer from the dreaming. It was as if we were stolen, put into a bag carried on the back of a whiteman who pretends to own the earth and the sky. In the sack were all the people of the world. We fought until there was a hole in the bag.

JOY HARJO, "A Postcolonial Tale"

In the end it is all a question of human relationships.

ROBERT FLAHERTY

CONTENTS

ILLUSTRATIONS

PREFACE

I got off a plane in Montreal a few years ago, hopped into a taxi with too many notebooks and not enough luggage under my arm, and asked the driver to take me to the offices of the National Film Board (NFB). With a pensive frown and an old-world twist of his mustache, he put the car into gear and adjusted the mirror to give me a glance. Not a few seconds passed before he was compelled to ask why I was going *there*? The Film Board? On a sunny day? It didn't seem like very much fun for an American tourist to visit a sprawling bureaucratic maze so far from the cafés and sights of *Vieux-Montréal*.

I laughed and explained that I was meeting a filmmaker named Alanis Obomsawin. Because documentary filmmakers tend to labor under a shroud of semiobscurity, I was prepared to add that she was an important Abenaki filmmaker who had been at the NFB since the 1960s and had made more than twenty films, some of them classics. I assumed I would have to throw out a few film titles like *Kanehsatake* and *Rocks at Whisky Trench* to evoke a glimmer of recognition, at least after an awkward pause in which I would begin to wonder about the relevance of what I do for a living. But I had no such need.

"*Mademoiselle Alanis!*" he exclaimed with delight, his voice thick with a French Canadian accent as he wove through the light mid-morning traffic. "*Oui* . . . I watched one of her documentaries on television last night."

"Really?" It seemed so improbable—Obomsawin's films had almost never appeared on television in the United States.

"Oh yes," he said, grinning in appreciation. "Ah . . . *Mademoiselle Alanis . . . Elle est magnifique!*"

At that moment my suspicion was confirmed: Alanis Obomsawin was not the usual documentary filmmaker. In the few years since this exchange with the taxi driver, it has come to seem emblematic of how she is regarded by those who know her work. Other stories come to mind: The student photographer who saw Obomsawin shooting footage behind the razor wire at Oka and was inspired to become a documentary filmmaker. The soft-spoken Métis woman, hardly out of college, who glowed whenever her cinematic mentor walked into the room. The prominent Native artist who gushed about how Obomsawin had cleared a path for subsequent generations of indigenous mediamakers. The list goes on for quite some time before a dissenting word is heard, and even then it is muted in nature.

Indeed, by virtue of her myriad accomplishments and lofty reputation, Obomsawin could be considered the grande dame of Canadian documentary filmmaking, if not the Canadian film industry in general. Still one of Canada's most distinguished filmmakers at the age of seventy-two, she has made almost two dozen documentaries about the lives and struggles of Native people in North America. All these films have their roots in her childhood experiences on the Abenaki reserve called Odanak and in French Canadian towns such as Three Rivers, where she spent her difficult adolescence. Then as now, creativity was her salvation. After a stint as a fashion model, she found widespread acclaim as a traditional Abenaki singer and storyteller on the folk circuits of the early 1960s. With friends such as the novelist and songwriter Leonard Cohen, she became a fixture in bohemian Montreal until her Native activism prompted the NFB to hire her as a consultant in 1967.

Within a few years of joining the NFB, she seized an opportunity to direct her first film, *Christmas at Moose Factory* (1971), a study of life in a small northern settlement based solely on children's drawings. From that point forward, her career at the NFB blossomed, and she added one of the first Native voices to the complacent Canadian media landscape. Over the following decades, she has produced titles such as *Mother of Many Children* (1977), *Incident at Restigouche* (1984), *Richard Cardinal: Cry from a Diary of a Métis Child* (1986), *No Address* (1988), and *Kanehsatake: 270 Years of Resistance* (1993), one of four films she made about her seventy-eight days behind the barricades in the armed standoff known as the Oka crisis. Although she has not received the audience she deserves in the United States, her films have won numerous awards at film festivals in Canada, Europe, and Asia, and *Kanehsatake* was shown on Japanese television to an estimated audience of eighteen million. All her films have appeared on Canadian television and in hundreds of schools and universities.

Few would dispute her stature as one of the leading figures in indigenous filmmaking in the world—save, perhaps, Merata Mita in New Zealand, no one has been as successful and influential over the past decades. Obomsawin was one of the first Native filmmakers inside the gated community of cinema, however it is defined, as well as the first Native staff filmmaker at the prestigious NFB, perhaps the greatest center of documentary production in the history of the medium. Since breaking the barrier that kept Native people from the power of the mass media, she has become one of the most prolific and interesting documentary filmmakers of any age or background in North America. With a reputation that extends well beyond Canada's borders, she has been the subject of interviews and film retrospectives from Auckland to Barcelona. Somewhat to my surprise, then, is the fact that this book is the first one about this extraordinary filmmaker—even more perplexing that it is the first book about *any* indigenous filmmaker. How can this be true in the era of blossoming indigenous media? In the era of *Smoke Signals* and *Atanarjuat: The Fast Runner*?

I can understand this lacuna in the United States. Despite honored appearances at Sundance and various American universities, Obomsawin remains little known within a self-satisfied nation for whom its northern neighbor seems to exist primarily for stand-up comedy punch lines and rustic beer advertisements. Add to that the enduring metaphysics of Indian hating, and the result is a terminal neglect of all things Native in the United States, unless routed through dusty

Costnerian operas or Michael Eisner's animated minions. If colorful, soft-focus Indians are always welcome in the European American imagination, real Native people, especially those with inconvenient desires and sharp-edged politics like Obomsawin, are not.

The absence of a book on Obomsawin, or any other First Nations' filmmaker, is more difficult to understand in the Canadian context. In recent decades, Canada has gained a reputation—perhaps not fully deserved, as Obomsawin's films make clear—for casting a more sympathetic eye on its indigenous inhabitants. On a personal level, I know that driving north and crossing the border from Washington State into British Columbia has brought this home to me. Moving north through the Northwestern United States, one finds that the Native presence is muted in general and utterly silent on state and federal property along the main highway. Then, when passing into Canada on the way to Vancouver, the first thing one sees is a totem pole and other symbols of a strong First Nations presence, even on federal land. Because such symbolic moments are not uncommon, American tourists such as myself are often surprised by how enlightened Canada appears in regard to its indigenous peoples, almost seeming to have an appreciation for Native cultures that is rarely found in its southern neighbor, not even in havens for Native fetishism like Sedona or Santa Fe. In view of this general state of affairs above the Forty-ninth Parallel as well as Obomsawin's prominence in the Canadian media, it is harder to understand her relative absence in Canadian film studies, unless one remembers the nature of that particular subfield. "Given the fragmented, and underdeveloped, state of Canadian film studies," Zuzana Pick has observed, "the contributions of Native filmmakers have yet to be documented."[1] Yet the literature on Canadian cinema, like that on indigenous media, has been growing the last few years, enough so that it was, I suspect, just a matter of time before a dissertation or book like this one came along. After all, Canadian writers jump-started the serious interest in Obomsawin's work in the 1980s and 1990s, producing a few articles that illuminated the path I would take in this longer study.

Indeed, years before I began to contemplate this book, Canadian scholars working in film studies had made a strong case for Obomsawin's significance. Jerry White praised her as "a true social film-maker" whose work is "among the most vibrant and organically po-litical in Canadian cinema."[2] In another outstanding article, Zuzana Pick claimed that Obomsawin's films "constitute a compelling and politically important contribution to a family album where the sto-ries of First Nations people in Canada are told, where their setbacks and victories are recorded with anger, compassion, and respect." Not-ing the impact of Obomsawin's efforts, Pick added that the filmmaker "has been successful in altering common perceptions. . . . [H]er films have fundamentally altered the way in which the cause of First Peoples has been communicated to non-Native Canadians."[3] In a similar vein, when Obomsawin was awarded the Governor General's Visual and Media Arts Award in 2001, a Native writer celebrated, in a brief but thoughtful article, how much her "sensitive, intimate, and poignant" documentaries have "changed perceptions of Native peoples."[4]

Observers in the United States have not been entirely blind to Obomsawin's accomplishment. One of the few exceptions has been Bird Runningwater, who, as the programmer for the Native Amer-ican Initiatives at the Sundance Film Institute, has gone on record about the importance of her cinematic project. "If you look at the history of the Native image in film, the vast majority of it has been created without the consent and most often without the control of the Native person whose image is being taken and utilized in media," Runningwater has said. "I really believe Alanis is using a medium to provide a voice and a story for a lot of people who historically have not had that opportunity."[5]

Despite these moments of acclaim, Obomsawin has not yet re-ceived the attention that she deserves in the United States or even in Canada, and this may be a symptom of her commitment to docu-mentary film, not exactly the most glamorous of métiers. The success of *Smoke Signals*, *Atanarjuat*, and a handful of other fiction films notwithstanding, nonfiction has been the medium of choice for Na-tive filmmakers in general and Native women filmmakers in particu-lar. Since the late 1960s Native filmmakers have produced dozens of documentaries, creating a significant body of nonfiction work that has never received the critical attention paid to Native literature, basketry, painting, and sculpture—all of which might seem in synch with the cultural traditionalism to which non-Native scholars have often been attracted, even to the detriment of understanding new facets of indigenous artistry and culture. I hope that this book will be useful to scholars and Native communities because it offers the first in-depth look at a key figure in the development of indigenous media across the United States and Canada. I want to show that Native cinema is more than *Smoke Signals*—that it possesses an unacknowledged history going back to the 1960s, one with Alanis Obomsawin at its center. Yet, even within the small world of "indigenous mediamakers," Native women have been slighted. For instance, the respected Hopi director Victor Masayesva bills himself as the first Native filmmaker, despite the fact that he was many years behind Obomsawin.

At the most personal level, I hope that my research will give Obomsawin the credit that is her due. In an old-fashioned sense, then, this book is an exercise in feminist canon busting that should prompt readers to wonder why this woman has been ignored while new books on Ford and Hitchcock crowd onto library shelves with every passing week. I want to celebrate the new points of view that her work brings to the cinema, and I hope to capture in prose something of Obomsawin's unique cinematic vision. Studies like this one can, I think, reveal how Native cinema has become as vital and interesting as traditional art forms that have received far more attention and resources. I don't mean to have the last word. There is always more to be said about an artist of Obomsawin's caliber, and I hope that this book will continue the conversation about her work until the next scholar takes an interest. The same is true for other indigenous mediamakers across North America: so many of them deserve the careful appreciation that has been afforded visual artists with European roots.

Let me say a few words about the shape of the book so that the reader knows what to expect. Although I have used the wildly disparate writings of Patricia Zimmermann, John Grierson, Richard White, Eva Garroutte, Mario Vargas Llosa, and Leonard Cohen to make sense of one of the great unheralded careers in nonfiction cinema, the book follows a rather traditional chronological sequence. Here in the preface, I describe the goals of the book and the motivations behind it. I also introduce the notion of *Other Visions*, which alludes, not just to *other* accounts of the past, but also to the pernicious process of cultural "Othering" that Obomsawin has fought against. Much of this is yet to come.

Then, in chapter 1, "Abenaki Beginnings," I examine the formative influences that brought Obomsawin to the screen, providing the first careful look at her difficult experiences on the Abenaki reserve at Odanak, before she found success as a model, singer, and traditional storyteller in the early 1960s. I make creative use of her friend Leonard Cohen's fiction in order to glimpse something of her adolescence.

Chapter 2, "Early Films," explores *Amisk* (1977), *Mother of Many Children* (1977), and Obomsawin's other half-forgotten films from the 1970s and 1980s, using them to explore the emerging thematic preoccupations of the filmmaker: the vulnerability of Native children; the importance of pan-tribal solidarity; and the continuing toll of Native-white conflict on First Nations. In addition, I attempt to demonstrate that her filmmaking practice has deep roots in the Abenaki oral tradition in which Obomsawin was raised.

Chapter 3, "A Gendered Gaze?" considers what Obomsawin was bringing to the screen in addition to a Native storytelling aesthetic during her first two decades of filmmaking. So much attention has focused on her groundbreaking role as a Native filmmaker that it is tempting to overlook the specific nature of her accomplishment, as if being "first" and "most prolific" were prizes enough. This chapter attempts to tease out the nuances of her vision in one crucial area: the gendered position of her filmmaking and how it relates to aboriginal women filmmakers, not just in North America, but also in other settler-states such as Australia and New Zealand.

Chapter 4, "Documentary on the Middle Ground," gives an account of Obomsawin's seventy-eight days behind the razor wire at Oka, one of the great unacknowledged acts of courage in the documentary tradition. After showing the importance of Native filmmakers as witnesses in moments of political crisis, I examine the four films about the Oka crisis that occupied Obomsawin's creative energies in the

1990s, using them to make some larger points about her media practice. Transposing ideas that have been influential in history and anthropology, I show how Obomsawin has functioned as a cultural broker between Native and white on the "middle ground" of the Canadian mass media and discuss the reasons why documentary might provide an ideal meeting place between contemporary cultures—something I explore at greater length in the following chapter.

Chapter 5, "Why Documentary?" asks a deceptively simple question. In these pages, I hope to show why Obomsawin has relied exclusively on nonfiction to share what she calls the *voice of the people* and explore why Native filmmakers in general have turned to documentary. Moving beyond issues related to indigenous media, I then engage Mario Vargas Llosa's recent "Why Literature?" to show how common assumptions about literature's role in transmitting ennobling human values might also apply to documentary cinema as practiced by filmmakers such as Obomsawin.

Chapter 6, "Cinema of Sovereignty," provides the first examination of Obomsawin's most recent work, exploring two documentaries, *Is the Crown at War with Us?* (2002) and *Our Nationhood* (2003), that deal with bitter disputes over the natural resources of First Nations. In this final chapter I set out the notion of a *cinema of sovereignty* to describe the representational strategies that Obomsawin has developed for Native people.

In the conclusion I provide some thoughts on the state of indigenous media in 2006, before considering Obomsawin's future projects (such as a film on Abenaki history), her place in the current Abenaki renaissance, her influence on various Native filmmakers who have benefited from her pathbreaking career, and the wider significance of projects such as hers in the current media environment. The book ends with a bibliography, two filmographies, and information about how to obtain the films under discussion.

More than hubris would suggest that the timing is right for this project: indigenous media is a topic of increasing interest, not just to First Nations hoping to convey their concerns to the world, but also to the film studies, American studies, Native American studies, and visual anthropology communities. Several books have appeared in the past five years on Native American film specifically, but they tend to focus on fiction film rather than the much larger arena of Native American documentary expression—and certainly none have highlighted questions of gender, documentary per se, and the larger mediascape as I intend to do. One very partial exception was Beverley Singer's *Wiping the War Paint off the Lens*. For those who do not know it, let me say that Singer's brief book, along with Jacquelyn Kilpatrick's *Celluloid Indians*, is a good starting place for anyone interested in Native film.

I would like to think that I am well positioned to pick up where Singer and Kilpatrick left off because, in addition to having written about Native artists such as Leon Polk Smith, I see my research on indigenous media as a natural extension of my *Emile de Antonio*. An outsider artist working to create an alternative, cinematic history of the United States, Emile de Antonio (1919–89) was often on a track parallel to those of Obomsawin and other Native filmmakers struggling to bring tribal points of view to the larger public. Both de Antonio and Obomsawin's films represent acts of resistance against the homogenizing effects of the global media, which have little left very little space for unauthorized points of view. Both provided independent thinking in their cinema—an increasingly rare quality as *independent film* has become a sloppy moniker that covers some art and a lot of junk. Nowadays, low-grade emulations of Hollywood product have appropriated the term as an honorific for no reason other than taking cash from somewhat smaller corporate entities or in somewhat smaller quantities. Sadly, true independent visions have become a rare commodity even in nonfiction cinema, where the "documentary conscience" once thrived in opposition to the abuses of the state and private enterprise. Perhaps the unprecedented success of Michael Moore's *Fahrenheit 9/11* (2004) will help reinvigorate this part of the documentary tradition, although I fear that that film will remain the exception that proves the rule (of Fox, ABC, CNBC, etc.)—after all, mounting pressure has been brought to bear against the public articulation of dissent in the past two decades. The media theorist Patricia Zimmerman cites "arts defunding, public television retrenchments, attacks against cultural difference, and conservative assaults against interventionist public discourses" as the factors that have gnawed away at the public space where documentary thrives.[6] Thankfully, working well beneath the radar of those who had never paid much attention to documentary before the media frenzy attached to *Fahrenheit 9/11*, Native filmmakers like Obomsawin have been giving life to this endangered species called *independent documentary*, restoring public space for something more than sound bites and slogans, and offering thoughtful counterpoints to the meretricious wares of the global media. Unlike the craven producers who abuse the term in order to sell their film into an attractive niche market or even the programmers at the not so Independent Film Channel, Obomsawin is a real independent in spirit and practice, an ironic fact given her position inside a government institution. Somehow, from within the bureaucratic confines of the NFB (and in many ways *because* of her place there), Obomsawin has shot back at the homogenizing narratives of nation and carved oppositional practices into Western mediascapes. Somehow she has found independence where others might have found dependence and despair.

Geoff Pevere has claimed that writing about Canadian cinema involves "stepping into the very heart of the country's conflicted soul."[7] I have not dared to probe into the essence of nationhood above the Forty-ninth Parallel, preferring to leave such inquiries to writers with the depth of knowledge that comes only from long experience. As a U.S. citizen who has never lived north of Brooklyn (and even then as a baby no less!), I can look into such matters only as a spectator and, perhaps, only when accompanied by the likes of Obomsawin, a thoughtful person who has stared into the grim paradoxes of the Canadian soul, sometimes against her will, for seventy-something years. I see as much as she is willing to share in conversations and onscreen, although I try to look around the edges as much as possible, hoping to glimpse the fundamental processes at work.

Up front, I promised modest aspirations for this book. Now I have to backtrack somewhat to give this project one more frame, one that will, I hope, not seem absurdly gilded and ostentatious: I want the book to make a contribution to the emerging scholarship

FIGURE 1. Obomsawin in 1971. Courtesy of the filmmaker.

on documentary expression now growing within American studies, media studies, and elsewhere. In exploring the politics and poetics of Obomsawin's documentary practice, I touch on larger questions about media and society such as: What can indigenous documentarians teach us about carving out a democratic space for difference, for dissent, in the postmodern mediascape? And what can we learn about how to tell complex, critical nonfiction stories, about representing other North American "realities" that enable us to create a democracy based on justice, equality, and inclusivity?

Answering these kinds of questions is more than intellectual curiosity. Despite the best efforts of Obomsawin and others like her and even the anomalous success of Michael Moore, we have lost sight of what it means to have a vibrant and independent documentary culture in the United States and, to some extent, in Canada as well, even though the wrong kind of documentary is everywhere we look today. With the ascendancy of television "reality programming" such as *Joe Millionaire*, *Survivor*, or *Big Brother*, we are living through an era that thrusts the pseudoreal in our face at every turn, and in the years to come documentary expression will become even more important in shaping our vision of North American "reality" as well as other realities—personal, local, tribal, national. And understanding this documentary expression, critiquing it, re-creating it, as scholars, students, and citizens, will be essential to making our way through the wilderness of dissent. In the spirit of great Abenaki outdoorsmen like her father, Alanis Obomsawin provides an ideal guide for examining this bitterly contested ground.

Skeptical observers might ask what importance a single filmmaker could have to the grim panoply of big media corporatism and official distortion. I would like to think that Obomsawin embodies alternative media practices that could have a broader significance for sustaining democratic values across cultural boundaries. I have high hopes for what I call a *cinema of sovereignty*, a forum where cross-cultural communication can occur without one of the parties being ignored, silenced, distorted, *Othered*. As the media theorist John Fiske has suggested, cross-cultural communication is becoming ever more important for a peaceful planet, and we must ensure that the less powerful culture in the equation is able to represent itself, rather than being the mere object of representation.[8] Whenever possible, we must learn to listen to difference without exoticization, to witness it without objectification. Obomsawin has done this exceedingly well.

This ability to listen in peace, to contemplate what is being said, is more than a luxury in the new century. More than most of us realize, the electronic media have become the essential mechanism for a global process of measuring our common ground with people far from home, literally and metaphorically, and making judgments about who *they* are to *us*, however those fields might be defined. Indigenous filmmakers working to reinscribe the image of the Native in the Western imagination (as well as in various tribal imaginations) are just one example of this process. So often stereotyped and exploited by mainstream media, Native peoples have shown how cultural and political self-determination is intertwined with representational self-determination—*representational sovereignty*, as I call it in the final chapter. The Hopi documentarian Victor Masayesva has said that indigenous media offer a journey for "tribal people to consider and reflect on the White man's most seductive and reductive invention for conception and representation which we have today: film and television."[9] I would suggest that it goes well beyond what Masayesva describes, that it may offer a path toward a degree of cultural and political autonomy that few indigenous people have known in the past century.

Several decades ago, Tillie Olson opened her classic *Silences* with a dedication to "our silenced people, century after century their beings consumed in the hard, everyday essential work of maintaining human life. Their art, which still they made—as their other contributions—anonymous, refused respect, recognition; lost."[10] I loathe the idea of creative lives lost or neglected, and, in the case of someone as gifted as Obomsawin, the shame is twofold: we have as much to gain as she from the act of recognition. Without question, Obomsawin is one of the relatively few figures that can be discerned in the long fog of cultural invisibility that has engulfed First Nations people and their artistry, like indigenous people almost everywhere. She is a portal to something more than mere stereotype, as I hope this book will demonstrate.

I turn first to the acknowledgments when I pick up a new academic book—it is often the one place where a personal voice intrudes on the official tone of the overeducated, the tone that conveys a great distance covered, reams of pages scanned, infinite angles pondered, but not, usually, a beating pulse. So it is with some relief that I spill out some acknowledgments of my own, both of the conventional and of the unconventional sort.

In the first category go the notes of appreciation. To scholars across the United States who have informed and encouraged my thinking through their words or writing—Bill Stott, Bill Nichols, Doug Kellner, Ari Kelman, Norman Stolzoff, Jason Jackson, Patricia Zimmermann, Thomas Waugh, Alice Nash, and many more. To my colleagues in the Honors College of the University of Oklahoma as well as the Film and Video Studies Program, where the ebullient Andy Horton and other faculty members have offered continuing support of my work. To the scholars, staff, and friends of the School of American Research, most especially Kehaulani Kauanui, Gerald Vizenor, James Brooks, Cam Cox, Nancy Owen Lewis, James Faris, Lawrence Cohen, Jessica Cattelino, and others who challenged my thinking on this topic during my nine months as a research associate there. To Veronique de Silva and the other wonderful people at the National Film Board in Montreal. To Jerry White and Jacquelyn Kilpatrick, who reviewed the manuscript for the University of Nebraska Press and helped me strengthen my arguments. And, finally, to the loves of my life, Circe Sturm and our daughter, young Miranda Sophia, who give me reasons to hope for a brighter future. What little I know about Native American studies comes from talking with Circe and people to whom she has introduced me over the years, whether in Tahlequah, Oklahoma, Davis, California, or Santa Fe, New Mexico. Yet it goes without saying that none of this project's foibles were due to her—I am quite able to cook up such things on my own.

In the second category go the less obvious sort of acknowledgments, the ones that reveal where I'm coming from and how I got there, where I fulfill the inevitable curiosity of the reader, where Abenaki speakers may wonder: *Awani gi ya? Who are you? Is he Indian?* The short answer is no. I am pure interloper on Native ground— there's no getting around that, even if the long answer has its hems and haws. Basically, I share with Carol Kalafatic the feeling that "my family hasn't told all the stories that would make my autobiography possible" and have no clue what has been half erased from our genealogical charts in fits of Southern shame (although I have some suspicions).[11] I can only go off lived experience and family narratives to stake this claim: I am most likely the result of rank strangers on the continent, some now happily ensconced in various postcolonial contexts between New Jersey, Texas, and California, others still blundering in circles as if the proverbial boat were rocking over their shoulder (put me in the latter camp out of solidarity with the unconsciously deracinated). For my father's parents, the longshoreman and the maid who immigrated illegally from Liverpool and Glasgow in the 1930s, the boat was quite literal. For my mother's parents, the illiterate logger and the kindly mother of twelve living deep behind the pine curtain of East Texas, the boat had long since receded from view—nine generations of Southern living tends to do that to white folks, who are generally eager to forget their relatively recent arrival and sometimes invisible dispossession of Native people in the name of something (often quite risible) called *civilization*.

Fortunately, blood and history do not an ideology make, at least not in every solitary case. As much as a maneuver of disavowal is possible, I would like to imagine that *I'm not from here*, save birth and culture and public school indoctrination and what now passes for community bonds under the present military-industrial regime. In this regard I am eager to fabricate a space for *post-American* and *post-Canadian* musings, in the sense that these terms have stood for exclusivist projects of subjugation and manipulation. I hope to explore this emerging space for cultural critique through the lens of Obomsawin, who has been expanding it into the cinema for thirty years, and to do so without glossing over the white/male privilege that follows me into cafés, parking lots, classrooms. I cop to that.

So why are we here? Well, in lieu of a clichéd statement of positionality, whose tropes I have already exploited to decent effect, I can at least explain something about the motivation behind this project (which, in some cases, is more important than roots). In writing as an interloper on Native ground, the best compensation I can offer is a hopeful spirit, a blend of critique and cautious optimism, that infuses the project at hand. If it is not presumptuous, I want to share Marianette Jaimes-Guerrero's belief that "a more inclusive Indigenous movement is opening to the human spirit," especially in the classrooms of our high schools, colleges, and universities.[12] If this book helps educators bring Obomsawin's decolonizing perspective into the classroom as a companion to her films and helps students appreciate what she is doing, I will have accomplished something. I claim no reward in terms of bank account for this book, perhaps no great sacrifice in the semisolvent world of academic publishing, but something nonetheless. For this reason, I have assigned all author royalties to the small Film and Video Studies Library at the University of Oklahoma, where the large and diverse Native student population has produced too few filmmakers thus far. I have asked that the money be used to purchase the work of Native filmmakers such as Obomsawin, which can inspire the next generation of indigenous artists and activists.

For me the real compensation is personal—getting to know Alanis, getting to learn new cinema tricks, hanging out with the sleek *cinemarobothèque* at the Montreal NFB, home to a well-oiled research assistant who never complains about fetching another film for professorial amusement. Writing this book has been pleasure enough. It has given me time to explore work I consider fascinating and underappreciated and to do so with the modest desire of sharing it with new audiences, fully aware that, after pointing folks in the right direction, I can recede from view and let Obomsawin's *other* visions startle and illuminate in ways to which my prose can only allude.

1

ABENAKI BEGINNINGS

> Canada became a royal colony of France in 1663. Here
> come the troops led by le marquis de Tracy, lieutenant-
> general of the armies of the king, here they come march-
> ing through the snow, twelve hundred tall men, the fa-
> mous *regiment de Carignan*. The news travels down the
> icy banks of the Mohawk: the King of France has touched
> the map with his white finger.
>
> LEONARD COHEN, *Beautiful Losers*

> The last thing they wanted was an Indian to document
> anything.
>
> ALANIS OBOMSAWIN

Early Years

Alanis Obomsawin does not know the exact place of her birth, only
that she was born somewhere near Lebanon, New Hampshire, on
August 31, 1932, and that, when she was an infant, she slipped into
a deep coma that neither her parents nor the local doctor could
explain. As the illness drained the life out of her, the doctor threw up
his hands in frustration and warned the family not to touch the sick
child. Death would not have been a surprising outcome to parents
who had lost two boys and two girls, none of whom had survived
their first year.[1]

Yet the story is far from over: in a scene that seems ripped from the pages of mythology, an old Abenaki woman flings open the door and dashes inside, grabbing the ailing child in a thick woolen blanket, and then evaporating into the night. Frightened and worried, the parents huddle together and discuss what is happening, deciding at last that they must respect the mysterious actions of a tribal elder, who, as they later learn, has taken their daughter north to a small shack on the Abenaki reserve not far from Montreal. "She kept me for six months," Obomsawin marvels. "Nobody knows what she did to me, but I survived."[2] It would not be the last time Obomsawin defied expectations.

Reunited with her parents for at least part of her tender years, Obomsawin grew up an only child on the tribal reserve at Odanak, speaking Western Abenaki as her first language.[3] A small tribe with only a handful of fluent speakers today, the Abenakis have never been the object of the obsessive attention that social scientists have directed toward certain tribes located on the plains or in the desert Southwest. Even within New England, their powerful Iroquois neighbors tended to overshadow the Abenaki, leaving these so-called people of the sunrise to live without much fanfare on lands in present-day Vermont and New Hampshire as well as north across the Canadian border toward Montreal. For centuries they had resided in the great interior of New England, fishing and hunting in the Champlain Valley, the Green Mountains, the Connecticut River valley, the White Mountains, and the Merrimack River valley. Much of their lands were thickly treed with white pine, red spruce, northern hardwoods, and hemlock, and wild animals were abundant—moose, deer, wolves, black bear, muskrat, mink, raccoon, foxes, and skunk. Hunting these animals would remain central to their lives well into the twentieth century, owing in no small measure to the cold climate. Most of their land was covered with snow for four or five months each year, leaving a short growing season of 140 days, which did not encourage the sort of farming practiced by their tribal neighbors to the south.[4] The traditional homeland would remain important to Obomsawin throughout her life, even as it seemed to disappear under her feet: "Long ago when our people, the Woban-aki, lived on our land in what is now called Vermont, a woman was washing clothes in the river. There came a beaver, who sat on a rock. He began to sing, 'I see you Woban-aki losing your land . . .' The woman ran to the village and told the others. They did not believe her. But it really happened. When the English came, they took *all* of our land and called it New England."[5]

For Abenakis, these moments of loss would continue long after the initial contact with French and English colonists. As a small child in the 1930s, Obomsawin grew up during a period in which the traditional Abenaki ways of life were being transformed, challenged, and regulated. Even though she spoke the language, lived in an Abenaki village and, later on, an official reserve, and bore a distinguished Abenaki name, she lacked federal recognition. Like many Abenaki people, she fell between the cracks in the Canadian bureaucracy for Indian affairs, which disenfranchised many tribal citizens who went south into the United States for a period of time without making extraordinary efforts to preserve their "band status" north of the border. It was one of many arbitrary rulings about who could claim official Abenaki status in the eyes of the Canadian government, whose policies also included such strange notions as an insistence on patrilineal descent—for much of the twentieth century, only those whose fathers had Abenaki blood were eligible for band status.[6] If such official discourses of indigeneity were painful reminders of colonial power in their midst, Abenaki families like the Obomsawins went ahead with their lives, often in very traditional Abenaki terms, in full awareness of who they were regardless of government edicts. "I never had any rights," Obomsawin complained later. "I never knew that story—registered or not registered—all I knew was that I was Indian, and that was that."[7]

Like many Abenaki men before him, Obomsawin's father was a hunting and fishing guide, in his case laboring for wealthy whites who owned a private lake and hunting lodge in the province of Quebec. Seventy investors from the United States and Canada purchased the lake and brought in men like her father to guide, cook, and maintain the elaborate lodge, which was like "a small hotel with big fireplaces," as she recalled.[8] When her father was working, the family did not

FIGURE 2. Obomsawin at a celebration in Odanak in 1969.
Courtesy of the filmmaker.

have much opportunity to see him, getting to spend only a few days visiting with him at the lake before having to return to the reserve. This was not an unusual situation for an Abenaki family at this time. During the 1920s and 1930s, men in the tribe turned their backwoods prowess into modest commercial enterprises, earning a reputation as the best outdoor guides that wealthy white sportsmen could hire. Yet preserving their traditional ways was a challenge in this tumultuous period in the life of the tribe. In the years between the world wars, even more than in previous decades, cultural continuity mixed with sudden transformation for the Abenakis. "If the tarpaper shack and Winchester rifle replaced the wigwam and bow, the time and place of deer camp and the respect for the game remained unchanged," the Abenaki scholar Frederick Matthew Wiseman has written, and "stories from the Indian past and lessons about how to navigate on the river and lake were repeated over flickering campfires."[9] Obomsawin seems to support this observation: even today, she can recall the sights, sounds, and smells of traditional Abenaki life from her childhood in the 1930s. "In those days everybody made baskets and canoes," she recalls. "They worked with the wood from many trees—especially the ash, spruce, birch, and pine—and sweet grass was an important part of everyone's daily life." As she remembers, every house on the reserve had the fragrance of sweetgrass and ash splints curling and drying from the ceiling.[10]

Despite such picturesque scenes, the years between the wars were a dangerous time for Abenakis in New Hampshire and Vermont, far more so than for their brethren across the border in Canada. Although affluent American whites had long enjoyed the rich hunting on Abenaki lands and the healing properties of their medicine springs, they were now looking at their guides and healers through a disturbing new lens of white ethnonationalism and eugenics.[11] Many had decided that northern New England offered the last pure spot of genuine Americana, even if this belief conflicted with the presence of thousands of dark-skinned residents in the forests and valleys of New Hampshire and Vermont. The latter state, in particular, became the "great white hope" of New England, a mythical preserve of white Yankee virtue, which encouraged some observers to wish away the

Native presence. For example, the popular writer Dorothy Canfield Fisher depicted Vermont as a "no-man's land without permanent Indian residents."[12]

Even worse than this burgeoning racist discourse were new government policies that affected the Abenaki. In an atmosphere in which the Ku Klux Klan was active across New England, the state of Vermont began its "Eugenics Survey" under the guidance of Professor Henry Perkins of the University of Vermont. State officials screened rural families for "bad" genetic traits, with the result that many Abenaki children were taken from their parents. As late as 2001, Wiseman could note that the theft of children and "the hatred emanating from the burning cross and Ku Klux Klan rallies" were still alive in the memories of Abenaki elders.[13]

Despite this general atmosphere of racism, some whites continued the old relationships with the Native inhabitants of New England. Obomsawin recalls that her parents could make traditional medicine to cure sicknesses and that this knowledge was prized in the informal economy extending well beyond the Abenaki community. "It was against the law," she recalls, "so it was an underground kind of thing." In some ways, working in traditional healing was akin to running a speakeasy, especially after her mother became known for helping people pass kidney stones. Strange white customers would show up at the door, frightened about a surgical procedure that Western medicine demanded, and nervously ask her mother if "you savages have medicine?" Her mother would give them a bottle of something, tell them to come back in several days, and often "their last trip would be with the bag of stones," the filmmaker remembers with a chuckle. Her mother stored them in old tomato soup cans, which Obomsawin played with as a young girl.[14]

If the Abenaki people were useful sources of medicinal information for local whites, this did little to protect them from the ill will of state and federal legislators across New England. The nadir for the tribe, at least in the modern period, came in 1931, when "An Act for Human Betterment by Voluntary Sterilization" was passed in Congress,[15] resulting in the not-so-voluntary sterilization of over two hundred Abenaki women, a significant portion of the small tribe. In a climate of terror and shame, some Abenaki families chose to forsake their heritage and pass into the most plausible white ethnic group they could manage. "The safest ethnic refuge during the 1930s," Wiseman has written, "was the French Canadian community, since they shared our religion, economic status, and other social and geographical traits."[16] Rather than attempting to pass into some form of whiteness (which their appearance probably made impossible), Obomsawin's mother and father decided to pack up and leave Lebanon, New Hampshire, for Odanak, the Abenaki reserve in Canada, following a pattern of border-crossing that had long characterized Abenaki life. Obomsawin was just six months old, having spent most of that time in the hands of the Abenaki elder who saved her life, and now her family was joining her north of the Forty-ninth Parallel.

Founded on the St. Francois River not far from Sorel, Quebec, in the early eighteenth century, Odanak quickly became the largest Abenaki settlement in what was then New France, and by the 1930s it was a well-established tribal reserve. Although Obomsawin's parents were reunited with their infant daughter in Odanak, the family did not live under one roof: Obomsawin lived with her mother's sister Jesse Benedict and her husband, Levi, who had six other children with whom she spent long pleasant hours playing outside, even in the dead of winter. She has never said why she was not living with her parents for much of her childhood, but, because her father was struggling with tuberculosis, he may not have been able to care for her. We do know something about her time in her aunt's house. Aunt Jesse kept a garden and fruit trees, which meant there was no shortage of food, one sign of the resourcefulness that sustained Jesse on the reserve when the Indian Act of 1876 required her to forfeit Native status for marrying a white man.[17]

Other kin in Odanak also left their mark on the young Obomsawin. "In my early years," she reports, "I was very fortunate to have two good friends, my aunt Alanis and an old man, Théo, my mother's cousin."[18] Her aunt showed her how to make baskets, while Théophile Panadis taught her the old ways of the Western Abenaki, including the songs and stories that would become a central part of her later work. A fluent speaker of his language, the retired woodsman was one of the most conservative traditionalists in the tribe. Panadis was such a treasure-house of cultural knowledge that scholars began seeking him out in the 1920s, regarding him, along with two other family members, Ambriose Obomsawin and Siegfroid Robert Obomsawin, as the best source for information about the Western Abenaki.[19] Between Panadis and her Aunt Alanis, the young Obomsawin had a wealth of traditional knowledge at her fingertips, something she appreciates to this day. "Those two people gave me something special and strong," she remembers. "It was the best time."[20]

The good times did not last for long. In 1941, when Obomsawin was nine, her family left the reserve and moved to Three Rivers, a French-speaking town just up the river. "That's when the trouble began," she remembers. No other Native people lived in the town, and she was forced to learn French as quickly as she could. "I attended a French school in the town's slums," she says. "That's when they told me that I was poor, that I was dirty, that we were savages."[21] The French Catholic children seemed unable to see the merits of a real Abenaki girl in their midst, even though, at the very same time, another Native girl from a neighboring tribe, the saintly Mohawk Kateri Tekakwitha, was becoming the object of intense fascination, even adoration, among North American Catholics. In 1940, Tekakwitha's devotees prepared an elaborate dossier that summarized the reasons in favor of her ultimate canonization, writing in terms that reveal the gender and racial biases that Obomsawin had to confront as an Abenaki girl. In describing Tekakwitha's devotion to Christ, the dossier paints the Iroquois as a "warlike" people, whose "savage girls" are "foolish and very fond of beads" even at the age of eight. After noting the rarity of Tekakwitha's "unsullied purity" and "love of virginity" among her peers, the dossier praises this "Servant of God" as a "genuine redskin, the first of that great and sorely tried human family to be presented to the Sacred Congregation of Rites as a candidate for the honors of the altar."[22]

If the white schoolchildren in Three Rivers could believe that Tekakwitha had been a "small wild olive-tree . . . growing so well that it would bear beautiful fruit,"[23] most were unable to extend their sympathetic vision to the world around them, where present-day

Native girls like Obomsawin sat in their churches and classrooms. Indeed, the early 1940s were a difficult time to be Native in general and Abenaki in particular. As a small, fragile population on the Canadian border that most European Americans had forgotten or would have preferred to forget, the Abenakis were never the first choice of dime novelists or Hollywood producers looking for "Injuns" to populate their reactionary fables. In some ways this neglect throughout the first half of the twentieth century had been a blessing. Given the treatment of Native peoples in popular culture even until quite recent decades, the Abenakis were better off without the attention of the screenwriters and directors responsible for films such as *The Massacre* (D. W. Griffith, 1913), *The Vanishing American* (George B. Seitz, 1925), *Drums along the Mohawk* (John Ford, 1939), and *Allegheny Uprising* (William A. Seiter, 1939).[24] Their good fortune, such as it was, was shattered in 1940, when Obomsawin was an impressionable eight-year-old.

Hollywood Abenakis

As Hitler's tanks raced across Europe and Japanese pilots trained for their raid on Pearl Harbor, MGM studios set its sights on an older foe, one whose on-screen defeat would remind European Americans of their ability to crush even the most bloodthirsty enemies of progress and civilization. Only months before the Nazi and Japanese armies were confirmed as the new "savage" Other on which European Americans must set their sights, Hollywood turned its Technicolor gaze on the original Other, focusing in particular on a small tribe that had escaped its notice in the past. In the popular *Northwest Passage* (1940), the Abenaki people became the sudden target of one of the most racist films ever released. If less notorious than nasty screeds like *Birth of a Nation* (D. W. Griffith, 1915) or *The Searchers* (John Ford, 1956), *Northwest Passage* deserves recognition as their ideological equivalent as well as a black mark on the career of its director, the erstwhile progressive King Vidor.

Northwest Passage starred Spencer Tracy as the colonial military leader Robert Rogers (1731–95), whose "Rangers" had burned Obomsawin's childhood home, the Abenaki settlement of Odanak, in 1759. During the Seven Years' War (1756–63), Rogers's men were supposed to serve as faux Indians after most of the real ones sided with the French, but, instead of mastering the art of woodlands warfare and passing stealthily into symbolic redness, most of them were no match for the highly skilled French *marines* or Native warriors who engaged them in the forests of New England. That Rogers ever became an Anglo-American hero is a tribute to the power of cultural mythologies to displace and dominate the historical record. As one historian has tartly observed: "What Rogers lacked as an irregular, he made up as self-publicist."[25] In London in the mid- 1760s, his boastful and inaccurate *Journals* became a literary sensation, obscuring the real facts of his "adventures" with self-aggrandizing half-truths that did not quite conceal the grim realities on which they were based. Here is how Rogers described the fateful morning of October 4, 1759, one of the seminal dates in the historical imagination of Obomsawin and many other Abenakis: "At half hour before sunrise I surprised the town when they were all fast asleep, on the right, left, and center, which was done with so much alacrity by both the officers and men that the enemy had not time to recover themselves, or take arms for their own defense, till they were chiefly destroyed except some few of them who took to the water. About forty of my people pursued them, who destroyed such as attempted to make their escape that way, and sunk both them and their boats. A little after sunrise I set fire to all their houses except three in which there was corn that I reserved for the use of the party. The fire consumed many of the Indians who had concealed themselves in the cellars and lofts of their houses."[26]

Somehow, this massacre of semi- and noncombatants became a defining event for Anglo-American culture in both the United States and Canada, and, over the centuries, as Rogers was wrapped in layer after layer of hagiographic gauze, he became an ideal subject for a Technicolor epic. Yet, because Hollywood producers do not read obscure primary documents, Rogers's leap to cinematic prominence required the intermediate step of Kenneth Roberts's best-selling 1936 novel *Northwest Passage*. In crafting his "historical" narrative of the raid, Roberts expended little effort in disentangling Roger's mélange of fact and fancy, but this did not keep the book from being treated as a factual account. As the novel sat atop the best-seller list for almost two years, the *Atlantic Monthly* exclaimed that it was "a great historical document, which historians will acclaim," while the *New Republic* endorsed its vision of the past for "anyone interested in the making of the nation," including, rather sadistically, "present-day Indians."[27] I could not find a single contemporary reviewer who expressed concern about the treatment of Abenaki people in the book.[28]

Despite the unsavory nature of Roberts's narrative, MGM was quick to capitalize on the success of his novel, lining up a respected director (Vidor) and an A-list star (Tracy) to begin production in 1939. Ignoring the quest for a "northwest passage" that consumed much of the novel, the film version focused on the raid on Odanak and the glorification of Major Rogers. In a green-fringed Robin Hood getup that would supposedly let him pass as "Indian" in the cold forests of New England, Spencer Tracy's Rogers is one in a long line of white protagonists who is even more Native than the Natives. One of his men brags: "The smartest Indian alive can't think half as much like an Indian like Major Rogers can." However, the filmmakers' judgment about "Indian thinking" seems clouded when Abenakis are depicted with an absurd trampoline-sized drum on which the major struts while giving a triumphal speech. The movie is filled with such freakish inaccuracies, yet one aspect of the original event does filter through even the lens of Hollywood: the brutality of the raid, even in a film with a celebratory point of view, still seems far from heroic.

Northwest Passage is one of those rare texts in which everything is laid bare unintentionally, thereby allowing the secret history of colonialism to seep through the celluloid and compete for recognition with the "official version" that the filmmakers intended to honor. In other words, the text is easily inverted from its normative mode. For example, the film is drenched with extreme expressions of bloodlust on the part of the colonists that seem like warrior machismo in one light and mental illness in another. Explaining to new recruits that his men eat like kings when prowling the north woods in their green stockings, Major Rogers declares: "Of course, now or then they have to stop eating to kill an Indian or two." Perversely, one of his men even manages to combine the two activities, wrapping the head of a slaughtered Abenaki warrior in a leather bag and then gnawing on pieces of it to curb his hunger. He even shares bits of the head with fellow Rangers (who, to be fair, do not realize what he is feeding them until later).

Perhaps because of the cannibalism and several scenes of or-giastic killing inflicted on Abenaki people, *Northwest Passage* takes great pains to legitimize their slaughter through didactic speeches and asides that must have been especially hurtful to Native young-sters of Obomsawin's generation. In explaining the need for attack-ing Odanak to his military superiors, Major Rogers reminds them how the Abenakis had "hacked and murdered us, burned homes, stolen women, brained babies, scalped strangers, and roasted offi-cers over slow fires." Throughout the film, Native people in general are described alternately as "dirty," "red hellions," "red skunks," and "weasels" fit for being "burned alive" or "skinned" if "their pelts were worth it," but the Abenakis are singled out for special opprobrium, suggesting to audiences that somehow the Abenakis are the ultimate enemy. In several melodramatic speeches, the audience is told that the Abenakis had flayed and dismembered captured officers, even pulling out their ribs one by one while the tortured men's hearts still beat and then "playing ball" with their heads. The unpleasant dismemberment fetish runs throughout *Northwest Passage*, as the director returned over and over to the vast quantities of white scalps that the Abenakis had supposedly taken, including one scene of over "seven hundred scalps" blowing in the wind near their wigwams just before the raid on their village.

For audiences in the early 1940s, I suspect that this alleged bar-barism would provide a symbolic link between "historical" Abenaki violence and contemporary fascist aggression overseas, one that is more than a product of my overheated imagination or presentist orientation to the past. As the film scholar Jacquelyn Kilpatrick has pointed out, when *Northwest Passage* was released in the United States, the Department of Secondary Teachers of the National Education Association recommended it for classroom use because "the success of this hardy band of early pioneers symbolizes our own struggles against bitter enemies in the modern world." Another teacher's guide endorsed the film for illuminating everything from geography to art (one of the Rangers painted *and* killed Abenakis), claiming that, through the "fine assortment of types" among the minor characters, "we glimpse early American characteristics of which we are rightly proud."[29] Presumably, this "fine assortment" did not include the Ranger who descends into cannibalism, as the guide made no mention of him.

In a recent book, the Abenaki writer Joseph Bruchac writes that he saw *Northwest Passage* as a young boy in upstate New York and still remembers the trauma of hearing some of the final words of the film. "Sir, I have the honor to report that the Abenakis are destroyed," Major Rogers tells his delighted superiors. While the rest of the audience cheered these words, young Bruchac sat silent in the theater, suddenly fearful. "That movie had made me afraid," he said. The connection between Bruchac and Obomsawin is more than tribal. The filmmaker grew up a few hours north across the Canadian border from the best-selling writer, whose Abenaki family name, Bowman, is an Anglicized version of Obomsawin, making them distant relatives.[30] For both of them, the popularity of *Northwest Passage* suggests a great deal about the general culture of Indian hating in which they grew up as well as the specific degradation of Abenaki culture that they were forced to witness around them in the 1940s. It is no wonder that both would devote their lives to getting Native perspectives into wider consideration, whether through writing, as in Bruchac's case, or through cinema, story, and song, as in Obomsawin's. "In hindsight, we can easily say that the native people of North America were oppressed by three major forces," Chief Leonard George, a First Nations leader, recently said. "These were the government, religion, and Hollywood."[31] For Alanis Obomsawin in particular, her creative work would be a constant rebuke to the first and last of these forces, government oppression and Hollywood distortion, undercutting the Abenaki people.

Beautiful Losers

Obomsawin had other challenges in her preteen years aside from the Abenaki bashing that *Northwest Passage* promoted. Because of her family's cultural isolation and meager income, her life was already filled with uncertainties when in 1944, after several agonizing years in and out of the sanatorium, working odd jobs when he could manage, her father succumbed to tuberculosis. On her 1988 album *Bush Lady*, she sings an Abenaki song called "Nzi Waldam" that seems to reflect her situation at this upsetting time in her youth. The song is about a young girl who hides in a ravine during Rogers's raid on Odanak, an event taught to generations of Canadian schoolchildren as a moment of military heroism much like what was presented in *Northwest Passage*. Although popular culture had for centuries romanticized the raid, the young Obomsawin also knew the tale from another source, Théophile Panadis, a living link to the historical event. Abenakis who were alive at the time of the raid has passed their stories to Panadis's grandmother (born in 1830), who then passed them to Panadis and he, eventually, to young Obomsawin. Nonnative historians used to doubt the accuracy of such oral transmission, but an ethnohistorian writing in the 1960s noted that among the Abenaki such stories "seemed to have been passed on by an aged person carefully and deliberately training young children until some of them knew the old stories verbatim, as an American child of my generation might know *The Night Before Christmas*."[32] In this sense, only three long generations—in fact, just three human voices—separated Obomsawin from a searing event in the mid-eighteenth century, which may explain why it seems so alive in her music.

Returning to the decimated village after the raid, the girl in Obomsawin's song looks around and then cries out:

> I am lonesome
> Where are my friends?
> Where are the trees?
> Odanak is gone.

Odanak was not gone forever, not in 1759, and not for young Obomsawin, although the world of her childhood was shaken by violence and loss. Soon after her father's death, she endured another traumatic experience that would affect her as much as the absence of her parent. "I remember the exact change," she says, thinking back almost six decades to the beginning of her dark times at Three Rivers. Having started school late, she was the tallest in her class but was beaten up almost every day. After her father's death she vowed that it would stop. One night she sat alone at home, thinking about the teacher, Mlle Réault, a stern woman who grabbed her arm and dug long red fingernails into her flesh, who talked to the white children about "savages" committing "massacres" throughout Canadian history, and who glorified events like Rogers's raid on Odanak. "I was the lone tall savage at the back of the classroom," Obomsawin wrote sardonically. "When I grew older, the same people who had beaten me up for years and years started flirting with me. It was strange. It took me a long time to lose the hate."[33]

Fighting back was the key to her transformation, a lesson that would echo throughout her later work as a filmmaker and storyteller. She remembers how she responded to racial slurs: "I never believed what I was told I was. I knew that there was a lot of wrong there. Every time I tried to do something they would tell me, 'Oh you can't do this, you're an Indian!' The more they said that to me, the more I said, 'Well I am going to do that anyway.' I was just a fighter. I just wanted to make changes."[34] She was tired of hiding her face behind her textbook when the children glared at her during history lessons; she was tired of children ganging up on her when she came onto the playground for recess; she was tired of planning secret routes to get home without being followed, taunted, and struck. Suddenly one night, she fixed on a plan: she would watch the entire classroom of thirty-two children and pounce on the first one who turned around in hate, planning to make an example that the others would not forget.

"It seems to me I had eyes all around my head when I went back that day," she remembers. When her classmates launched into their inevitable harassment, she leaped on the first girl who locked eyes with her, grabbing and punching while the nun watched in mute astonishment. "I had her on the floor and she got so nervous she peed," Obomsawin recalls, "and the nun was so shocked she didn't react." Nobody reacted even though the white girl was screaming. With the child at her feet and the nun frozen at the chalkboard, Obomsawin stood up, glared at the class, and demanded: "Who's next?" All of them turned back to their studies, seeming intimidated by the tall

Abenaki girl in the back row. "I made my stand there," Obomsawin remembers, telling the story like she had told it many times, "but then there were many places that I had to make my stand."[35]

Another place was the schoolyard, where she tried out her new strategy of resistance. Over and over she had heard the taunt of *sauvagesse* while standing on the edge of the games that the white children played. Emboldened by her outburst in the classroom, she positioned herself with her back flat against the brick wall so that no one could sneak behind her and waited for someone to call her "dirty savage." She counted the insults . . . one . . . two . . . three . . . four . . . She knew that five was an arbitrary number, but she had decided that "when they say it five times I'm really going to get mad." As soon as a white girl uttered the fifth insult, Obomsawin said: "Come closer, I can't hear you. Can you repeat that?" When the girl foolishly obliged, Obomsawin struck her with her fist. "It was like plugging an iron in the wall," she remembers. "I would get so mad, I'm telling you, so mad. Five times, and then the fight would start." Even after this second eruption against the intolerance of her peers, she faced the same old taunts on the way home, although the beatings started to taper off. "I was very skinny," she says. "I wasn't a big girl, but that is how I got them to stop beating me."[36]

Today, when asked about her childhood and the suppression of her most basic rights, Obomsawin tells her interviewers a few representative stories. When pressed for more than what she normally provides, she pulls back, saying: "I don't like to talk about that time because it was very bad." Perhaps we can glimpse something of her adolescent experience through creative refraction, through the wild lens of her friend Leonard Cohen's imagination. Like Obomsawin, Cohen, a Jewish bohemian, was a cultural outsider in white Christian Canada. After he switched from writing celebrated novels and poetry in 1966, just before Obomsawin began her turn from singing to filmmaking, he morphed into a counterculture icon the likes of which Canada had never seen. Emerging as something along the lines of the Bob Dylan/Jack Kerouac of the Great White North, he received international attention for his morose, half-spoken love songs such as "Suzanne" and "So Long, Marianne." Although his songs have a lyrical richness that seems out of place in contemporary popular music, it is in his creative writing, not his songs, that we can find traces of Obomsawin.

In more ways than one, Obomsawin's childhood memories were at the root of Cohen's most important novel, *Beautiful Losers* (1966). Born in 1934, just two years after Obomsawin, into a traditional Jewish family in Montreal, Cohen had gone to prestigious McGill University, formed a county-western band called the Buckskin Boys, and then won major awards for his poetry and prose with works carrying titles such as *Let Us Compare Mythologies* (1956) and *Flowers for Hitler* (1964). A glamorously brooding figure often seen in a cape and beret, Cohen was intertwined with half of Montreal's sizable milieu of artists and intellectuals, earning a reputation as a "lover of women and eternal hipster . . . the Rock and Roll Lord Byron."[37] He knew Obomsawin quite well during this period, well enough to spend a fair amount of time at her apartment. On one occasion he noticed an old book about Kateri Tekakwitha, that seventeenth-century "lily of the Mohawk" who, as noted earlier, was the first Native woman selected for beatification en route to sainthood in the Catholic Church. Taking Obomsawin's copy of the rare book with him on a trip to Greece, Cohen used it as an important source for *Beautiful Losers*, along with a farmer's almanac, Longfellow's *The Song of Hiawatha*, and, I believe, conversations with Obomsawin.[38]

The last is an angle on *Beautiful Losers* that has not been explored, in part, I suspect, because it does not reflect Obomsawin without the distortion that novelists find necessary to execute their own idiosyncratic visions. The alterations were so great that, when Obomsawin is asked in interviews if she served as Cohen's inspiration for fleshing out the dead saint, the subject of the narrator's agonized musings over redemption, Obomsawin's cryptic response is to laugh and say, "You'll have to ask Leonard,"[39] which might obscure the fact that her connections to the Tekakwitha character are slight. Granted, Cohen seems to have used her stories about the town of Three Rivers, where Tekakwitha's mother had been baptized and educated: "a lousy town for an Indian girl," Cohen writes, explaining in an aside that he had just been told this by "a young Abénaqui who went to school there."[40] But this is small piece of the puzzle.

The novel is stocked with telling references to Abenaki life that seem to have come from Obomsawin, although Cohen has never said as much, even in the guise of his narrator, an unnamed anthropologist who is an "authority on the A——s, a tribe I have no intention of disgracing by my interest" (BL, 4). Much is kept confidential in *Beautiful Losers*, yet much is revealed if one looks in the right direction. Rather than the saintly Mohawk with whom Obomsawin is sometimes linked, it is the narrator's twenty-something wife, Edith, who was, the narrator "confesses," an "A——" (BL, 20), with whom she has far more in common. Confusion between the two female characters that Cohen has imagined is understandable: he spins between them with jump-cut velocity, describing historical facts about the seventeenth-century saint in one sentence, then imploring Edith to kiss him in the next (BL, 96). Yet much more of Obomsawin's influence is apparent in Edith than in the dead saint on whom the narrator is fixated. While interviewers never fail to mention the filmmaker's striking looks, Tekakwitha is described as "not pretty." Edith, on the other hand, was a "lovely" modern women with hair "black, long and smooth" and eyes with a "solid depthless of black that gave nothing away (except once or twice), like those sunglasses made of mirrors" (BL, 23). Cohen paints Edith as young, stylish, and living in Montreal—just as Obomsawin was when Cohen met her and began taking mental notes for *Beautiful Losers*, his obsessive rumination over the twisted threads of Indian and white histories.

I think that the connections between Edith and Obomsawin are more than appearance. Just as Obomsawin lost her father at the age of twelve and was educated in an abusive setting, Edith was described as a "beautiful thirteen-year-old Indian orphan living with foster Indian parents. . . . She had been abused by schoolmates who didn't think she was Christian" (BL, 58). Just as Obomsawin and other Native girls in the 1940s were brutalized with taunts of *sauvagesse*, so was Edith in the novel. Just as Obomsawin would work as a swimsuit model when barely out of her teens, Edith possessed a sexuality that did not go unnoticed by the local French Canadian men. In his novel,

Cohen imagines the Native female body as a symbol of cultural and political conquest in his surreal allegory of intercultural violence. In describing the kind of violence that Edith was forced to endure, Cohen seems to have drawn on stories that Obomsawin told him about a painful period of her youth, the one she refuses to discuss in interviews except to say "I don't like to talk about that time." Cohen fills in the blank with archetypical moments of violent exploitation, horrific events that unfold while French Canadian men "laughed and called her *sauvagesse*, ha ha!" (BL, 60).

Such abuse may not be the literal story of Obomsawin, which, given her silence about this unhappy period in her youth, I have neither the ability nor the right to record here. I can find the "truth" of her tale in the pages of her old newspaper interviews no more than Cohen's narrator can find the truth of his so-called Mohawk saint of the seventeenth century. "I have been writing these true happenings for some time now," he complains to the reader of the novel, with the narrative careening between gruesome details of imperial conquest and sordid adventures in 1960s Montreal bohemia. "Am I any closer to Kateri Tekakwitha?" he asks in despair, before answering his question with metaphor: "The sky is very foreign. I do not think I will ever tarry with the stars" (BL, 95).

Likewise, I am modest in my aims, all too aware of the elusive nature of biographical reckoning. Still, I can look for the telling refraction, the place where something of Obomsawin appears in the fun-house mirror of Cohen's imagination. I suggest that he pulled something from his conversations and intimacies with Obomsawin that runs parallel with, and perhaps even intersects, the biographical truth of her early life—and, if not her, then certainly more than a few Native women of her generation. I turn to the symbolic truth of *Beautiful Losers* when I cannot (and should not) access the literal truth of Obomsawin's life in a difficult period, about which the practiced storyteller falls strangely silent. My intention is this: that the tenor of the story, as well as certain details, provide a rough sense of her past, something formative in her worldview, something that sheds light on her later work as a filmmaker. So I return to her novelist friend and share his bitter musings. "Who can track the subtle mechanics of the Collective Will to which we all contribute?" he asks in assessing the ways in which local whites had discriminated against Native girls like Edith (BL, 60). At one point, Cohen's narrator speculates on the origins of this "Collective Will" to oppress the racialized Other in the form of innocent Native girls like Edith and puts the blame on something larger than individual hatred: "French Canadian schoolbooks do not encourage respect for the Indians. Some part of the Canadian Catholic mind is not certain of the Church's victory over the Medicine Man. No wonder the forests of Quebec are mutilated and sold to America. Magic trees sawed with a crucifix. Murder the saplings" (BL, 58).

All of white Canada is responsible for the mistreatment of this Abenaki girl, Cohen suggests, just as it bears responsibility for the long-term violence against Native people. "O Tongue of the Nation! Why don't you speak for yourself?" the narrator asks, holding up the white male racists as representative figures from the dominant culture, as case studies in understanding the mechanics of a more sustained onslaught.[41] In one episode that Edith must endure, her abusers are bent on fulfilling the destructive "Collective Law" of white Canadians rather than obeying the "Natural Law they felt" in the presence of Indian innocence, and Edith can do nothing more than cry out to Saint Kateri Tekakwitha for a salvation that does not come. As if in response to her psychic wounds and those of other Native girls, Cohen infuses the book with a desire "to hammer a beautiful colored bruise on the whole American monolith. . . . I want History to jump on Canada's spine with sharp skates. . . . I want two hundred million to know that everything can be different, any old different" (BL, 187).

Although Obomsawin's influence on this classic novel, and the ways in which it embodies aspects of her sentiments and experiences, has never been delineated, I have to reiterate a fundamental point: Cohen's creative process was too messy to allow for simple links to the lives of his friends. With an ample supply of pep pills and hashish, he wrote twenty hours a day to create a novel that his publisher described as "a love story, a Black Mass, a monument, a satire, a prayer, a shriek, a road map through the wilderness, a joke, a tasteless affront, an irrelevant display of diseased virtuosity, a Jesuitical tract, an Orange sneer, a scatological Lutheran extravagance—in short a disagreeable religious epic of incomparable beauty." All this appeared on the original dust jacket and might have seemed an odd way to sell a novel were it not such an accurate appraisal of its contents. Cohen's book unfolds in as many directions as Joyce's *Ulysses*, yet at its center is always a question of repression, both political and personal, and the subjugation of historical memory, both of which would become great themes in Obomsawin's films.

On the question of history, Cohen asks how French Canadians could feel loyalty to the English, who had "conquered and humiliated them" (BL, 7). At a heated political rally in mid-1960s Montreal, a Quebecois filmmaker from the National Film Board (NFB), wearing his "violent leather jacket," gives a speech to a crowd chanting "Give us back our History! The English have stolen our history" (BL, 118). The imaginary filmmaker exhorts the crowd into a nationalist frenzy. "History decrees that there are Losers and Winners," he tells them. "History cares nothing for cases, History only cares whose Turn it is" (BL, 119). In her own work at the NFB just a few years later, Obomsawin would take a less aggressive posture toward the power of the Canadian state, but it would be no less firm in the resistance it offered. Ultimately, her stance would prove far more intelligible to the thousands of white Canadians living outside the bohemian quarters of Montreal, the thousands who would ignore scabrous novels like *Beautiful Losers* yet watch her films for their first Native impression of their collective history and culture. Her desire to teach, even reform, the white Other from a position of compassion, just like the tenacity of her resistance, was the product of her youthful experiences. "I have a drive," she says, "from every bit of memory I have from my childhood."[42]

As Obomsawin grew older into adolescence, the grim scenes of her youth were repeated in new forms that would shape her mature thinking as an artist. "You watch the drinking, the people sleeping on the sidewalks, being abused, and you hear the language," she said, remembering a ragged sidewalk where Native faces were twisted with alcoholism. "It's a snake pit." She had long been aware of the oppression shadowing her people and wondered how she could escape the stereotypical fate that Canadian society seemed to reserve for Native women. "How much can you take and how long do you go on until you finally believe what they're telling you: that you're no good, that your parents are no good, that your language is no good, that you don't have a culture, that you don't belong?" She had seen her parents drinking themselves into a terrible state, and she had experienced her own moments of looking into a mirror with despair. She understood the pain that drives the drinking and the alley fights, the turmoil and the self-doubt that ruined the lives she would later encounter in making films about Native homelessness and substance abuse. "There was a time in my life when I was told that's where I should be," she recalls, before emphasizing her struggle not to succumb to this fate, not to fall into the easy traps for poor Native women growing up in 1940s Canada. Success, however, could not mean separation: she never wanted to isolate herself from the problems besetting Native peoples at the time or to sever her ties to vulnerable communities. Instead, she developed the sympathetic eye of a social worker and a deeply held view that "they're not separate from me" that would propel her throughout her later film career.[43]

Performance

This sensitive view of the world was taking root in her teens, but Obomsawin was not immune to the effects of living in the midst of a hostile dominant society: "As I grew older I was always made to feel that I should be selling myself, or that I should be someone's maid, but I always found a way to fight back."[44] On *Bush Lady*, she mocks the white male voice that tried to achieve her objectification: "Hey bush lady / Look at her! / Isn't she beautiful? / Yeah. / She's my lady. / She's all mine." She dedicated the song to "all my sisters who live in despair in the skid rows of North America," the sort of women she would document in her 1988 film *No Address*.

Obomsawin knew something about objectification on a personal level: as young as age fifteen, she began finding work as a model in Quebec and Montreal. At first it was occasional work, requiring her to take other jobs such as one in a Three Rivers dry cleaners where she

FIGURE 3. Portrait of the filmmaker, ca. 1970. Courtesy of the filmmaker.

befriended local children: "There were a lot of poor children of the *quartier* who would come around because I would sit on the steps and tell them stories."[45] A few years later, modeling took her to Florida, where a two-week trip turned into two years working for a company called Catalina Bathing Suits, whose salesmen needed "mannequins," as Obomsawin puts it, to present their lines of swimwear to department store representatives.[46] Because the money was not enough to live on, she took a second job as a nanny in the home of a local family. Working with these children had a side benefit that made the Florida experience worthwhile: by her early twenties, she had learned English from reading to the children in her care. It was her third language after Abenaki and French, and it was the one that she would use for most of her film career.

After her experience in swimwear, Obomsawin returned to Canada and took up residence in cosmopolitan Montreal for the first time. If Odanak was not more than an hour's drive to the east, it was a far different world than the one she was entering. By the late 1950s, Montreal was nurturing a small renaissance of oddball creativity that was pushing a larger cultural transformation soon to sweep Canadian culture, a so-called Quiet Revolution against the conservative strictures of Catholic teachings in education, women's rights, and other issues that had made the late 1940s and the 1950s into a *grand noirceur* (great darkness) of repressed conformity.[47] Kicking back against this darkness with youthful optimism, Obomsawin found herself immersed in a talented milieu with the likes of Leonard Cohen, the sculptor Mort Rosengarten, the graphic artist Vitorio, the filmmaker Derek May, the photographer John Max, and an assortment of other black turtlenecked characters with something provocative to say. "They were very cultured people," she remembers, "and I learned a lot from them, their way of being."[48] Her friends were at the core of Montreal's bohemian scene, whittling away hours in hipster hangouts like the Bistro and the Swiss Hut, arguing about how to reinvent the world, or at least the slice they could glimpse out the window, where the pressing blandness of mainstream Canadian life swirled like never-ending winter. To her friends, Obomsawin was a welcome relief from this cultural snow-blind. "With her glistening eyes and jet-black braids," one journalist wrote, "Obomsawin cut a striking figure around town, singing and telling stories at parties and coffee houses."[49]

Singing was the key to the next stage in her life. With stage fright limiting her performances to parties and other small occasions where there were sympathetic ears in the audience, she had never planned to sing for anyone aside from friends. Yet, by the end of the fifties, she was becoming known around Montreal as a singer of beautiful songs in Abenaki, French, and English. Then, in 1960, she received a call from a promoter associated with Folkways Records in New York City, who asked her to perform traditional Abenaki songs in a major production entitled *Canadiana* for Manhattan's Town Hall. The invitation came as a shock, and she responded with a firm no, but the promoter kept calling until she relented. For someone who had sung only for friends at parties, the big night was a terror. "It was hard getting up on that stage," she said, remembering that she was so nervous she thought she might faint. Her mother was in the audience watching as she walked to the center of the stage, opened her mouth, and made not

FIGURE 4. Obomsawin in 1971. Courtesy of the filmmaker.

even a whisper for a painfully long moment. "You know on stage a minute is like an hour?" she has asked, seeming amazed that she was able to find her voice and finish her performance.[50] Afterward there was a riot of applause, but it was not enough to spark her interest in facing down stomach-churning stage fright on future occasions. However, as the praise kept pouring in, she soon changed her mind. Her performance had caused such a sensation that she began getting calls from all over North America and Europe, asking her to sing at colleges, schools, and folk festivals, and she eventually relented.[51]

Obomsawin was now a professional singer, touring across Canada with a growing set of traditional songs and stories. It was a good life, although it did not free her from the demeaning attitudes that she had endured as a child—no doubt, her performances were tinged with exoticism in the minds of many white Canadians. When she sang at the Guelph Spring Festival in the early 1960s, the local paper covered her appearance in a way that revealed the kind of attitudes that she was confronting in mainstream Canada. In a patronizing article, the male staff writer describes a "very attractive woman with a rich, melodious voice filled with feeling." After gushing about her singing and storytelling ability as well as her "charming" stage presence, he shares some comforting news with white Canadian readers: her "folk-lore stories illustrated the legends and history of her people, while pointing out regardless how materially poor the Indian people may be, they are never unhappy." Echoing what is heard in white descriptions of African American performers of the nineteenth century (and beyond), the writer searches for reassuring signs of this happiness in the face of the oppressed, noting in addition to her stereotypical Native beauty and "timidness" that "each of her songs was punctuated with a warm, enveloping smile."[52]

The journalist would have fallen out of his chair had he learned the truth: beneath this smile was a cultural critique (if one too subtle for him to detect). Obomsawin designed her performances to subvert the stereotypical views of Native people, and she alternated songs with stories to make sure that her points were clear. Feeling like a "walking museum," she told stories about her tribal history and about the animal world, the latter being of special importance to the

FIGURE 5. Obomsawin singing onstage in Montreal in 1976. Still from *Amisk* (1977). © 1976 National Film Board of Canada. All rights reserved. Photograph used with the permission of the National Film Board of Canada.

lifelong vegetarian. Performing in schools for both white and Native children, she began to find her voice as a teacher, often using her animal stories to explain Native ethics. "Animals have sorrow just like human beings," she said in many performances before teeming crowds of eight-year-olds, before explaining that hunting could be done with respect, as she had seen her father and other Abenakis approach creatures in the woods and rivers. "I explain[ed] to them about the skin and hair and how everything from an animal must be used," she recalled, "so [they] will develop an understanding that our people's lives are very different from what they hear."[53]

Even as she was touring Canadian schools, universities, and concert halls, Obomsawin was considering other means to convey her message of cross-cultural understanding, but she would never give up her self-identification as a singer. "No matter what I do, I will always sing," she said much later. "It's what I do in film, but in a different form."[54] As tiring as it was, touring across Canada had a long-term benefit for her: in learning how to tell stories about Native life to a diverse audience, she was getting a foundation that would serve her well as a documentary filmmaker. Her performances also brought her to the attention of the NFB, one of the most prestigious institutions of its kind in the world and the place that would be her creative home for decades to come.

Joining the NFB

Obomsawin almost backed into her job at the NFB, which in the 1960s was not the sort of place that a Native woman would expect to join, especially not in the prestigious role of staff filmmaker. A documentary would change all that, although it was not one that she made. Several years before she was putting together her own films, she appeared on the other side of the camera, as the star of a documentary called *Alanis!* a half-hour black-and-white film that aired on the CBC in a prime-time slot in 1966. This profile of a young Abenaki singer with an evident passion for Native rights caught the eye of several producers working for the NFB, one of whom was Robert Verrall. "We were about to make a film on a remote Indian reserve and felt clueless about how to proceed," recalls Verrall, a key player in the development

INTRODUCING
ALANIS
O' BOMSAWIN

FIGURE 6. Obomsawin interviewed on Canadian television about the proposed canonization of Kateri Tekakwitha, ca. 1966. Courtesy of the filmmaker.

of the NFB. Along with another colleague, Joe Koenig, he sensed that Obomsawin was someone who might be able to help. Setting up a meeting, the producers solicited her advice on making documentaries about Native people. Obomsawin replied with characteristic candor: "Well, I've seen Film Board films dealing with Aboriginal people, and we never hear the [Native] people speak." Impressed, Verrall asked her to join the ranks of the NFB. "She could have been a jet setter," he later said. "There's no doubt, if she had wanted to go in that direction, she would have found the support for it [based on her talents and charm]. But her commitment to her people was so real and so genuine."[55] In 1967 she accepted his offer and came to work at the NFB, an ideal place for someone who wanted to shape public discourse in Canada, even if it was far from a welcoming home for a Native woman with strong political views. The Canadian government had created the board in 1939 under the guidance of an influential Scotsman named John Grierson, whose charge was to "make and distribute films designed to help Canadians in all parts of Canada to understand the ways of living and the problems of Canadians in other parts."[56] The reality of the institution had never matched its high-minded rhetoric, especially when it came to Native issues.

Almost from the moment of its founding in 1939, the NFB aimed its collective lens at the Native people of Canada, producing in the 1940s and 1950s such films as *NorthWest Frontier* (1942), *Totems* (1944), *Caribou Hunters* (1951), and *Land of the Long Day* (1952). Until the launching of Native-dominated Studio D in 1991, as Marie de Rosa has pointed out, NFB films on Native issues were the exclusive province of non-Native filmmakers, who had racked up more than a hundred titles on the subject. Obomsawin would become the great exception, the lone staff filmmaker with a First Nations background until Gil Cardinal joined the ranks in the 1980s.[57]

Things were difficult at first for Obomsawin, as they would have been for almost any Native person in the same situation. In 1967, the year that she joined the board, the NFB produced a handful of films for the Department of Indian Affairs, which one might expect to have been aimed at Native audiences and interests. The films included such fascinating titles as *Duck Identification Loops* ("a series of 8mm loops to assist hunters in carrying out improved duck-species identification"), *La Grand Hermine* ("a record of the restoration of Jacques Cartier's ship"), and *Northern Affairs Programme: Resources, Transport and Communications* ("a series of films to encourage more investment in the development and exploitation of the non-renewable resources of northern areas"). Not surprisingly, Native people had not participated in the making of these films, nor would many Native people benefit from their existence. The politely entrenched racism and sexism of the NFB would not change until Obomsawin fought her way into film production, becoming the first indigenous artist on staff at the most important documentary film production unit in the world.[58]

Although she was the first Native filmmaker on staff and may even have been the first Native person making her own film at the NFB, Obomsawin did not finish her first project for several years after her arrival in 1967, during which time Willie Dunn (Mi'kmaq) became the first Native director of an NFB project with his short film *The Ballad of Crowfoot* (1968; 10 minutes, 18 seconds), "an impressionistic, haunting, often bitter account of the opening of the Canadian West, presented through still photography and the words and music of [the filmmaker]."[59] A year later, in 1969, the NFB could celebrate what it called the first film "made by an Indian film crew," *These Are My People* (Willie Dunn and Roy Daniels, 1969), "a short examination of longhouse traditions that George Stoney produced as part of the Challenge for Change program on the St. Regis Reserve (Akwesasne)."[60] Along with a slew of other titles such as *You Are on Indian Land* (Mort Ransen, 1969), Challenge for Change marked a new day at the NFB in terms of what was possible for Native media producers. "The astonishing characteristic of these films, produced with government funds," writes the film scholar Richard Barsam, "is that they present the subject's, not the government's point of view and are critical of government policies and practices."[61] It was a model that Obomsawin would take to heart in the late 1960s, although it was not the only one a minority filmmaker would find worth learning at the NFB.

Obomsawin has rightly been honored as the first Native filmmaker on staff at the NFB, but it is important to note that she was not the first nonwhite filmmaker to work there. One of her predecessors was the great director William Greaves, an African American who headed up to Canada when his acting career hit the wall of Hollywood racism. From 1952 to 1960, Greaves stopped acting to learn filmmaking at the NFB, working on dozens of nonfiction projects, in which he was schooled in the intricacies of film production, and even participating in the beginning of cinema verité in North America. When he returned to the United States in 1960, he had become a skilled filmmaker who quickly made his presence felt in the world of nonfiction, with creative profiles of Booker T. Washington, Frederick Douglass, Muhammad Ali, and other figures that he produced for public television and government agencies. Although Greaves broke a number of barriers in his long and influential career, one that continues to unfold after five decades of work, and has been hailed as "the leading Black documentary filmmaker in the United States today," his accomplishment has not received the attention it deserves.[62] In this regard, Greaves and Obomsawin have shared a common fate, one that plagues even the best filmmakers working in nonfiction cinema (especially when their work has a political edge or comes from a minority position in terms of race), and their similarities extend beyond the lack of appropriate recognition. Obomsawin's career has followed a path that Greaves first laid out at the NFB: the cultural outsider who joins the state-sponsored media institution almost as a token presence, learns the cinematic trade from some of the best craftspeople in the business, then reappropriates the ideological tools of the state for Other purposes in time to support the various liberation movements of the 1960s and 1970s.[63] It is a brilliant maneuver to undertake, although not one for the faint of heart.

Obomsawin may have envisioned this path from her first moments at the NFB (she is too modest to say as much), but she must have glanced at her lily-white surroundings and sometimes wondered if she were in the right place. Of course, the glass ceiling had been installed above her head with the utmost politeness, as befitted the reigning liberal culture of the NFB, but even polite barriers were not easily moved. The patronizing, even fawning attention that she received could itself become an obstacle to advancement. For example, when John Grierson returned to the NFB in a consulting role after a long tenure overseas, he became fixated with the attractive Abenaki newcomer. With more than a hint of Orientalist fascination, he praised the wondrous "dream magic" that she spun into the drab world of the NFB. "Listen to this woman and pay attention," he lectured his younger colleagues, who gathered in awe of their founding father. "You will hear wisdom! Not the wisdom of Plato, Dante, Shakespeare, Tolstoy—but wisdom from another realm. *Dream-magic!*"[64]

Despite such encomiums from above, Obomsawin was not given the chance to make her own films during these first years at the board. Instead, she served as a consultant on various projects dealing with Native people. For example, when the veteran producer George Pearson screened a test print of *Cold Journey*, a feature about the challenges confronting a young Native man in mainstream Canadian society circa 1970, the audience was resoundingly unimpressed. Some of Pearson's colleagues at the NFB considered dropping the film from theatrical release, but Robert Verrall, now director of production at the NFB, thought that Obomsawin might have some ideas and arranged a private screening for her. As Verrall must have anticipated,

FIGURE 7. Obomsawin at the National Film Board, ca. 1975. © National Film Board of Canada. All rights reserved. Photograph used with the permission of the National Film Board of Canada.

her response was very different from the largely white test audience's. "This film is too important to kill," she told him. "There's just too much in it that has to be shown and discussed." With her encouragement, the film was recut and then released into theaters across Canada in 1972. Although the final product did not set the box office afire, it accomplished what Obomsawin had hoped: it was successful in "bringing whites and Indians looking at the same film together," as Verrall said, and, perhaps with this cross-cultural value in mind, he later asked her to edit down a half-hour version for children's educational television.[65]

Just as important as Obomsawin's consulting work on films such as *Cold Journey* was her work with a different sort of media—educational kits about Native people designed for Canadian teachers. For someone who had been mistreated in the education system, it was a tremendous opportunity to challenge the curricular shortcomings that she had experienced throughout her youth. In preparing innovative kits for national distribution, she was crafting stories as part of the overall lesson plan and creating filmstrips with Native languages and music, both of which took her another step in the direction of

34

FIGURE 8. Obomsawin during the making of *L'Ilawat educational kit* for the National Film Board, ca. 1975. © 1975 National Film Board of Canada. All rights reserved. Photograph by: Robert Van Der Hilst. Photograph used with the permission of the National Film Board of Canada.

nonfiction film. What was most exciting to her about the kits was getting Native people involved in the development of such classroom resources, often for the first time in Canadian history. "Just to think that now a teacher would actually use *our* material and *our* voices for teaching," Obomsawin later said with astonishment. "It was such a victory."[66] Although the kits were intended for use in primary schools, they were soon popping up in universities and other unexpected settings, in part because they were well made, and in part because of the paucity of "Native voices" then available in instructional media.

While Obomsawin was working at headquarters in Montreal in the late 1960s, busy with the kits, her consulting work, and other projects, she remained eager to preserve her tribal connections. When not preoccupied with NFB business, she raised money for the Odanak Reserve with singing performances and even modeling jobs, which must have been one of the few instances of high-fashion paychecks ending up in Native hands. And she finally got an opportunity to move behind the camera, finishing her first film, *Christmas at Moose Factory*, in 1971. It was a pioneering work of Native cinema that, like much of

FIGURE 9. Obomsawin in Yellowknife at a conference on education, ca. 1971. Courtesy of the filmmaker.

her work, has not received the attention it deserves, even though it was one of the early films that set the pattern for her more celebrated projects. Like all her artistic work, her first documentary had its roots in the painful lessons of her early life: a profound sensitivity to cross-cultural affliction and how it shapes the lives of Native people as well as the possibility of transcendence through creativity, communication, and compassion. In stepping into the realm of documentary film production at the tail end of the 1960s, Obomsawin had found the ideal place to test these lessons.

2

EARLY FILMS

Christmas at Moose Factory

The coloring is inside the lines, more or less, and the picture is a bright splash of red, blue, and green on construction paper. The lens is close enough to reveal an unsteady line, the product of a small hand still learning to manage the pencil. As the seconds slip past, we see nothing but drawings, seemingly the work of many different hands. On the sound track a dog barks through howling wind, two lonesome sounds that emerge again and again in the fourteen-minute film. Like Robert Coles's work with the drawings of African American children bruised by racial discrimination, this creative documentary is built from crude drawings that carry more power than any professional illustration, simple drawings that capture an unjaded vision of life in the winter of 1967–68 at Moose Factory, a residential school for Northern Cree children. When we eventually hear Obomsawin on the sound track, she is subtle in her narration, explaining how "these children speak with their drawings about life around them and how they feel when Christmastime comes." The camera swoops across the drawings, accentuating particular details as they flip past like a slide show, accompanied by a rich collage of sound: dishes clattering; a Skidoo revving; a child talking about seeing a black bear; a mother's shopping expedition; and Santa placing gifts underneath the holiday tree.

FIGURE 10. Publicity photograph from the making of *Christmas at Moose Factory* (1971). © [1967–1968] National Film Board of Canada. All rights reserved. Photograph by: Ben Low. Photograph used with the permission of the National Film Board of Canada.

In rapid succession, Obomsawin shows us several drawings of a conventional Christmas star, before she mixes in cultural difference, suddenly but unthreateningly, through peals of laughter and two-dimensional images familiar to every parent, uncle, or aunt. As a drawing of an angel appears on-screen, several young voices are quick to tell us that it is no ordinary angel—it is an "Indian angel," we learn. In a similar maneuver, Obomsawin gives us a standard Christian hymn breaking through the howling wind, before cutting to a Cree-language sermon and a mournful Cree voice singing over acoustic guitar. Conventional expectations for a white Christmas have been gently complicated, allowing Obomsawin's universalist message to ring through: *How different are these children from your own?* The message is too subtle to dip into the sentimental treacle that is often slathered across Other children on television, such as those who appear before bloated American celebrities encouraging us to pledge our support for a Cambodian orphan for "the price of a cup of coffee per day."[1] Instead, Obomsawin provides a more artful evocation of empathy, collective decency, compassion, one that does not cast the children in the role of ill-fated victims.

The drawings continue to flip past, and the voices continue to murmur happily, lulling the viewer into a state of relaxed bemusement before Obomsawin gives us a surprise ending: real photographs of the child artists from Moose Factory, many smiling, mostly girls, real children, real Native children, not kids reading from a script, not disembodied voices that we can let drift off into abstraction. Then a final poignant image: a thirty-something Cree man in flannel shirt and jeans, his arm around his son and his dog, all their eyes closed in contentment, a male version of Madonna and child, a far cry from the 1970s stereotype of the Native male as social threat, angry activist, broken addict—or, alternately, noble shaman of the natural world. Instead, he appears ordinary, decent, loving, a good father. *Deserving.* Obomsawin leaves us with this powerful symbol of shared humanity, an image to which almost all viewers can relate, and then cuts to the credits, which announce: "Written and directed by Alanis Obomsawin." In 1971, almost four years after she captured the audio, the National Film Board (NFB) released her first film. Her humane universalism had leapt from song to screen without a stumble, and at the age of thirty-nine she had become the first Native woman to make a film for the NFB. It was a good beginning.

In this chapter I want to write with some care about *Christmas at Moose Factory* and Obomsawin's other early films because they are almost unknown, largely unstudied, and certainly underrated—reason enough to give them some consideration here. I believe that these films are important in establishing the ground on which Obomsawin was working as well as the goals that she was attempting to accomplish. Through her pathbreaking early work, we can see her thematic preoccupations, her strategies for dealing with power inside and outside the NFB, and her personality as a visual artist as it takes shape. In a flurry of activity between 1977 and 1988, she released six hour-long documentaries on the heels of the aforementioned *Christmas at Moose Factory*: *Mother of Many Children* (1977); *Amisk* (1977); *Incident at Restigouche* (1984); *Richard Cardinal: Cry from a Diary of a Métis Child* (1986); *Poundmaker's Lodge: A Healing Place* (1987); and *No Address* (1988). With each of these, she seemed to be developing a greater sense of what was possible with documentary cinema

FIGURE 11. Obomsawin in 1967 during the production of *Christmas at Moose Factory* (1971). © [1967–1968] National Film Board of Canada. All rights reserved. Photograph by: Ben Low. Photograph used with the permission of the National Film Board of Canada.

and, in the process, demonstrating the nascent power of indigenous media to Canadian viewers. Because of her early experiences with racism, she had always been ideologically opposed to the reigning systems of thought governing the lives of Native people in North America, but, in the late 1970s and 1980s, she was finding an extraordinary means for combating them. As the political theorist James Scott once wrote: "The main function of a system of domination is to accomplish precisely this: to define what is realistic and what is not realistic and to drive certain goals and aspirations into the realm of the impossible, the realm of idle dreams, of wishful thinking."[2] During the productive decade beginning in 1977, Obomsawin would show that her documentary agenda for Native people was more than an idle dream, that her traditional Abenaki storytelling voice could be transformed into the realm of cinema, and that indigenous resistance to the orthodoxies of the mass media was both feasible and necessary. The process would begin with her first substantial project, a wide-ranging look at Native women in Canada called *Mother of Many Children*.

Mother of Many Children

Obomsawin has never used the term *feminist* to describe herself, fearing somehow that to do so would limit her to women's issues. When asked about the term, she tries to transcend it without rejecting it, explaining that she opposes all injustice facing "men, women, children": "I don't care who it is; I'm going to go there and stand with whomever, even if I have to stand on my own."[3] Perhaps because of her childhood experiences with racial taunts and abuse, she is hesitant about labels of any sort, even ones with positive connotations for many of us.

Nevertheless, her films are the undeniable product of an interest in revaluing the work and lives of women (something I'll address in more detail in the next chapter). After making *Moose Factory*, Obomsawin turned her attention to Native women in her second film, *Mother of Many Children* (1977). Now the mother of her own young daughter, Kisos, whom she adopted at the age of one week, Obomsawin wanted to "pay homage to women at home, who survive, who take care of children—people that you don't really know." Her goal was to represent the broad spectrum of Native women living across Canada in 1977—a fine subject for a film, she thought, although she was hard-pressed to find support for it. "I have letters saying 'Forget it,'" she recalls. Initially less than enthusiastic, the NFB expected her to find external funding for the project, and one of the most likely outside sources, the Department of Indian Affairs, expressed no interest in funding a documentary about Native women. Almost ready to give up, she thought: "That's crazy: I've spent my energy on this, and I'm going to do it." The next morning she started drumming up support the hard way, by what she calls "standing up in a canoe." She took the train from Montreal to Ottawa and made personal appeals in various offices, finally getting a small amount from the secretary of state, just enough to film one sequence. Each time she finished a sequence, she returned to Ottawa to plead her case once again, eventually getting enough to finish an almost hour-long film. When the final results were screened in Ottawa, she got a letter from the secretary of state saying it was the best investment in a film his office had ever made, and she remembers that, ironically, "the man in charge of Indian Affairs also wrote me a fantastic letter."[4]

The film that received this praise, *Mother of Many Children*, is a subtle document of female empowerment. It begins with an epigraph claiming that there is no *he* or *she* in Native languages, gently establishing a feminist theme that is inherent rather than overt. No one in Obomsawin's films talks about *rights, gender oppression, political activism,* or *glass ceilings.* No one utters a catchphrase of 1970s activism like *the personal is political* or a bumper-sticker slogan like A WOMAN NEEDS A MAN LIKE A FISH NEEDS A BICYCLE. Yet Obomsawin's message—that women are an essential force within Native cultures in Canada—comes through with indelible clarity.

Mother of Many Children works on a horizontal plane: rather than diving deep into one or two subjects, it moves around the Canadian landscape every few minutes, pausing to focus on a woman of interest, to take in her story, before moving to another interviewee, often someone quite different.[5] The result of this lateral movement is a feeling that all these women are connected, despite differences in language, tribal affiliation, educational background, and geography. A young Ojibway[6] woman at Harvard and a traditional Inuit throat singer are presented as relatives of a sort, as much as the nineteen-year-old Cree woman giving birth in the Fort George James Bay hospital is literally in the same family as the Cree elder shown in a wigwam six hundred miles away, singing in anticipation of his grandchild. Benefiting from the skilled editors with whom she worked at the NFB, Obomsawin maintains this elegant horizontal structure throughout the fifty-two-minute film, moving seamlessly between old ways and new challenges, traditional ways and contemporary issues.

At the beginning of the film, soon after the childbirth scene, a Cree elder tells the camera that women were "more powerful than men" in their traditional society: women were the ones who taught art and ideas to the young, the ones responsible for transmitting tribal knowledge between the generations. As if to underscore the strength and autonomy of Native women, Obomsawin cuts to a long shot of several Inuit women walking on lichen-covered rocks near the Arctic Circle, picking year-old berries that have been preserved in the snow, before she moves to a closer shot of women fishing through the ice. Next the scene shifts south toward the Forty-ninth Parallel, to an Ojibway grandmother making a doll from leaves that will turn colors with the seasons and a young woman remembering how she was included in the backwoods hunting and trapping of her father's world.[7]

Always rocking back and forth between her emphases on autonomy and oppression, Obomsawin then cuts to Marie Williamson, an elderly Ojibway who provides a history lesson about the abuses of Canadian residential schools. She remembers back to 1914, as she and her siblings were taken from their family when Williamson was nine, bound for the supervision of the priests at a school called St. Anthony's (later St. Mary's). Williamson's grandmother was afraid she would never see them again, as Williamson tells the camera before adding: "And we never did see her again." She then describes the rigors of residential school life, with Obomsawin explaining in voice-over that the last such school was in operation until 1969 at Moose Factory, the site of her previous film.

Mother of Many Children does not dwell for long on the tragic before moving to a new scene in which Mohawk teachers have taken over a former residential school and Native children explain how grateful they are to have one another in the classroom, rather than finding themselves lost in a sea of non-Native faces. One young girl talks about the abuse she suffered from white children in the past, but now an easy smile seems to reflect a feeling of comfort that she has discovered in the tribal school. Once again, Obomsawin's message is subtle but clear: Vulnerability can be overcome through solidarity and resistance. Start your own schools; launch your own lawsuits; tell your own stories.

The filmmaker then takes us to the far north, to a young I'ilawat woman named Marie Leo who describes her coming-of-age in her rural village. Just as the filmmaker did in *Moose Factory*, here again she uses the rough drawings of a child, this time to illustrate Leo's time in the traditional menstrual hut at the age of eleven. Here, as in the rest of the film, the voices are paramount, especially Native voices. Throughout the film Obomsawin mixes the English translation at a lower level than the original Native speakers. While English speakers might have to work to hear the translation, Native language speakers would have no trouble deciphering the original voice on the sound track.

Next the film moves to Harvard University, where we see an Ojibway woman named Wilma Salmon in a seminar. An African American professor is talking about the burden placed on oppressed peoples: they must endure the oppression and also take the lead in overcoming it. It seems unfair, he suggests, but inevitable because no one else can do it for them. After talking about the difficulty of going back to her village from a place like Harvard, Salmon displays some of her artwork to the camera, which is a perfect segue to the next scene, in which Inuit women are sitting behind the microphones of a radio station, talking about their work, local events, and cold weather. "Everything happens through the radio station," Obomsawin explains to the viewer as we see Inuit women making prints from carved stones to be sold at a tribal co-op in Montreal. The Inuit sequence ends with a beautiful shot of female throat singers, who will also appear in her next film, *Amisk*.

Mother of Many Children takes a more political twist in the next two sequences, where a speaker at the National Native Women's Conference tells the audience that they have to take a more aggressive posture and give "static" to those who impede their progress. "It takes women to get things going," the speaker says into the microphone. Obomsawin then cuts to a young woman—Jeannette Corbiere Lavell—contesting section 12.1.b. of the Indian Act, which caused Native women to lose their legal status as tribal members on marrying white men. This articulate young Ojibway woman describes her lawsuit against this injustice, which brought her into contact with a low-level judge who said, "You should be grateful that a white man married you," before ruling against her. Although his ruling was overturned at a higher level, the Supreme Court of Canada finally voted five to four to uphold the discriminatory act, which had disenfranchised this women and thousands like her. Still, Lavell does not express bitterness, instead choosing to emphasize the value of the failed legal effort in bringing attention to the cause. She seems to have been right: in 1979, an Aboriginal Women's Walk from Oka to Ottawa expanded international awareness of this provision of the Indian Act, leading in 1981 to an official condemnation from the UN Human Rights Committee. Finally, in 1985, an embarrassed Canadian government remedied the situation with the repeal of section 12.1.b and the passage of an accompanying bill (C-31) ending federal authority over tribal membership.[8] One historian described the repeal as sounding "the death knell of the official policy of assimilation."[9]

After giving an overview of this contemporary legal and political controversy, Obomsawin goes back to the old ways, showing an older Ojibway woman threshing rice into a canoe with two long sticks, seeding the river at the same time she collects rice. A man steers the canoe as the woman sits in the back harvesting the rice, while in a voice-over an Ojibway woman speaks about the power of women in tribal councils. Obomsawin then interviews Lillian Potts, the first woman to serve as Cree chief, who talks about her daughters needing to be independent and educated "even if they are girls."

The filmmaker continues to interweave her celebration of the endurance of traditional ways with her analysis of social and political problems besetting contemporary Native people. In an isolated Métis town called Vogar, she meets with a woman who complains that the young people are drinking too much. Three caskets appear on-screen, and Obomsawin tells us that these young Métis people met a violent death, although the exact cause is not specified. (Out of respect, she uses still photographs taken during the short funeral sequence rather than disturbing the proceedings with a camera crew). The penultimate scene takes place inside the Portage Correctional Centre in Manitoba, which incarcerates Native women whose lives have taken troublesome turns. Some of the women interviewed have as many difficulties after prison as they did before. "You feel kind of sad leaving this place," says one woman in silhouette, before describing how Native women are released from jail in a manner that seems designed to encourage a return trip.

Again Obomsawin balances her presentation of the hurdles facing Native women with an evocation of their collective, creative power, cutting to a rehabilitation center where Native people are helping one another with substance abuse, the same subject of her later film *Poundmaker's Lodge*. In doing so, Obomsawin is not glossing over a grim reality: one woman tells the camera, "We don't have a chance being Indian," another talks about being mocked as a "pagan," while a third, in an echo of the filmmaker's own experiences, describes the pain of seeing her girls taunted and beat up on the way home from school.

To end her film, Obomsawin returns to her emphasis on the power of tradition even in the face of the new. The emblematic figure here is 108-year-old Agatha Marie Goodine, a Cree woman who walks down a rural path with various female descendants in tow, all of them linked arm in arm. She does not seem like a person from another century, but in a sense she is: Goodine is old enough to have been listed on an important treaty from 1876.[10] A warm, humorous presence, Goodine tells the camera: "Life was so beautiful then. . . . We thought it would go on forever." She is also the source of the film's title, explaining: "The Great Spirit created a woman and made her the mother of many children." With that, the film ends, having taken us from the birth of a child to the last years of old age.

Amisk

Far north: a river winds through land frozen in a way that suggests the proximity of the Arctic Circle. The camera sways with the movement of the oars, gazing down at the icy river, the tip of the traditional canoe in center frame. Then a long shot—again, beautifully composed—of a man in snowy woods, dwarfed by snow-covered pines, talking through translation about hunting and trapping being his way of life, one that has kept him out of the white man's schools. In the opening moments, Obomsawin is creating a portrait of her father's world, the snowshoe world of an Abenaki guide in the 1920s, which remains very much alive in another Native context, much further north, fifty years later in James Bay, Canada. Very much alive, and very much at risk, we soon learn, as Obomsawin describes the vast hydroelectric project threatening the traditional Northern Cree way of life. As she establishes these stakes, she does so without forcing the connection between the controversial project and the slender canoe in the water, instead letting the viewer make the link. Although a welcome relief from the doctrinaire tone of some political documentaries of the

1970s, her gentle handling of the material may obscure the significance of the proceedings, in terms of both the cultural threat of the engineering project and the Native response to the project. The Cree and Inuit resistance was "unprecedented," according to one historian, who described the Canadian government's tendency to ignore Native concerns when making use of Native land, even for what, in the case of James Bay, was the largest project of its kind in North America to that time.[11]

After the opening sequence, the filmmaker appears on-screen, welcoming Native performers to Montreal for a benefit concert that will "raise money in support of the cause of our people in the North," as she says. Several clerks, all of them older white women, check the paperwork of the arriving performers, who are coming from as far off as Alaska, and they seem surprised to be able to communicate with the dark-skinned men and women. "Oh, they do speak English," one woman says with relief. Obomsawin forefronts this exchange as if to make her overarching point. "They know *nothing*," she has often complained about white Canadians with regard to Native cultures.[12]

Then Obomsawin cuts without comment to outside the grand concert hall, before sharing one of the performances inside, a Dogrib drum circle from the Northwest Territories performing with intense passion. Unlike other films that document benefit concerts in the 1970s, such as the *Concert for the People of Kampuchea* (Keith McMillan, 1979), which starred Pete Townsend and other white celebrities charged with entertaining white teenagers for the benefit of far-off brown people, *Amisk* has a Native filmmaker capturing Native performances before a mixed audience, performances that she intersperses with Crees talking plaintively about the loss of their land. In a moment of particular poignancy, a Cree elder complains to the camera about white geologists and surveyors who will not even answer questions about what they are doing at James Bay. In such stories the old patterns of colonization seem very much alive, and no one in power seems to respect what the essayist Wendell Berry has called the *first political principle*: "that landscape should not be used by people who do not live in it and do not share their fate."[13]

Despite such quiet, reflective moments, *Amisk* still revolves around concert footage, and among the many fine performances in the film is one by the filmmaker herself. About halfway through the fifty-two-minute film, Obomsawin appears onstage in a red dress to sing a lullaby in English but with a traditional Abenaki inflection, making it obvious why she was such an acclaimed performer. Hers is one of several stellar moments in the film, which provides an excellent forum for Native creativity. The production values here, as in most of Obomsawin's work with the NFB, are high: smart, professional camera work and crisply recorded sound, during the performances as well as the interviews. At one point, the camera slowly zooms in on Inuit women standing nose to nose in an astonishing display of traditional Inuit throat singing (the same women who appear in *Mother of Many Children*). The energy of the moment is in stark contrast to the political desperation expressed in the interviews with various Cree people—yet, if their position is desperate as the Quebec authorities move forward with preparations for the dam, their demeanor is not. These calm-spoken, almost wistful accounts of the grim political situation contrast nicely with vivid demonstrations of Native cultural vitality onstage, including in the heart of the film a number of nontraditional performances by Native folksingers. In sharing only those individuals with whom she expresses solidarity, Obomsawin steers clear of the conflictual situations that enliven her later films, making the voice and face of officialdom noticeably absent from *Amisk*. Yet this suits the goal of the film, as stated just before the closing credits, when Obomsawin describes the success of the performances to packed houses over the course of a week. "For the first time ever in Montreal, people became aware of the strength and richness of our culture," she says, "and we became aware of the unity of our people." During her final words, she cuts from the concert hall back to the traditional canoe moving through the icy waters that we saw in the opening moments. Now it seems to be moving faster—an inspirational image that seems to signify a new assertiveness for Native peoples launching into the cold waters of modern Canadian politics. *Amisk* is more than a *concert film*, a somewhat pejorative designation in nonfiction cinema. Rather, it is a testimony to cultural survival and creativity. Indeed, Obomsawin captured what was in many ways a turning point for Native resistance against government arrogance and white Canadian ethnocentrism, using the concert as a microcosm of the larger perspective in which unique Native voices would talk back to white Canada and, for the first time, be heard.

Incident at Restigouche

In 1981 the Quebec provincial police conducted a monumental raid on the Mi'kmaq fishing town of Restigouche, seeking to impose new regulations on local salmon fishermen. When Obomsawin heard about the crisis on the news, she immediately wanted to head to Restigouche with a crew, but the NFB was never designed for rapid response. "That's the problem for many documentary filmmakers," she complained. "When there's something important happening, there's no way of getting there fast." Her institutional home, often a great benefit to her, was now forcing her to wriggle through bureaucratic channels for several weeks before she could get funding for a small crew. By then the police had mounted a second raid on the Mi'kmaq reserve, but Obomsawin was there soon afterward, finally on the scene with a camera crew to document what she would describe as "the biggest and most violent action in Canada versus Indians in fifty years."[14]

Because she could sense the importance of the unfolding events, Obomsawin was irritated at what she had missed, later claiming that the film would have been very different if she had been able to start shooting right away. "I had a very hard time making that film," she told one reporter. Having missed much of the action, she had to rely on footage from the CBC and stills from a freelance photographer and from L'Aviron, a Campbelton newspaper. After shooting some interviews soon after the second raid on the town, she went back to the NFB to get permission to conduct more interviews, including one with the minister of fisheries, Lucien Lessard, the official who ordered the raid. The response from the NFB administration was dispiriting. "Well, I don't think you should interview the whites," she was told in no uncertain terms. "Racism and prejudice exist at there [at the NFB] like anywhere else," she complained in 1987, expressing a bitterness

FIGURE 12. *Incident at Restigouche* (1984). Directed by Alanis Obomsawin. Produced by Alanis Obomsawin, Andy Thomson. © 1984 National Film Board of Canada. All rights reserved. Photograph courtesy of *Journal l'Aviron de Campbellton.*

that she rarely made public. "My history at the board has not been easy," she added. "It's been a long walk."[15]

Obomsawin's response was savvy: she held her tongue, left the NFB meeting, and proceeded to do exactly what she wanted, conducting the interviews she needed, including a remarkable exchange with Lessard. When confronted about her disobedience, she shot back at her superiors: "Now I'm going to tell you how I feel." "Nobody is going to tell me who I'm going to interview or not interview," she said.[16] She pointed out how often white filmmakers had interviewed Native people in NFB films and how the opposite had never been true. By the 1980s such representational inequities had become blatantly indefensible, as her superiors soon realized. Having won her point, Obomsawin now had the space to make her film in relative peace, a reflection on her growing power within the NFB. With every passing year she was acquiring greater authority and autonomy to make documentaries as she saw fit, eventually reaching the point where she was willing to defy her superiors to create what she envisioned as necessary and true.

The result was a far more aggressive form of political documentary than anything Obomsawin had attempted before, from the opening frames: three black-and-white stills of billy-club-wielding cops in riot gear, accompanied by the ominous thud of jackboots on the pavement. Then, suddenly, we see a kindly looking old man in a brown felt hat, apparently a Mi'kmaq elder. Bathed in the afternoon light, he almost seems shot in sepia as he describes the first raid on his town. Then, with a protest song about Restigouche on the sound track, Obomsawin cuts back to the black-and-white photographs, her only visual evidence of the first raid, including an image of a cop with his boot on the neck of a unarmed young man. To viewers who know little about the crisis, it is hard to imagine that all the trouble is over salmon, and Obomsawin seems to anticipate our wonderment. In what at first seems like a mistake, she lets a mawkish folk song run on the sound track while cutting to crude drawings of old-time Mi'kmaq life, with banal images of men on boats, salmon in the water, salmon fighting their way upstream. To demonstrate the historical importance of fishing, she even appears to sentimentalize the salmon's life cycle, but the whole sequence is redeemed at its close with a clever cut from salmon eggs to a Mi'kmaq newborn crying. Her point is plain: the life cycle of this tribe is linked inextricably with this fish. That is why the Mi'kmaq fishermen are resisting the government's encroachment on their fishing ground; that is why fishing rights are seen as essential to tribal sovereignty.

A title flashes on-screen: "The First Raid, June 11, 1981." Obomsawin shows photographs of the three hundred provincial police and ninety game wardens who descended on the town after cutting the local telephone service to preserve the element of surprise. The onslaught looks nothing if not military in nature, and we hear from a Mi'kmaq teenager who headed into the melee with his camera, recalling that there were "so many cops I couldn't get them all on film." Next we hear from a tribal councillor who tried to keep violence from erupting when Mi'kmaq fishermen refused to leave the banks but was told to shut up. "You don't represent nobody," the cops told him. "We're the bosses, and we're taking over now." The cops shout orders in French, a language that many locals do not understand, and then lash out with nightsticks when the fishermen do not respond or, even more dangerously, try to prevent them from shredding the nets that constitute their livelihood. Overhead a chopper helps the police track down a single Mi'kmaq man who has taken off running, until he is grabbed by the hair, thrown to the ground, and stomped. It is a vile scene, and Obomsawin does an excellent job of conveying the drama and chaotic energy of the day, although she is working only with photographs and reminiscences.

Obomsawin then cuts to an interview with the man who ordered the raids. "Virtue was not necessarily just on one side," concedes Lucien Lessard. Seated in front of a lace curtain, he sports his weekend clothes, a wide-lapel leisure suit that gives him the appearance of a 1970s game-show host, although he is anything but jaunty as he reels off justifications in fast-paced French. "One must not think that just because they are Natives," he says, "that all is pure." In her shifting back and forth between Native and white accounts of an event, juxtaposing versions of "the truth," we can see how Obomsawin was beginning to use what Zuzana Pick describes as a "reflexive strategy that exposes the tension between one regime of knowledge, which is embodied and localized, and the other, which is imaginary and deferred (the discursive and representational archive of colonialism)."[17] A turning point in many ways, *Incident at Restigouche* marks the beginning of this powerful aesthetic strategy, one that will characterize most of Obomsawin's later work (most notably, her Oka films of the 1990s and Mi'kmaq films of the new millennium).

In the next sequence of *Incident at Restigouche*, Obomsawin leaves Lessard in his chair for the time being and moves on to the second raid, nine days after the first, showing how the locals were determined to prevent the humiliation of June 11 from happening again. With pan-tribal supporters arriving from as far away as Alaska, the Mi'kmaq people seem prepared for rubber bullets, tear gas, and whatever else the police will throw at them. Obomsawin cuts back to her interview with Lessard, now wheeling defensively, explaining that the Mi'kmaq would never have accepted the government's new fishing regulations without the violent confrontation at Restigouche. "I ask you, Mademoiselle Alanis, would it have been possible [to solve the situation in another way]?" The camera pans with agonizing slowness across the lace curtains to the figure of Obomsawin, who sits across from the minister looking profoundly unimpressed with his rationalizations. A thundering silence. Then, after some intervening footage of the minister in Restigouche trying to broker an agreement with the Mi'kmaq tribal leaders, she fires back at him: "I was outraged by what you said to the [Mi'kmaq] band council. . . . It was dreadful." He seems taken aback as she dresses him down about the importance of Native sovereignty, a topic he appears never to have entertained seriously. Herein lies one of the themes of the film: the irony of Quebecois resentment toward the hegemony of Anglo-Canadians, given their own a history of oppressing the Native people in their midst.

After listening to her impassioned defense of the sovereign rights of First Nations, Lessard asks in disbelief: "Are you telling me Montreal belongs to you?" The proposition seems absurd to him but not to the filmmaker, who shoots back: "Of course, all of Canada belongs to us!" She leans over and explains: "We always shared, and you took, took, took. Instead of being proud of us, you talked about '*your* Canada.' " In response he tries to suggest that six million French Canadians in the province almost necessitate some kind of dominance over smaller tribal populations, but he seems shaken and eventually half apologetic about what he has wrought at Restigouche. Yet, if Obomsawin was furious with him for what he had done, she still appreciated his willingness to talk with her on camera. "I stuck to my guns and he stuck to his, but I admire somebody like that," she later said about an exchange that a Canadian film magazine described as "one of the strongest we've ever seen in documentary."[18]

In the final segments of the film, Obomsawin describes the aftermath of the two raids, including arrests and trials of Mi'kmaq fishermen who were alleged to have resisted capture. When the local judge chooses to discount photographs taken at the scene because they came from a Native photographer and then decides to "make an example" of one man, the local women are not surprised to find the legal system stacked against them (although the conviction was overturned on appeal). Obomsawin also talks to elders who say that the raids were traumatic events in the life of the reserve that will be remembered for generations, a sentiment that will be borne out in her subsequent Mi'kmaq films, *Is the Crown at War with Us?* (2002) and *Our Nationhood* (2003), almost twenty years later. As if to anticipate her continuing commitment to Mi'kmaq sovereignty as a microcosm of Native rights in general, Obomsawin expressed her concern about the long-term impact of the incident, the brutality of which took her aback: "During the raids Lessard ordered, the cops shouted at the Mi'kmaq, '*Maudit sauvage*, you fucking Indian, you fucking savage.' When you hear that, you ask, 'Who are the real savages?' I'm not saying that the Mi'kmaq were angels. But you know, with 550 policemen there, I think [the Mi'kmaq] behaved in a way that [was] more than dignified. And to have the children watch that! It's not something that people are going to forget."[19]

After all her difficulties with the NFB over the production, the response to her finished film was surprisingly positive. Peter Katadotis, then the director of English-language production, was "very excited," she recalls. "At the end, he really liked the film, and he told me so." Her faith in the NFB was restored over time, enough so that in 1987 she could say: "The Board is the voice of the country—people sometimes forget this. . . . They make films that could not be made anywhere else. Who would allow the people to tell their stories?"[20] Yet Native people had not been "allowed" to tell their own stories at the NFB until Obomsawin started making films there in the 1970s. In her rhetorical question, she almost appears to forget that she was the one who gave the grain of truth, at least from a Native perspective, to the NFB's high-minded rhetoric.

After *Incident at Restigouche*

In the late 1980s and early 1990s Obomsawin made several other films that were natural extensions of the positions and practices she had already expressed in her work. In 1986 she made a small documentary, one of her most poignant, about a ward of the state who was shuttled twenty-eight times between foster homes, often in abusive conditions, until he committed suicide at the age of fourteen. *Richard Cardinal: Cry from a Diary of a Métis Child* is told through snippets from Richard Cardinal's diary, creative reenactments of boys running in

FIGURE 13. *Richard Cardinal: Cry from a Diary of a Métis Child* (1986). Directed by Alanis Obomsawin. Produced by Marrin Canell, Alanis Obomsawin, Robert Verrall. © 1986 National Film Board of Canada. All rights reserved. Photograph used with the permission of the National Film Board of Canada.

fields, and interviews with those who knew Cardinal. We hear Leo Crothers, Cardinal's last guardian, describing the boy who hanged himself from a tree in his backyard only forty-two days after his arrival. "He was a good worker," Crothers says. Obomsawin follows the story beyond the boy's death, taking on an activist role when she mails a gruesome suicide photograph to government officials to condemn their inaction in the case as well as their general inattention to the needs of Native children. In sharp terms she describes the astonishing gaps in social services, including a failure to share records about Cardinal's suicidal past before it was too late. Psychologists, social workers, doctors, administrators—all these functionaries of the state failed this articulate, emblematic Indian child, as Obomsawin paints it, and the results of a government hearing seem to support her claims, describing "serious inadequacies" in the boy's care, and noting that he "never got what he needed most . . . to go home." As the film would have it, the most attention Cardinal ever got from the state was at his funeral, and Obomsawin wants her documentary to challenge this status quo. Her desire was that this thirty-minute film prompt a change in attitude toward Native children under the care of the state. She said: "I want people who look at the film to have a different attitude next time they meet what is called a problem child and develop some love and some relationship to the child, instead of alienating him."[21]

Some viewers might have had this response, but more measurable was the change at the official level: as a result of the film and the publicity surrounding it, Canadian law was changed to improve the situation of Native children in the foster-care system. Obomsawin's film was a rare example of a social-uplift documentary actually bringing about political change in a demonstrable manner, although it is important to note that it did not spark policy change in a vacuum. Instead, it was another example of documentary film building on the momentum of an existing social movement or organization, in this case the work of Métis living within the province of Alberta. Numbering well over 100,000, the Métis live all across Canada but are concentrated in the prairie provinces such as Alberta, where they have had their greatest success in acquiring political rights and influence over issues such as foster care. In no small measure their influence is a result of having secured their own land base in Alberta, which has not happened for Métis elsewhere in Canada. In enacting provincial laws such as the Métis Population Betterment Act (1938) and the Métis Settlement Act (1990), Alberta became the only province to establish Métis settlements within its boundaries—and the only one to attempt to forge a legal definition of Métis identity.[22] The Métis seem to have the most tangled history in terms of identity formation of any Native group in North America, but as one scholar has noted: "This complex history does not alter the fact that today the Métis are recognized by the Canadian constitution as a single, holistic aboriginal group."[23] And their growing power as such in Alberta in the 1980s provided the ideal conditions for Obomsawin's film to make a difference in terms of public perception and policy.

Obomsawin followed *Richard Cardinal* with two more films designed to prick the conscience of viewers who knew little about the most vulnerable subgroups of the Native population in Canada: substance abusers and the homeless (two groups with a significant

FIGURE 14. *No Address* (1988). Directed by Alanis Obomsawin. Produced by Marrin Canell, Alanis Obomsawin. © 1988 National Film Board of Canada. All rights reserved. Photograph by: Audrey Mitchell. Photograph used with the permission of the National Film Board of Canada.

overlap). In *Poundmaker's Lodge: A Healing Place* (1987), Obomsawin presents a rehabilitation center where the therapeutic value of returning to tribal customs and community is emphasized. The film includes a number of moving interviews, always one of the filmmaker's strengths, as well as quick historical surveys of the damage done by alcohol to Native lives. Then, in 1988, she released *No Address*, which depicted the horrific conditions facing the estimated twelve thousand homeless people living in Montreal at the time. Working in a classic mode of documentary, Obomsawin exposes an overlooked social problem and reveals how ordinary Native men and women have become orphans of the city. She profiles young Native women who leave their reserves and find themselves on cold urban streets, disconnected from family, tradition, and even social services that might help them—the title refers to the inability of the welfare system to even locate many street people. In an image of dark irony that upends a normally complacent symbol of holiday cheer, we see homeless men sleeping under Christmas trees.

Trying to figure out what is happening to these Native men and women, Obomsawin conducts interviews on the streets, in mobile soup kitchens, in the office of compassionate social workers. She talks to women who lament their descent into drugs and prostitution. "I want to go back to my family," they plead to the camera. As always, Obomsawin hints at the solution toward the end of the film: cultural self-help in the form of the Montreal Native Friendship Centre, community radio, and other institutions that promote Native solidarity. Wielding the image of the solitary Native person cut off from the tribal community and abandoned among the glass towers of the city, the film provides a powerful metaphor of contemporary Native life in Canada, where Native people can endure both a literal and a figurative homelessness in a white-controlled economy and political system. *No Address* is a thoughtful film, softer in spirit than the more aggressively political work Obomsawin would dive into in the 1990s, and one that leaves the audience in a hopeful mood. As Zuzana Pick has observed, the film "constructs a social and psychological framework for hope through solidarity and empathy," two qualities that are, I believe, always at the heart of Obomsawin's cinematic vision of the world, two qualities that she possessed well before she began making movies for the NFB.[24] Their origins lie in the traditional art of storytelling that she learned as a child in Odanak and later performed on stages across Canada, one that depends on the creation of empathy and solidarity among a community of listeners. Perhaps more than any single quality, her profound knowledge of the Abenaki oral tradition would set her apart from other filmmakers and give subtle, if often overlooked, form to the work she was creating at the NFB. In the final portion of this chapter, I want to explore how her documentary aesthetic has its roots in this older art form, whose mastery has long been associated with members of the Obomsawin family.

Storyteller

In almost all her films, Obomsawin tells stories that are political in subject and activist in origin, and, as a result, it is not difficult to situate her work within one of the main frameworks for political documentary. Almost two decades ago, in an edited collection called *Show Us Life*, Thomas Waugh wrote about what he termed *committed documentaries*, nonfiction films that were designed to spark social change rather than being content merely to record it.[25] Unlike the cozier armchair accounts of the world's troubles that often appear on network television, "committed documentaries" function as media interventions in what is happening on the ground. For example, Obomsawin's purpose in making *Amisk* was to take part in the protest against the James Bay hydroelectric project. "This is why I make films," she says. "To go for changes."[26]

Another writer, Cameron Bailey, has set out a more recent version of Waugh's idea under the eloquent term *cinema of duty*, a cinema that he describes as "social-issue oriented in content, documentary realist in style, [and] firmly responsible in intention." According to Bailey, a film of this sort "positions its subjects in direct relation to social crisis, and attempts to articulate solutions to problems within a framework of centre and margin, white and non-white communities."[27] No doubt, Obomsawin fits this definition as well. Not only does she work on social crises that the federal "centre" seems to be inflicting on the Native "margins" of Canadian society, but she also uses the same language as Bailey to describe her motivation. "I love what I do. It's like a duty," she says. "I am really at the service of my people."[28]

Yet, as simple as it is to slot her work into these general definitions, it is much harder to figure out the particulars of her filmmaking practice and uncover the unique aesthetic that was emerging over the first two decades of her career. The difficulty comes in part, I believe, from her development of a more subtle aesthetic than what we see in the work of celebrated documentarians like Errol Morris, Michael Moore, or Marlon Riggs, artists who forefront their own personality through some combination of ironic juxtaposition, idiosyncratic editing, musical punctuation, and cinematographic flourishes. Unlike these filmmakers' styles, Obomsawin's can sometimes wash over viewers without their awareness or appreciation.

D. B. Jones, the main historian of the NFB, is one such viewer. Jones has dismissed Obomsawin's formal accomplishment even as he expressed admiration for what she is doing. For example, he praises her for avoiding the "oversimplification of issue and technique," "crude tendentiousness," and "over-reliance on words" that tarnished more than a few well-meaning political films in the 1970s and 1980s. Yet, even as he hails the strong filmmaking in her "personal and self-effacing" projects in one sentence, he sniffs about them "lacking in artistic breakthroughs" in the next.[29] This is an uncharitable reading of her work, one that glosses over its understated richness.

One of the few scholars to see the depth of Obomsawin's work has been Jerry White, a film and media studies professor at the University of Alberta. White concedes that, on an initial viewing, her films might seem unremarkable in formal terms and might even be written off as mere appropriations of an older, pedantic NFB house style to Native ends. The filmmaker even contributes to this narrow interpretation at times, such as when she told White in an interview: "I like to make it as plain as possible, so that the attention has to be on the work and what the people are saying. . . . I don't like to do fancy things where your attention is on other things." Rather than accepting her modest words at face value, however, White studied her films and found "a significant transformation of documentary aesthetics" in her ongoing project. In a brilliant summation of her stylistic accomplishment, he writes: "She takes what she finds valuable from the Canadian tradition of documentary (low-budget production, fusion of as opposed to choice between interviews, observational techniques, and voice-over), and adds what she needs for her activist project (emphasis that this is *her* speaking in the voice-over, that these films are foremost for 'our people,' secure in the knowledge of who that is). The mixture of forms associated with such contradictory impulses as nation-building and activism/agitation looks a little strange on first glance. But when the films are considered together, and in the context of Obomsawin's activist priority, the sheer consistency of her aesthetic mixture makes it clear that these films occupy a complex social and cultural space."[30]

If at first glance Obomsawin seems to offer a Native gloss on the orthodox NFB style, the truth is, I think, closer to what Merata Mita once said about working as an indigenous filmmaker in New Zealand: some artists manage to "express their peculiarly Maori experience in the language of the oppressor."[31] No doubt Obomsawin picked up the "language of the oppressor" to some degree, becoming well versed in NFB conventions over her first years as a filmmaker, but that did not mean she lost her unique vision as a Native artist and activist in the bureaucratic haze. "I've certainly learned much from the Film Board," she says, "but I have my own way."[32]

What is the Obomsawin way? Unlike the pure realist narrative found in the most straightforward nonfiction cinema, including the NFB didacticism that put Canadian schoolchildren to sleep in the 1950s, her films have several important qualities that set them apart. First is a clear sense of subjective authorship—her subtle but strong presence in voice-over is just one way in which her creative hand is emphasized in almost all her films. Second is a willingness to make sudden poetic diversions into song or artful images, such as the surprising cutaways to fish spawning in *Incident at Restigouche* or the canoe slicing through the icy river in *Amisk*. Third is a storytelling technique that is measured and at times almost meandering, using what White has characterized as a "non-narrative, elliptical documentary ethic."[33]

FIGURE 15. Obomsawin performing traditional Abenaki stories and songs, ca. 1970. Courtesy of the filmmaker.

The contemplative pace comes, in part, out of the Abenaki storytelling tradition that Obomsawin learned from relatives such as Théophile Panadis, who had such a profound influence on her. Known as "The Storyteller" throughout the Abenaki woodlands, Panadis related traditional narratives to audiences that included the wide-eyed young filmmaker as well as other tribal children and even folklorists and anthropologists who had made the trek to Odanak.[34] Surely it is a coincidence that Obomsawin joined the NFB in 1967, just a year after Panadis's death, but one can imagine her desire to continue his work at least in some symbolic fashion. By the time she started working at the NFB, she had already begun to return the gift he had given her by touring folk festivals and universities to perform Abenaki songs and tales. The oral tradition was an essential part of her childhood as well as the first place she found success as an artist, and for this reason it may have made its way into her film career at some level. That is what I want to explore in the coming pages.

So what does an Abenaki story sound like? I can give one example from the filmmaker's own family. In January 1959, an elderly great-aunt, Olivine Obomsawin, spoke in her Native language to the Dartmouth College anthropologist Gordon Day, sharing with him a rare

Abenaki version of Roger's 1759 raid on Odanak that she had heard as a little girl from her own grandmother. I quote it at length to provide a sense of the way in which Abenaki narrative would deal with a violent clash between Native and non-Native cultures, something that would occupy Alanis Obomsawin for much of her cinematic career, and to suggest that such stories about Abenaki history were the foundation for her work as a filmmaker. This is the story that her elderly relative told the anthropologist, who translated it as follows:

> And the Indians at that time in the fall were dancing. Already the harvest was all gathered. . . . And they danced and some-times celebrated late, dancing and sometimes going out be-cause it was a nice cool night. They rested, some went to smoke and rest. And one, a young girl, a young woman, she did not immediately go in when the others went in. When they went into the council house to dance again that one, the young girl, the young woman, did not go in because it was cool and she stayed outside. She remained longer outside, and it was dark, and when she was ready to go in at the start of the dancing inside the house, when she was ready to go in, then someone stopped her. He said, "Don't be afraid." In In-dian, you understand, he said, "Friend. I am your friend, and those enemies, those strange Iroquois, they are there in the little woods [planning] that when all [the Abenakis] leave for home they would kill them all, their husbands, and burn your village, and I come to warn you." And surely the young woman went into the council house, the dancing place, and she warned the other Indians what he told. She warned what she had been warned. And some did not believe her, because she was so young, because she was a child. Some of them stopped and went home to see about their children and get ready to run away. And some of them did not listen to that young girl, the young woman. . . . And some Indians at once hurried home. They stopped dancing and went home, and they went to see about their people, their children, in order to run away as soon as possible, so they could hide. . . .

[F]ather gathered everyone—it was dark, of course—in the dark[;] no one kindled a light. They gathered their children in the dark, you can be sure. And they left to hide somewhere where they could not find them. Of course it was night at that time and they hid—in a big ravine where they could not find them. And that man, the old man, they counted their children to see if they were all there there where it was deep. And one had been left! My aunt's grandmother was the one who was missing! And she did not know that she was alone in the house, but already she was awake, and she was sitting at the foot of the bed and she was looking out of the window leaning on the window sill. She was singing, she was calmly singing [to herself]. She did not even know that the others were gone. Suddenly then her father quickly entered in the dark, entering quickly, and he took her—he found her singing, this one. Right away he took her and left as quickly as he possibly could to the ravine—the big ravine that is where Eli Nolet's house [now] is, that's where the ravine is, At the Pines, that's what they call it at Odanak, At the Pines. And there they hid, the Indians, the Abenakis. And my grandfather, the Great Obomsawin, the Great Simon, he crossed the river, just as the sun was rising. Just as the sun is seen first. He didn't arrive soon enough, and just at that time he is almost across the river when the sun showed. And his hat—something shone on his hat, something [bright] that he wore. And there he was shot down on the other side— he was the only one [to get across]. All that were with the houses—well, that was when they burned the village—the others, surely many were killed of the others, all that were with the houses.[35]

Alanis Obomsawin the filmmaker has a great deal in common with Olivine Obomsawin the storyteller. Like her relative, she zooms in on moments of extreme crisis between Native and white to provide a marginalized perspective on a critical historical event. Like her relative, she uses children as key figures in her narratives, either as passing images, as in *Incident at Restigouche*, or as the main subjects, as in *Richard Cardinal*. Like her relative, she highlights the calming influence of Native song. And, finally, like her relative, she emphasizes Native people helping one another across tribal lines.

Interestingly, one of the few other Abenaki versions of this pivotal event comes from Théophile Panadis around the same time (ca. 1960), and it seems probable that Obomsawin heard one or both versions in her early years. One piece of evidence supporting this supposition is that the lone girl in her song about the raid resembles the girl who gives the warning in the Abenaki version of the attack and that this noteworthy figure does not appear in the standard English and French sources. Moreover, the filmmaker made no secret of her reverence for the Abenaki stories she learned as a girl, even dedicating her song about the "massacre of our people in Odanak by Major Rogers and his men" to her Uncle Théophile and her Aunt Alanis.[36]

Obomsawin's fondness for the oral tradition was not unusual for someone who cherished her ties to Abenaki communities and saw herself as an educator at heart. As Michael Dorris has written, the oral tradition is "the vehicle through which wisdom is passed from one generation to the next and by which sense is made of a confusing world. It is responsible in large part for the education, entertainment, and inspiration of the community."[37] Abenakis seem to have been unusually scrupulous about their stories—scholars have argued, for example, that they were "very tenacious" about their oral tradition, which they regarded as an indispensable tool for the transmission of cultural values and knowledge."[38] Despite the cultural dislocation that affected many Abenakis of her generation, Obomsawin fit this older pattern. Telling stories was the centerpiece of the Abenaki education that she received from her relatives, and she never abandoned the storyteller's art, always relying on the power of the spoken word in her creative expression as a performer, a creator of educational kits, and rare filmmaker who listens before she looks. "I am very fussy about sound," she says. "I come from a place where hearing and listening to people is important."[39]

In the hands of someone like Obomsawin, documentary film becomes an extension of traditional storytelling, which often used vocal inflection, facial expression, and dramatic gesture in a protocinematic manner. "Film is a way of seeing very like the oral tradition," Leslie Marmon Silko has pointed out. "It operates on a highly refined, simultaneous, personal level. . . . Film gives the feeling that we get going for a walk, experiencing many things at once in a simple elemental way."[40] It is important, I think, to see the connections between the two art forms for someone steeped in both, but to do so without shading into the reductivist mind-set that brings all Native artistry back to nature. I do not see Obomsawin's work as "simple," and, if it does have an "elemental" power, that power does not come out of the natural world.[41] Rather, it comes out of an imagination honed by the art of Abenaki storytelling, a specific cultural practice as constructed as an Elizabethan sonnet or a trompe l'oeil painting. It is not a birch tree or a hedgehog stumbling toward the dawn. It is an art form at the core of her cinematic practice, one that warrants scrutiny as a key influence on her documentary work.

Obomsawin's careful attention to the spoken word, its cadences and nuances, is unusual among documentarians, and it begins in the first moments of her filmmaking. Long before proposals are written and cameras are in place, she heads alone into the field with her tape recorder to do nothing more than talk to people. "It's not the image," she stresses. "It's the word that is most important. It is what people are saying. . . . It's the people themselves who tell me what they are and what the story is. And . . . if it means listening for 15 hours with one person, I'll do it."[42]

When she returns with a camera crew to capture the same person on film, Obomsawin still honors the spoken word, refusing to cut off the storyteller—as much as the high cost of film will allow. Her willingness to listen even continues into the editing room. As Jerry White has suggested, the people in her films are allowed to complete thoughts, to pause for a moment's reflection, to stumble in their wording before finding their way, all of which slows the pace of the film to a point that is quite unusual for nonfiction cinema. Not only does she break with "rhetorical norms of documentary, such as focus or concision," White observes, but "it's clear, just as she says, that she wants your attention to be on what the people are saying: that her films feel a little slow and rambling, and formally stripped down, is a testament to how little conventional documentary really does this."[43]

An older rhythm is at work here, one more leisurely than what commercial television demands. With her background in the patient art of storytelling, Obomsawin seems to create a space for contemplation, conversation, and reflection, qualities that have been squeezed out of the global media marketplace. "No contemplation is possible," Jean Baudrillard has complained about contemporary cinema. "The images fragment perception into successive sequences, into stimuli toward which there can be only instantaneous response, yes or no—the limit of an abbreviated reaction. Film no longer allows you to question."[44] With its casual pace and nuanced point of view, Obomsawin's filmmaking harks back to an older mode of narrative, one that implies respect for the audience and the sense that the listener is a kindred spirit, not a mere agent of consumption, a demographic target. Obomsawin is telling the story, of course, but she is not alone in her self-imagined field of discourse; she is not communicating *monologically*, as the mass media tend to prefer.[45] Rather, she is talking *with* us in her films, allowing us time to reflect, consider, and question.

Obomsawin is not alone in this conversational impulse. If she was one of the first Native people to bring a storytelling aesthetic into cinema, she certainly was not the last. In her wake, Native filmmakers have become quite explicit about using cinema for the older art of telling stories. Carol Geddes, the talented Tlingit filmmaker, has described the crucial connections between filmmaking and Native oral traditions. "Visual media such as film and video," she says, "are uniquely appropriate to cultures which have traditionally relied on the spoken word, music, and drawings to communicate."[46] Similarly, Loretta Todd, a Métis filmmaker, has written: "I see myself in the same way as the storyteller, except my way of telling the story is different. The storyteller, the artist, has a role to play in the health of the community. Even though there is no word for 'art' and 'artist' in most communities, there is a word for people who tell stories. There's a word for people who make things and help people with their dreams."[47] Dreams are not irrelevant here, although the subject might seem more appropriate to fiction filmmakers like Fellini or the Coen brothers than a nonfiction realist like Obomsawin. Yet Obomsawin has a deep interest in dream states, which seem to provide her with imaginative connections to places we need to go, taking us between here and there. "As a little girl, I used to have very fantastic dreams," she remembers. "I think dreams have meanings for sure. They could be bringing messages."[48] They are, perhaps, the most fundamental form of storytelling, one that has long informed the indigenous oral tradition (as it has certain elements of modernist literature in the Western tradition).

The popular Abenaki writer Joseph Bruchac tells a traditional story about the significance of dreams in the matrix of conquest. In this story, an Abenaki man dreamed that he saw a white man, his neighbor, wearing a fine white shirt. When he woke up, he went to his neighbor's house and described what he had seen to the white man, who was attentive and polite. "I understand," he said, well aware of the importance of dreams to the Abenakis, and then he went inside his house to retrieve the white shirt and give it to the Abenaki man. The Abenaki man took the shirt with appreciation and returned to his home. The next day, his neighbor appeared at his door with a loaded rifle in hand. "I had a dream last night," the white man told him. "In my dream, you gave me all of this tract of land, this wide valley where you and your family hunt." The Abenaki man glanced at the rifle and at the expression in his neighbor's face. "I understand," he said at last. "The land is yours. But let us no longer tell each other our dreams."[49] Obomsawin has defied this logic, choosing instead to share her personal visions with the other side, something that I address in chapter 4, which describes documentary as a "middle ground" between cultures. For Obomsawin, the camera is the equalizer between cultures: it is the mechanism to record stories of Native dreams (and nightmares) and share them with other people far and wide.

So that this notion does not seem like an imposition of stereotype, I want to give one example of how dreams have propelled Obomsawin's cinematic life. In 1988, while in Edmonton, Obomsawin turned on the news in her hotel room and saw an interview with a woman named

Crothers. The woman was talking about Richard Cardinal, who had lived for a short time as a foster child in the home she shared with her husband. As we have seen, Cardinal, barely seventeen, had hanged himself in their backyard not long after coming to the Crothers's. "I felt so bad," Obomsawin remembers thinking about the plight of these well-meaning foster parents trapped in an insane system that shuttled a Native adolescent from home to home with jarring regularity. "I didn't want these people to feel sorry that they had taken him in," she said. Just as a humane gesture, well before she was planning to make a film about the incident, Obomsawin got in her rental car and drove out to the Crothers's house, thinking she just wanted to talk to them about what happened.

The Crotherses gave her a warm response, seeming eager to meet someone who knew firsthand about the challenges facing Native youths. After a few hours of drinks and conversation that lasted well past the dinner hour, the filmmaker looked out into the night and saw a massive snowstorm gathering force, and she wished that she could stay the night rather than risk the drive back to Edmonton. When the Crotherses realized the severity of the storm and extended an invitation to her, Obomsawin replied: "Yes, I'll stay, but I want to sleep in Richard's bed." Rather than being taken aback, the Crotherses seemed open to this gesture of solidarity between two Native people and led the filmmaker upstairs to the attic, where behind a trap door were four beautiful bedrooms, one of which had been Richard's until a few days earlier.[50]

"I slept in his bed," Obomsawin recalls, "and that night I was really concentrating and talking to him, and wondering if there is something that I should do. And I had this really very weird dream, and I was asking him how he felt. And I dreamt that I was in a place lying on some pieces of iron—very, very big pieces. And as I was lying there a car came down on me. I woke up and I was choking—it was coming down on me and there was nothing I could do. And that was my answer, and I thought, 'I have to do something.' So that's when I decided to make the film."[51]

Dreams and stories: these elements from an older world have gone into Obomsawin's decolonizing cinema, one that would expose the government's mistreatment of Native youths like Richard Cardinal. I believe that these Abenaki influences are critical to understanding what Obomsawin does with cinema, but I do not want to bring it all back to some stereotypical sense of Nativeness (essentialized connections to the natural world, an innate talent for vision quests, an intimate rapport with animals, etc.). These factors are influential in the lives of some Native artists but completely irrelevant in others. It is too simple to ghettoize Native creative expression by labeling it *indigenous aesthetics* and denying the welter of influences in which modern artists must work. No doubt, Abenaki traditions made their mark on Obomsawin's imagination, shaping her cinema in ways that are only beginning to be unraveled here. But, as much as her narrative style comes out of indigenous poetics, it also heeds the properties of classic rhetoric. In an era in which the documentary filmmaker has become one of the great engines of public persuasion, Obomsawin has used her cinema for a classic purpose: to make arguments about the nature of the social world and how it might be improved. Like orators from the classical past, she speaks with eloquence about the urgent concerns of the day, illuminating the follies of the past, and envisioning solutions for the future. Her success is dependent on her ability to meet the criteria that Aristotle proposed as characterizing effective rhetoric: an argument must appear *credible, convincing*, and *compelling*.[52] And meet those criteria she does. The credibility of her work comes from the stature of the speaker, the moral authority that Obomsawin has earned over the decades. Its convincing nature comes from the evidence that she is able to muster as a documentarian. Its compelling quality comes from the passion in her cinematic voice. All these qualities were as critical to Théophile Panadis as they are to Alanis Obomsawin, but Obomsawin added something to the stew that her relative never experienced: a gendered position as a Native woman.

3

A GENDERED GAZE?

In our language there is no word for he or she.

ALANIS OBOMSAWIN

Is it significant that the cardinal figure in Native filmmaking is female? Yes, I think so, although in ways that are more complex than I initially expected. I went into this project with some unexamined assumptions about the way gender identity would play out on-screen for Obomsawin, and I fear that this could have overdetermined my reading of her films. Yet, if I have labored under some initial naïveté in asking how her gender position influences her cinematic production, I am not alone: film scholars have debated the meaning of this question, in various forms, for the past three decades.[1] In the pages ahead, I hope to explore the challenges of generalizing about the so-called female gaze and about what happens when a woman is calling the shots in documentary production.

We might begin by asking if it is even possible for Obomsawin to present a female gaze when she works so often with a male-dominated crew of National Film Board (NFB) professionals, from sound recordists to cinematographers to editors? Although her collaborative process would seem to complicate the picture, it is, I think, possible that her filmmaking gaze remains gendered. After all, it was

FIGURE 16. Obomsawin during the shooting of *Richard Cardinal* in 1983. Courtesy of the filmmaker.

her controlling intelligence that shaped her film projects from start to finish and made her a nonfiction auteur rather than a mere cog in the NFB machine—after all, among other duties, she conceives, researches, writes, narrates, directs, and coproduces almost all her films. And she brings, I believe, a particular intelligence to all these roles, one that reflects her experience as a gendered—as much as a racialized—neocolonial subject. Her choice of subject, her style of storytelling, and her way of interacting with interviewees all seem to come out of an implicit sense of sisterhood running throughout her work as well as, of course, her commitment to her Abenaki past and her First Nations future.

The feminist impulse is most obvious in a film such as *Mother of Many Children*, although it shapes all Obomsawin's work to some degree. As the reading of the film in chapter 2 should suggest, *Mother of Many Children* is a clear tribute to the underappreciated strength and diversity of Native women as well as a call to unity for reasons of sisterhood as much as race. As such, its gender politics are unmistakable. Then why does the filmmaker seem hesitant to talk about gender with the same passion and effusion that she brings to discussions of race? I suspect that her reluctance is less a failure of political commitment than a product of her generational and class background. As an Abenaki woman who grew up in an impoverished small town during the Depression and the Second World War, she did not come of age when *feminist* was a common term, nor did she have a chance to attend a university, where feminist theory or women's studies might have been taught. This lack of exposure may explain why she views a feminist position as a potential limitation, as if it would restrict rather than open up her field of vision, and why she has sometimes kept her distance from the most overt forms of gender solidarity. For example, when in the 1980s the NFB launched its film unit for women under the name Studio D, Obomsawin claimed to give it her full support even though she did not want to work there. "I didn't want to be closed in a frame like that because I was concerned about the whole family," she said. "I could not say that I would only work with women."[2]

If she shied away from some aspects of feminist discourse emerging in the 1970s, Obomsawin was never blind to the gender inequities of postwar Canada—far from it. If anything, the thematic preoccupations of her work suggest that she was acutely aware of these cultural biases. From her earliest projects (such as *Mother of Many Children*) to more recent work (such *My Name Is Kahentiiosta* [1996]), she has focused her lens on Native women at risk as well as on those in successful leadership roles as artists and activists. For her own part, she sees her path as "a long road" toward respect as a Native woman working in a white male world like the NFB and has never romanticized the fate of the twice oppressed. Some indigenous female artists have executed a judo move that turns double marginalization to their advantage, at least as an act of rhetorical bravado. "Swimming against the tide becomes an exhilarating experience," says the Maori filmmaker Merata Mita, in many ways Obomsawin's equivalent in the Anglophone Southern Hemisphere. "It makes you strong," Mita claims. "I am completely without fear now. . . . [F]or 90 minutes or so, we have the capability of indigenising the screen in any part of the world our films are shown."[3] Characteristically, Obomsawin has expressed her own triumph over patriarchal obstacles in more subtle terms, usually alluding to the challenges that she has faced, before quickly switching the conversation to other areas.

At best gender was a small, occasional advantage to Obomsawin as a filmmaker. Like the earliest generations of female anthropologists, she may have found that interviewees would invite her into their homes to talk in front of a tape recorder far more readily than they might a male visitor. Her gender might also have made her seem less threatening to potential interviewees in power, including the male politicians and army officers with whom she sometimes does battle. Even young female filmmakers today are aware of this apparent silver lining to the old cult of domesticity in which women were consigned to the home front. "In the field, as a woman, it's a great advantage," said the documentarian Liz Garbus soon after making her first film, *The Farm*, in 1998. "I think that people are used to talking to women. They've always talked to their mothers. That was the one person in their family they went to talk to. In this society, people are more used to talking to women within [their] families, so I think that's an advantage."[4]

These are rosy scenarios to contemplate, but the systemic burden of gender oppression on Native women cannot be minimized so easily. Indeed, the accomplishment of a Native woman such as Obomsawin is all the more remarkable when considered in the larger political context of imagemaking in the West. Over the past century, cinema has not proved itself a welcome home to Native women, either in front of the camera or behind it. Of course, most of the damage has come *in front* of the camera, where Native women (or white actresses in redface) have been pilloried, parodied, and perversely fetishized. With few exceptions, their representational fate has been a twofold simplification: dichotomization or dismissal.

In the first instance lies the split between maiden and squaw, a dichotomy that casts Native women either as willing martyrs to European American expansionism or as animalistic sex objects who, when not meeting the carnal needs of white men, become silent drudges in the seemingly ceaseless toil of their culture. It goes without saying that neither side of this dichotomy has resulted in on-screen historical accuracy. The myth of the Indian maiden has given audiences the soft-focus romanticism of Ramona and Pocahontas, while the squaw has made her appearance, largely mute, in a series of characters including the cruelly imagined Look in *The Searchers* (1956), the libidinous Running Deer in *A Man Called Horse* (Elliot Silverstein, 1970), and their orgiastic counterparts who flock to Dustin Hoffman's side in *Little Big Man* (Arthur Penn, 1970).

Most of the time, however, even the worst stereotypes have been absent: when it comes to Native women, the Western gaze has been dismissive, uninterested, or pointed in the wrong direction altogether. Even on the dusty trail of the cowboy movie, the one genre in which a Native face might appear without astonishing the audience into some kind of seizure, Native women have been rendered insignificant or invisible (with very few exceptions).[5] "Silence surrounds the lives of Native North American women," writes Laura F. Klein and Lillian A. Ackerman, two historians of the subject. "We never hear their voices and are never told their tales."[6] Whenever something of Native women's lived experience makes it on-screen, it is too often a distorting fragment, one that suits the needs of a producer hungry for something romanticized, eroticized, objectified—certainly, not anything resembling a real Native woman.[7]

Obomsawin was no stranger to these stereotypes, as the discussion in chapter 1 of her schoolyard abuse and later media objectification should indicate. Especially when her career was first taking off in the 1960s and 1970s, white audiences must have had a hard time *not* viewing her through the warped lens of cultural prejudice to imagine her as the embodiment of the Pocahontas/Indian princess myth, in which the attractive Indian maiden provided "an important, nonthreatening symbol of white Americans' right to be here, because she was always willing to sacrifice her happiness, cultural identity, and even her life for the good of the new nation."[8] Obomsawin defied such stereotypes from the moment she began her public life as an artist. Working in the face of persistent objectification, she confounded expectations of Native women as silent, sacrificial, or merely sexual. This was true in three main phases of her career: as a singer and storyteller in her late twenties; as an education consultant in her thirties; and, finally, as a filmmaker in her forties and beyond.

At first Obomsawin was sui generis. I have already suggested that, for more than seven decades of North American cinema, Native women had been the object of looking, never the agent. The sudden appearance of a Native woman calling the shots must have startled and even disturbed some non-Native viewers. As E. Ann Kaplan has suggested, the gaze of the Other can destabilize white subjectivities, especially for those unaccustomed to seeing alternative points of view on the screen.[9] In the 1970s and 1980s, when Obomsawin's films were first appearing in theaters, college auditoriums, and classrooms, her work must have seemed disconcerting to those whites who expected confirmation of their lived experience, one in which Native women were either absent or presumed to conform to media mythologies. Yet here was a Native woman telling powerful nonfiction stories from her own point of view, serving as the obvious link between the diverse perspectives in her films, functioning as the controlling presence on-screen and off. There was nothing subordinate about Obomsawin's public persona as a filmmaker—occasionally defiant, usually soft-spoken, but always in charge, never the mere mouthpiece for someone else's agenda. Watching her films, we see only what she wants us to see, although her very personal vision is neither confrontational nor off-putting in its idiosyncrasies (given the relative popularity of her films, I can assume that I am not the only one who feels this way). Indeed, her personal vision as a Native woman is so compelling and well crafted that it is hard to throw it aside in favor of opposing points of view, such as those of the male government officials in Incident at Restigouche. If multiple perspectives are always provided in her films, Obomsawin makes clear which one she endorses. She may be subtle, but she is never silent.

Perhaps it is not surprising that a Native woman would be the first staff filmmaker at the prestigious NFB or that she would become so prominent in the world of indigenous media as the decades passed. Native women have always been essential creative forces in their communities, although the outside world tends to overlook this fact. As one Native scholar has observed: "The value accorded their women by Indian cultures has been vastly underrated—historically and today."[10] If women's roles in Native cultures have been too diverse to generalize without caveat, their vast cultural influence is undeniable, especially in the area that Obomsawin knows best—education. In a keynote address at the National Symposium on Aboriginal Women of Canada in 1989, the novelist Jeannette Armstrong (Okanagan) talked about the continuing power of Native women as teachers even after the devastations of colonialism. "In traditional Aboriginal society," she said, "it was women who shaped the thinking of its members in a loving, nurturing atmosphere within the base family unit." According to Armstrong, the current challenge is to preserve the traditional role of Native women as "insurers of the next generation."[11] So much did Obomsawin's work seem to fit this mandate that the symposium featured a retrospective of her films.

In addition to extending the general role of Native women as teachers into new forums such as educational kits and documentary filmmaking, Obomsawin has also brought her specific background as an Abenaki woman to her creative life. Historians suggest that the Abenakis had long employed a gender division of labor that resembles European American practices, at least on first glance. While boys learned to hunt with their fathers and prepared for their solitary vision quest, girls were pushed into a more communal direction— planting and harvesting crops, boiling maple syrup, tanning hides, and cooking meals with other women. Although their lives did not include opportunities for political and military glory, Abenaki women were regarded with far greater respect than European American males ever granted the "guardians" of their own domestic sphere (romantic protestations from the nineteenth century or Phyllis Schaffley notwithstanding). Among the Abenakis, the words *mother* and *grandmother* were terms of great honor, and women's labor was celebrated for its physical dexterity and visual artistry, whether in decorating shirts, embroidering winter coats, making jewelry, or weaving baskets.[12] Interestingly, in her filmmaking practice, Obomsawin seems to have fused traditional Abenaki gender roles. While she continues the artistic and pedagogical legacies of her grandmothers, she has also pushed her way into positions of cultural and political leadership as an activist and even into nonviolent forms of military engagement (as will become clear in later discussions of her work at Oka and Burnt Church). Working as a teacher, a visual artist, and a cultural leader from the pulpit of cinema, Obomsawin has transformed traditional gender expectations, both Native and non-Native, in ways that are fascinating—although not without parallel.

In the broadest outlines, Obomsawin's path has some resemblance to that of a number of white Canadian women who entered filmmaking in the early 1970s. Moving in the same general circles as Obomsawin, Anne Claire Porter, Mireille Dansereau, Aimée Danis, Louise Carré, and Hélène Girard, among others, constituted the first wave of Quebecois women behind the lens, laboring for the most part under the NFB logo. Within a few years, Lea Pool, Micheline Lanctot, Paule Baillargeon, Brigitte Sauriol, and others began working with private funding rather than NFB support. The watershed year for Canadian women in film was 1975, just as Obomsawin was shooting her first substantial project, *Mother of Many Children*. In this "international woman's year," a number of Quebecois women made their first films and, in the process, created a body of work that tended to reflect the preoccupations of 1970s feminism: a concern about gender oppression; a valorization of women's labor; and an acknowledgment of the diversity of women's experiences. Like *Mother of Many Children*, these films were, according to Nicole Giguére, "not so much protest films as attempts to allow women's voices to be heard on topics of importance to them." Without claiming a "specifically feminine form of cinematographic writing," Giguére has noted some common traits in the first wave of feminist nonfiction in Quebec. These directors' films tend to feature women on-screen; their cameras tend to maintain a respectful distance that works against crude voyeurism or aggressive interrogation; and their approach to political issues is often through the personal, rather than going straight at the outbreaks of political violence and nationalist crises that captured the interest of their male counterparts at the NFB. According to Giguére, "every male filmmaker worthy of respect has at least one film that is focused upon the political situation [in 1970s Quebec]," whereas women tended to work on a more intimate scale.[13]

Obomsawin does not fit neatly within these generalizations. Unlike most of her white counterparts in Quebec in the mid-1970s, she made films with a strong protest component (*Amisk*, e.g., was, as we have seen, designed to raise awareness about the ill effects of the James Bay hydroelectric project). By the early 1980s, she showed little fear of interrogation when it came to government ministers stepping on Native rights, even if she otherwise treated her interviewees with uncommon courtesy. And, as her career progressed, she would show an increasing desire to confront political crisis in its rawest forms, taking her camera ever closer to moments of violent strife in places like Restigouche and Oka. Moreover, in the four films that she would create in the 1990s after her summer behind the barricades at Oka, she would work on an epic scale that her white Quebecois counterparts certainly did not attempt in the 1970s. Simply put, once we move past the broadest strokes, Obomsawin has relatively little in common with her white Quebecois peers.

To get a closer analogue to Obomsawin's filmmaking practice, gender and race must, I suspect, be considered in tandem rather than in isolation.[14] Rather than considering the white Quebecois women who worked down the hall at the NFB or elsewhere in Montreal, we need to look further afield, to filmmakers who are indigenous *and* female. For example, we might consider Obomsawin's creative connections to aboriginal women in Australia like Tracey Moffatt, Rachel Perkins, Sally Riley, Darlene Johnson, Erica Glynn, or Frances Peters, although, even when the factors of gender and race are considered together, we have to be cautious about making blanket generalizations that would cover these very different filmmakers. One scholar has wisely suggested that these women should be understood as individual artists, only then pointing cautiously at some common threads, including "disturbing readings of colonial history," "stark accounts of familial trauma and connectedness," and an "ability to transform Aboriginal traditions, such as the mythological tropes and orality into cinematic forms, in their duty as cultural activists and in their exemplary artistic and aesthetic gifts."[15] These descriptions could also apply nicely to Obomsawin, even if her films are less self-revelatory than the ones from down under.[16]

Bringing together race and gender also suggests a comparison between Obomsawin and the Maori filmmaker Merata Mita, the first Maori and the first woman to make a feature-length film in New Zealand. The two celebrated women followed a strikingly similar path into filmmaking, even starting in much the same place. "We were offered no choices, given no alternative; television made us invisible," Mita says about growing up in New Zealand in the 1940s and 1950s, just a few years after Obomsawin was coming of age in Three Rivers. Like the Abenaki filmmaker, Mita was raised in her traditional culture, got her foot in the filmmaking door as a consultant on someone else's project, worked her way into the state-sponsored film production unit, and then shattered the glass ceiling to make her own hard-hitting political films like *Patu!* (1983), which the London Film Festival hailed as a "major documentary of our time."[17] Both have channeled their political passions into their cinema; both have worked with indigenous children; both have challenged comforting stereotypes about race relations in their seemingly progressive nations.[18] The only interesting divergence is where they ended up: unlike Obomsawin, Mita has since delved into fiction film and worked as a screenwriter, following a frequent pattern of documentarians "graduating" from the form, something that Obomsawin has steadfastly refused to do.[19]

Better still, Obomsawin can be compared with indigenous women filmmakers closer to home, especially documentarians like Carol Geddes, Loretta Todd, Lena Carr, Arlene Bowman, Barb Cranmer, and Sandra Day Osawa, all of whom work in Canada or the United States. Despite differences based on personal backgrounds, creative aspirations, available technologies, and institutional settings, these women share some meaningful common ground with the prolific Abenaki filmmaker. All of them, I believe, have drawn on their experiences as neocolonial subjects in sexist societies to articulate a set of five practices (or some combination thereof).

The first thread that runs through the work of Obomsawin and her closest peers is that it challenges the formation of national public memory in the United States and Canada from a Native standpoint. This includes a desire to reinscribe on film what has been erased from the historical record, namely, the agonies of the colonial past and their continuing legacies in the lives of Native people. Almost all Obomsawin's mature work—including *Incident at Restigouche* (1984), *Kanehsatake: 270 Years of Resistance* (1993), *My Name Is Kahentiiosta* (1996), *Spudwrench: Kahnawake Man* (1997), *Rocks at Whisky Trench* (2000), *Is the Crown at War with Us?* (2002), and *Our Nationhood* (2003)—challenges the received wisdom about indigenous people and reveals the tragic interplay of past and present in Native struggles to defend themselves against the onslaught of state authorities and oppressive public ignorance. Other Native women, such as the Vancouver-based filmmaker Loretta Todd, have followed Obomsawin's lead in challenging public memory. In *Forgotten Warriors: The Story of Canada's Aboriginal War Veterans* (1996), Todd examines the neglected role of Native soldiers in the Second World War as well as the little-known story of how the Canadian government seized thousands of acres of land from these same veterans, who had served their country with distinction. "These men had never been present in the consciousness and memory of Canada," she says. "I wanted to actually infiltrate the Canadian cultural memory, to try and implant us, to create images that were timeless, to almost create our own archive."[20] Another filmmaker based in Vancouver, Barb Cranmer, has shown how traditional ways of life remain alive on the northwest coast in films such as the award-winning *Qutuwas: People Gathering Together* (1997). "It was important for me to get the truth out there from our own perspective, and do it with the respect and integrity that comes from our community," Cranmer says. "That's been a driving force for me."[21] In a similar vein just south of the Forty-ninth Parallel, the Seattle-based Sandra Day Osawa has produced films such as *Usual and Accustomed Places* (1998), highlighting the difficulties that the Makah nation has faced with regard to fishing and hunting rights over the past hundred years; likewise, Osawa's powerful *Lighting the Seventh Fire* (1995) explores the same issue for the Anishinabe people in the Great Lakes region.

The second thread is that the work of these women insists on the significance of individual Native lives—and often with a gendered twist. Although their filmmaking sometimes focuses on Native men—as in Todd's *Today Is a Good Day: Remembering Chief*

Dan George (1998), Osawa's *Pepper's Powwow* (1995), or Obomsawin's *Spudwrench*—it more often explores the lives of Native women as a means to challenge the masculinist assumptions of European American culture. For Obomsawin this impulse is most obvious in *Mother of Many Children* and *My Name Is Kahentiiosta*, although at some level it runs throughout all her work. For example, she celebrates Native women by emphasizing their voices in the most literal sense: all her films demonstrate the transgressive power of female voice-over in documentary as an accompaniment to visual evidence. As Christopher E. Gittings has suggested, a female voice-over "evicts the 'symbolic father' from the cinematic space of enunciation . . . [thereby] troubling the historical male monopoly on this transcendental, authoritative form of cinematic representation."[22]

Obomsawin is not alone in her reliance on female voices, whether in narration or interviews. Barb Cranmer uses female narrators in most of her documentaries, including *Laxwesa Wa: Strength of the River* (1995), *Qutuwas*, and *T'Lina: The Rendering of Wealth* (1999). So does Sandra Osawa, who narrates *In the Heart of Big Mountain*, her 1988 exploration of the life of the Navajo matriarch Katherine Smith, who lost her traditional lands in Arizona when valuable natural resources were discovered there. Carol Geddes also fits this pattern, with films such as *Doctor, Lawyer, Indian Chief* (1988), which follows five Native women who are successful in various professions. In *Navajo Talking Picture* (1986) and *Song Journey* (1994), Arlene Bowman made two fascinating documentaries that revolve around the experiences of Navajo women, serving in both films as narrator and on-screen guide to the unfolding events. In the first film her relationship with her traditional Navajo grandmother takes center stage, while in the second it is the filmmaker's desire to find a place for herself and other alienated Native women in male-dominated portions of powwow culture.[23] The female voice is also central to Loretta Todd's work. *The Learning Path* (1991) begins with an on-camera introduction from the actor Tantoo Cardinal (Cree), before we hear the filmmaker's voice narrating painful stories of Native education in Canada.[24] Finally, in Lena Carr's *Kinaalda: Navajo Rite of Passage* (2000), the filmmaker narrates her thirteen-year-old niece's experience of a sacred ceremony marking her passage into womanhood.

The third thread is that these filmmakers often depict the political resilience and cultural creativity of Native people, thereby complicating the stereotypical Western view of Native subjectivity as simple, primitive, or monolithic. On the cultural side, Obomsawin's *Amisk* presents Native artistry in both contemporary and traditional terms, while *Christmas at Moose Factory* shares a charming glimpse of youthful creativity. Barb Cranmer has produced a moving tribute to traditional female weavers on the northwest coast entitled *Gwishalaayt: The Spirit Wraps around You* (2001), perhaps inspired by Loretta Todd's *Hands of History* (1994), which explores the work of four Native women artists and shows "the central role that Aboriginal women have always had in their communities of origin and in determining the survival of their people."[25] Todd is also the creative force behind *Today Is a Good Day*, which profiles the actor, poet, and cultural activist best known for his role in *Little Big Man*. Carol Geddes profiled a more obscure artist in her *Picturing a People: George Johnston, Tlingit Photographer* (1997), which details the life of a young man from the Yukon community of Teslin who was one of the first Native photographers to become "a creator of portraits and a keeper of his culture," as the NFB catalog puts it.[26] Perhaps the most prolific filmmaker working on the subject of Native artistry is Sandra Osawa, who in addition to her more political films has produced the exploration of Native jazz music *Pepper's Powwow* and a hilarious look at the career of a Native comedian, *On and Off the Res with Charlie Hill* (2000). (Osawa is now at work on a film about Maria Tallchief, the celebrated Osage ballerina.) Finally, Arlene Bowman's *Song Journey* gives a sympathetic look at Native women excluded from certain public performances at intertribal powwows.

As for political resilience, Obomsawin has never ceased touching on this theme, whether it is the strong women activists who appear in *Mother of Many Children* or the various acts of Native defiance that form the backbone of *Incident at Restigouche*, *Kanehsatake, Is the Crown at War with Us?* and *Our Nationhood*. Resilience is also a great theme in Osawa's work, most notably in *Lighting the Seventh*

Fire, Usual and Accustomed Places, and *In the Heart of Big Mountain,* as well as in Barb Cranmer's *Laxwesa Wa.* Loretta Todd has also explored this theme: *Forgotten Warriors* culminates with the aging veterans coming together from across Canada to perform a healing ceremony for the benefit of their fallen brethren.

The fourth thread is a desire to expose the deceptions of federal, state, and local governments in their dealings with Indian nations as well as the generalized white racism that supports such conduct. Almost all Obomsawin's films fit this description, most evidently in the conduct of rampaging whites (soldiers as well as civilians) in *Incident at Restigouche, Kanehsatake, Rocks at Whisky Trench,* and *Is the Crown at War with Us?* Barb Cranmer has also worked in this vein, showing in *Laxwesa Wa* how the Canadian government has "managed" Native fisheries into a disastrous condition that Native people are struggling to overcome. Loretta Todd has been unflinching in her depiction of the failings of the Canadian state in *Forgotten Warriors* and *The Learning Path,* while Sandra Osawa has followed suit in an American context, with hard-hitting exposés of government failures and generalized Indian hating in *Lighting the Seventh Fire, Usual and Accustomed Places,* and *In the Heart of Big Mountain.*

Finally, the fifth thread is a belief in the importance of cultural continuity and pan-tribal solidarity. Obomsawin gives great weight to both themes in *Amisk, Mother of Many Children, Poundmaker's Lodge, No Address,* and *Incident at Restigouche* as well as in her later films about the Oka crisis, and her peers have followed suit. Geddes's *Picturing a People* stresses the importance of documenting the Native past, Todd's *Forgotten Warriors* celebrates the links between aging veterans, Carr's *Kinaalda* and Cranmer's *T'lina* underscore the necessity of maintaining traditions, and even the title of Osawa's *Lighting the Seventh Fire* honors a traditional Anishinabe prophesy signaling "a return to traditional ways."

Even when the connection to the past is bittersweet, these filmmakers present it as worth pursuing. In her controversial *Navajo Talking Picture,* Arlene Bowman shares her desire to connect with traditional Navajo life as well as her frustrations in failing to achieve it, while her follow-up project, *Song Journey,* shows her making a more satisfying connection with her roots (broadly defined) and her seemingly newfound enthusiasm for pan-tribal solidarity. In the narration to the second film, Bowman describes feeling a need to visit her ancestral Navajo land, where she would, she believed, be brought "back to [her] traditions." She admits that she does not "normally come out to the reservation very much," and that her interest in powwows had long been "dormant," but that making *Song Journey* gave her an opportunity to rekindle both these interests. At the end of the film, Bowman enters a crowd of dancers and experiences a moment of pure pan-tribal solidarity. "I felt a sense of wholeness dancing with the people of all nations," she explains.

Like Obomsawin, Cranmer, Carr, Geddes, and Osawa, Bowman idealizes the notion of solidarity among Native people regardless of geography and generation. Underneath this insistence on the vital connections between Native people is a willingness to suspend judgment of localized problems such as tribal mismanagement, disputes with other tribes, and gender relations within particular Indian communities (any autocriticisms are muted). All these Native women filmmakers seem to avert their cameras from divisive issues that might weaken resolve against the perceived greater enemy: government neglect of Native rights and white ignorance about Native people. Even when a film acknowledges intertribal strife, as does Osawa's *In the Heart of Big Mountain* regarding Hopi-Navajo land disputes, it does so gently, reserving its anger for the federal government and private corporations, which are behind the dispossession of Navajo families.

Although some combination of these five factors is at play in almost all Obomsawin's films as well as those of her Native peers, I hope not to fall into the notion that position explains production, that is, not to lapse into the simplistic formulation that the combination of Native and woman results in a predictable textual outcome. As I have suggested throughout this chapter, generalizing about gender cannot be done without frequent caveats. Because I have outlined a few broader propositions about Obomsawin's work based on her gender position, I worry, along with Trinh T. Minh-ha, that "what we 'look for' is un/fortunately what we shall find" in academic inquiry.

Trinh has taken some shots at certain scholars such as anthropologists whom she sees as inventing patterns rather than finding them, as projecting their own imaginings on the bodies of the Other, all the while aspiring toward Malinowski's goal for ethnography: to "grasp the native point of view . . . to realize his vision of the world."[27]

Can one look for a structure without structuring? It is a question for a humanist like me as much as for social scientists. Trinh asks this rhetorical question and answers it in the negative, noting how difficult it is for the academic mind to admit that "recording, gathering, sorting, deciphering, analyzing and synthesizing, dissecting and articulating are already 'imposing our[/a] structure,' a structural activity, a structuring of the mind, a whole mentality."[28] Even in looking for the gendered qualities in Obomsawin's cinematic gaze, I have, I realize, my own structures to impose on indigenous media, although I retain the faint hope that my impositions are more suggestive and less totalizing than the ones found in the work of the grand taxonomers to whom Trinh objects most stringently. Rather than essentializing what female Native filmmakers like Obomsawin are doing, I want to acknowledge the contradictions and paradoxes embedded within their work, even as I scramble up the interpretive hill to take in a wider view of the subject.

In closing here, I want to return to my original question: Is it significant that the cardinal figure in Native filmmaking is female? I think that it is, for the reasons stated above as well for one final reason: Obomsawin's gendered subjectivity seems to underwrite one of the fundamental qualities of her work, an ethos of social concern that is based on an attitude of profound compassion. Obomsawin often expresses sympathy in response to suffering, a heightened appreciation of human interdependence, and a willingness to sacrifice her own needs to assist society's most vulnerable members. Characterizing Obomsawin in this way might seem disturbingly close to endorsing the stereotype of the hypernurturing, self-sacrificing Native woman, but this ethos is something that the filmmaker places front and center in her own interviews, activism, and documentaries.[29] Qualities that might seem like patriarchal legacies are transformed into an expansive force in her work, a force that takes her far beyond the

FIGURE 17. Obomsawin during the shooting of *Mother of Many Children* (1977). Courtesy of the filmmaker.

essentialist role of nurturing kin to a larger political context in which compassionate filmmaking becomes a kind of public service. Obomsawin is not succumbing to some mythology of domestic entrapment when, throughout her work, whether as a filmmaker, an education consultant, or a performer, she talks about the importance of children. Rather, she focuses her attention on *any* child at risk, not just members of her own family, clan, or tribe. In films such as *Christmas at Moose Factory, Mother of Many Children*, and *Richard Cardinal*, she reveals a sustained interest in the vulnerabilities of young people that few male documentarians have ever developed, suggesting that true compassion goes well beyond one-on-one nurturing. Within her films, compassion is a larger social practice that can ameliorate the worst problems in Canadian society, whether an imperfect foster-care system (*Richard Cardinal*), homelessness (*No Address*), substance abuse (*No Address*), or the neglect of Native land claims and fishing rights (*Incident at Restigouche, Amisk*, etc.).

Although these subjects fit within the progressive documentary tradition that begins with John Grierson in the 1930s (and whose influence I will discuss later), Obomsawin's ethos gives her a different angle of approach than her male nonfiction forebears. Unlike male documentarians who have pointed their cameras at, say, underprivileged children or the ill-housed working class, Obomsawin does not look through the lens and see abstract symbols of oppression. Rather, she *listens* to the subject and allows even the most vulnerable child to speak and be heard as a distinct individual—even posthumously (in the case of Richard Cardinal). Can Native children at risk be the subject of respectful cinematic attention, attention that neither pities nor sensationalizes? Obomsawin was one of the first Native women to answer that question with a resounding yes in her caring films about those who have been silenced and neglected, employing an ethos of compassion that seems to have come, at least in part, out of her gendered position as a Native woman in Canadian society, a position that, like most everything else, is a historical and social construction but palpable nonetheless in how it has shaped her attitudes. Without romanticizing or essentializing the traditional gender roles assigned to women, Obomsawin reveals how what was once a personal/familial ethos can be transposed to a societal stage through her particular brand of *cinema engagé*. Whether this ethos originated in old-fashioned European American gender constraints or perhaps simply in an older Abenaki emphasis on human interdependence is immaterial. What matters is how she has turned it into a powerful form of social critique that animates all her creative work.

4

DOCUMENTARY ON THE MIDDLE GROUND

The spark was an unlikely combination of golf and greed. In 1989 an ill-conceived plan for sixty luxury homes surrounding an upscale golf course set off the most serious confrontation between Native people and government authorities in contemporary Canadian history, something that for U.S. observers might have evoked the deadly 1973 standoff at Wounded Knee in South Dakota. Histories of the Oka standoff have shown what Alanis Obomsawin would reveal in four films during the 1990s: that, as in all such matters, the underlying reasons for the violence had been sown in centuries past.

For more than two hundred years, Mohawks in the town Kanehsatake had endured the expansion of the adjacent town, Oka, whose largely white population kept spreading into lands that the Mohawks considered their rightful property. Beginning in the 1780s, the Mohawks had delivered a number of petitions requesting formal title to land they believed themselves to have been promised. Although the tribe had little success in their quest for official land rights over the next two hundred years, some outsiders, including figures within the Canadian government, were sympathetic to their demands. When apprised of the brewing conflict over the golf course in the late 1980s, John Ciaccia, the minister for Indian affairs in Quebec, wrote to the mayor of Oka, Jean Ouellette, about the Mohawk predicament: "These people have seen their lands disappear without having been consulted or compensated, and that, in my opinion, is unfair and un-just, especially over a golf course." Contemporary local politicians, however, were no more attuned to tribal concerns than their pre-decessors had been in the past. When asked at a municipal council meeting in March 1989 if he had consulted the Mohawks about his development plan for the golf course, Ouellette scoffed: "You know you can't talk to the Indians."[1] To the Mohawks this was the final insult in a long chain of abuses.

Having witnessed too many incremental steps toward the long-term erosion of their lands, Mohawk activists took a stand over a small tract of forest that included a number of Mohawk graves. At first these activists relied on peaceful protest to secure what they considered a sacred plot of land, working the legal and political channels with their scant resources. When the white city council continued to support plans for the golf course, they turned to more aggressive forms of dissent, culminating in their decision to arm themselves and take up defensive positions on the disputed land.

Furious, Ouellette ignored Ciaccia, who had requested that he not involve the provincial police, and called in the Sûreté du Québec (sq) to settle the matter once and for all. Its officers more often spending their time on country roads in pursuit of speeding motorists, the sq was not trained for military-style exercises against indigenous people or anyone else. But now dozens of officers showed up in the sleepy town with assault rifles and bulletproof vests, wielding billy clubs and tear gas, reminiscent of the situation that Obomsawin recounted in her 1984 *Incident at Restigouche*. Rather than inspiring confidence that the situation would soon be settled, their arrival created dread and tension among local people on both sides of the issue.[2] According to one observer, Mohawk children were asking their parents when, not if, the police were going to shoot them.[3]

Instead of giving in to the pressures of the sq, the Mohawk *warriors*, as they became known, began digging into trenches on the disputed land. "When it became clear that the sq was preparing to move in with armed force," one Canadian journalist wrote, "the Mohawk protestors decided to call in the Warriors from the larger communities of Kahnawake and Akwesasne."[4] In response to Mohawk defiance, the local authorities decided that it was time for bold action.

The morning of the raid was horrific. Police tried to rush into the woods along a narrow road, but, facing gunfire from the pines, they were forced to abandon their vehicles and retreat. Frustrated warriors pumped bullets into deserted police cars, ransacked them for weapons, and then piled them into a twisted heap of scrap metal to block further access to the road. The raid had begun just before dawn, with no more than thirty warriors stationed in the pines, but soon after it started supporters began pouring into the woods. Within hours of the first gunshots, seventy-five warriors had assembled and were taking stock of their collective arsenal—a few dozen shotguns and .22-caliber rifles, ten bolt-action .303s, a small number of pistols, and a disturbingly large number of assault rifles, including automatic CAR-15s, M-1 carbines, and even a Russian-designed machine gun known as an RPK. Although the warriors were still outgunned and outnumbered, they had some advantages: the SQ did not know the woods, did not know how many warriors it was facing, and did not know about the dozens of guns and thousands of rounds of ammunition.[5]

Surging into the woods in the early morning haze, the SQ soon discovered the seriousness of the opposition as Mohawk weapons began to fire. As one journalist described the scene: "A short, fierce gun battle erupted, and a bullet ripped through a seam in Corporal Marcel Lemay's flack jacket and pierced his heart." While it would later be determined that the bullet that killed Lemay probably had come from the warriors' position (even though the gun that had fired on him would never be found), at the time no one was certain whether the officer had been the victim of friendly fire or a warrior's rifle. The Mohawks denied responsibility, even though some recalled hearing one of their comrades shouting, "I think we got one," in the heat of battle.[6]

According to journalists' accounts, the situation got worse from there. "There's only one way we're going to be able to build the golf course," Ouellette had warned ominously long before the violence began. "That's with the army."[7] Yet, even after the SQ raid and the shooting of Corporal Lemay, bringing in the armed forces seemed unlikely. Federal Indian Affairs Minister Tom Siddon stood in the pines to reassure journalists and other observers: "This is a place of tranquility and great historical and spiritual significance to the people of the Mohawk Nation, and we respect that." Yet, just a few days after this public declaration, the Canadian armed forces were dispatched to replace the exhausted sq on the barricades.[8] With tanks, helicopters, and well-armed soldiers lining the razor wire that had now been strung through the forest, the standoff would last long into the summer, with the warriors eventually falling back to a building that housed a Native treatment center for addiction. They remained under siege in the treatment center until an agreement was reached, seventy-eight days after the initial raid.

No one living in Canada could have missed this dramatic crisis on the barricades between Native and white. Night after night, the news coverage had been extensive, if short on knowledge about the background of Native land claims. One Mohawk observer, Dan David, claimed that most journalists were unwilling to seek the truth, preferring to lose themselves in a haze of stereotype and simplification about "the shoot-out at the Oka Corral," as one British paper dubbed it. "To most of them, this was just a cop story," David complained about the journalists, adding that the standoff was painted as if "the police and soldiers were there to 'restore law and order,' to put things back the way they were." He believed that few outside journalists could appreciate the price of going back to the status quo, which he described as "a certain and steady ride down a one-way street to an oblivion called assimilation."[9]

Instead of seeking the truth, the news coverage often relied on government press releases and other one-sided sources. One Quebecois writer described the surreal scene that he witnessed on Canadian television during the two and a half months of crisis:

Like a succession of heat hallucinations, army tanks ground through a dappled Canadian forest at the height of summer; teenage boys in battle gear slowly encircled the Kanehsatake Mohawks with bale after bale of razor wire; and the armed

Warriors with their *noms de guerre* like Spudwrench, Wizard, and Lasagna jabbed heavily sedated TV viewers coming down from *Twin Peaks*. Eventually we saw a white mob in jogging shorts stoning cars filled with Indian old people and children. We watched as the Prime Minister, in his oddly platitudinous style, congratulated 'all members of the armed forces of Canada for their forbearance.' And we're still seeing the official media logo of the crisis: a poster-perfect soldier and a masked Mohawk warrior standing inches apart, eyeball-to-eyeball.[10]

This was the depressing media landscape that Obomsawin encountered in the summer of 1991, but she was in a rare position to do something about it. Never before had an indigenous person been armed with the tools of the electronic mass media when this sort of crisis was unfolding; never before had it been possible to create a well-funded portrait of state violence against Native people. The result was an extraordinary cinematic record of Oka that would challenge the ignorance and bias governing mainstream press coverage.

On the morning of the raid, in the middle of work on *Le Patro*, her short film about a Montreal community center, Obomsawin heard the news on the radio and knew what she had to do. Driving immediately to Oka, she surveyed the situation, realized the importance of what was happening, and sped back to Montreal to gather what she needed. Not wanting to sit through the endless hassles that had waylaid her efforts with *Incident at Restigouche*, she was firm in her resolve to outrun the bureaucracy this time. "I told the Film Board, 'I'm changing production and I've got to get there right now.' "[11] Ten years had passed since Restigouche, and now, with seven films and various awards to her credit, she was someone to be reckoned with at the National Film Board (NFB). When she got what she wanted, she headed out to Oka with a cameraman and an assistant, doing sound herself until another crew member joined her in the warriors' camp.

"Alanis Obomsawin did not spare the viewers," a reviewer would later write about her film, "just as she and her film crew were not spared a single sickening moment of the stand-off."[12] Her willingness to remain inside the barricades to record the unfolding events, not knowing what kind of violence might erupt, represents one of the great acts of courage in the history of documentary filmmaking. Even at sixty-one years of age, she was willing to endure near battle conditions as well as simple discomforts such as sleeping on the cold ground. For seventy-eight days she remained in place while her various crew members, mostly younger male technicians, were anxious to rotate out of harm's way—"some of them didn't want to stay there too long," she recalls without passing judgment. As someone with an antipathy to firearms, she had to steel herself to stay where everyone— warriors, police, soldiers—was heavily armed. Most nights she could barely sleep a few hours before a new emergency erupted along the razor wire and she had to run through the darkness to where it was happening, believing that her presence with the camera would have a restraining effect on the army. "I was told many times that the fact that I was there, especially as a Native person, [meant] that the police and army wouldn't do certain things there with the camera."[13]

Not that the warriors were getting special treatment from the media in general—far from it. In the long, slow hours between flare-ups of violence and tension, Obomsawin and the warriors watched the television coverage with a skeptical eye, comparing the slant of the CBC reports to what they could see happening around them. With so much of the mainstream coverage seeming to regurgitate the official line provided in army briefings and ministerial press conferences, the warriors were infuriated by their inability to get their own perspective to the Canadian public. For a long time, Obomsawin remembers, the few reporters inside the barricades were not allowed to send footage over the razor wire or even communicate with their own news organizations. When telephone contact was finally established across the barricade, Obomsawin listened to her NFB superiors pleading for her to cross to safety. Although supportive of what she was doing in principle, they were concerned about the considerable expense of keeping her crew in place, not to mention her well-being. Their fears were not irrational. "It was like wartime," she said, remembering the rumbling tanks on the perimeter, the army grunts sweeping the woods with search lights, the oppressive drone of helicopters over-

FIGURE 18. Obomsawin sleeping on the ground behind the barricades while making *Kanehsatake: 270 Years of Resistance* (1993). Courtesy of the film-maker.

head, the moments of uncertainty when the warriors would run out of their bunkers at 3:00 a.m. to confront soldiers, sometimes with insults or hurled eggs, while the angry soldiers fixed their bayonets in response.[14]

The worse it got, the more Obomsawin felt the need to stay. In the middle of the standoff, the CBC pulled its reporters out, meaning that, as Obomsawin recalls, "there was quite a bit of stuff that the CBC didn't have [on film] because they weren't there to film it." She was determined to remain in place, a Native witness to potential atrocities, no matter what her NFB colleagues told her, no matter what other observers were doing. Right until the end of the standoff, she stuck behind the barricades, leaving only the day before the warriors planned to exit. Waiting for her at the razor wire were the head of the NFB and her lawyer, both of whom were eager to prevent the confiscation of her footage (a number of journalists had lost their film to the soldiers in this manner). On the following day the warriors came across the barricades as she anticipated, and Obomsawin made the most of her frontline position to record what the warriors called their *exit* rather than their surrender. According to one review of her 1993 *Kanehsatake*: "Shocked and sickened viewers have to remind themselves that these are our valiant Canadian 'peacekeepers,' sanctioned by the Mulroney government, who are grinding people's faces into the pavement, roughing up women and separating them from their children."[15] Such painful scenes of Native exodus from the pines would be at the heart of a later film she would make about Oka, *Rocks at Whisky Trench* (2000), which she would release a decade after the crisis. But now her task was making the film that would be called *Kanehsatake: 270 Years of Resistance*, the first of her four searing documentaries about what happened that summer.

In the fall of 1991, she began working on the footage that she and her crew had captured at Oka, trying to shape a narrative out of the chaos that they had witnessed. Working with three different crews over the seventy-eight-day standoff, she had amassed over 250 hours of sixteen-millimeter film, a vast quantity, and one that did not even include another fifty hours of stock shots that would be added for consideration in the editing room. The amount of footage was overwhelming even to her award-winning editor, Yurij Luhovy, who said that it was far more than had ever been shot for an NFB film. "It was a huge project," he said. "Just to give you an idea of the magnitude, it took me six months just to view the raw footage and mark the best elements in the film. Then, two of my assistants would remove the selected elements from which I then made the first rough-cut assembly consisting of twelve of the best hours shot."[16] The results of all this work and struggle are impressive: a brilliant film of occupation and resistance that echoes with the sounds of crying children, grim-faced soldiers, high-velocity gunfire, and grinding tank treads—none of which a viewer would expect to see in the placid Canada of stereotype.

Reading *Kanehsatake: 270 Years of Resistance*

Obomsawin's epic document of state violence and indigenous sovereignty under fire begins, appropriately enough, with gravestones. Each one is carved with a Mohawk name from the 1820s, each one a testament to the tribe's deep roots in the woods around Oka. In voice-over we hear the calming tone of the filmmaker's voice as she provides a thumbnail sketch of the crisis. She tells us about the golf-course expansion while showing images of affluent whites on a putting green, then pans across a stand of majestic trees as she describes the encroachment onto "Mohawk land." Although in these opening minutes she has not expressed her explicit judgment of who is right and who is wrong, her use of this phrase, which elides the complex legal status of the pines, sets her squarely in the Mohawk camp on the most fundamental issue in the film.

As if to underscore her place in the Mohawk camp where she literally lived for those seventy-eight days, Obomsawin begins sharing sympathetic testimonials from the Native side, beginning with two Mohawk women, Ellen Gabriel and Kahentiiosta, both of whom were seasoned activists and veterans of similar conflicts (although the film does not acknowledge this fact, nor does Obomsawin's later film on Kahentiiosta). A well-spoken young woman, Ellen Gabriel tells the camera about the raid onto Mohawk land: "We were fighting something without a spirit—they were like robots." Cut to menacing images of gun-toting soldiers in gas masks, their faces utterly obscured, and simulated footage from a war zone: uncontrolled camera movements in the woods; the sound of gunfire; angry voices. Obomsawin then appears in the woods with "Mad Jap," as the Mohawk leader Robert Skidders decided to code-name himself during the standoff. "I think we tried to conduct ourselves in a very honorable way," he tells her, "because we did try to avoid violence."

In the first moments of the film, Obomsawin has cast her Mohawk subjects in a warm light while suggesting that the Canadian police and soldiers are inhuman cogs in a vast war machine. Other scholars, however, have detected a more ambivalent posture in the film. In an excellent article about *Kanehsatake*, Zuzana Pick has described the "contrast in rhetorical forms" that shapes the opening segment of Obomsawin's most important film. According to Pick, the filmmaker shifts between autobiography, interpretation, reminiscence, and chronicle like a practiced storyteller and, in the process, is able to "integrate affective, experiential, and interpretive modes of speech." As Pick sees it, the filmmaker's point of view is strong but not exclusive: rather than sanding off the edges of competing accounts in order to make them fit into a smoother narrative, she allows the various stories to coexist, rubbing against one another, jostling in juxtaposition for the viewer to sort out. Pick claims that this inclusivist vision "disrupts the unified position of the narrating subject" and subverts the possibility of a single "interpretative frame," but this strikes me as a mild overstatement.[17]

As in all her films, Obomsawin has a subtle but strong presence throughout the narrative, one that never leaves the viewer uncertain of who is telling the story (or why). Even when she strives for balance, which she often does in her coverage of Oka, Obomsawin leaves no doubt where her allegiances lie, as we can see in her fixation on the use of the word *savage*. "And they call us savages," one warrior tells the camera in disgust, referring to white Canadians and their military representatives. At several points in the film Obomsawin uses reference to that loaded word from her childhood in order to invert the stereotype onto its white perpetrators. Later in the first half hour of the film, she uses nighttime footage of rioting whites, some of them shirtless, burning an effigy of a Mohawk warrior and yelling "Savages!" because the Mohawks had shut down a bridge used by sixty-five thousand cars each day. The chaos of the French Canadians appears in stark contrast to the composure of the warriors being interviewed in *Kanehsatake*, a fact that seems even more striking if the viewer stops to contrast the reasons for their grievances: the whites are rioting in the streets because the Mohawks have closed a major bridge, resulting in longer drive times to work and shopping, while the Mohawks are taking up arms to defend their land after being cheated and deceived for three centuries.

Yet Pick is not the only scholar who sees Obomsawin's work as an "open text" with various voices in more or less equal competition. Another is Laura Marks, who writes about *Kanehsatake* in her recent *The Skin of the Film*. After mistakenly identifying the filmmaker as "Anishnabek," Marks then overestimates the democratic nature of the assembled voices in Obomsawin's greatest documentary, claiming that the filmmaker "does not put one Mohawk in the position of spokesperson, for that would merely mimic the authoritarianism of government officials." I agree: the film does not privilege the testimony of any one Mohawk; it privileges that of two, Ellen Gabriel and Kahentiiosta, whose eloquent voices begin and end the film, and whose sane and thoughtful commentary provides a touchstone for the narrative at a number of points. Marks also argues that the filmmaker is interested in Native voices whose claim to the pines "cannot be expressed in the terms of legalistic, territorial discourse," but that too strikes me as wrong. For the past two centuries, the warriors have developed a "territorial" discourse all their own, talking about their land claims in a manner that is mythic and even sentimental but also quite legalistic—the latter quality has been developed out of necessity in the Canadian courts where Mohawks have pressed their claims since the eighteenth century. Contrary to what Marks implies, their discourse is not naturalistic, and their claims are not spoken into the wind between the trees for the exclusive benefit of songbirds and beavers: Mohawks have used the courts, political action, civil disobedience, and occasional violence for 270 years of resistance, as the title of the film suggests. Obomsawin makes clear that she is part of this long path of resistance, yet Marks believes that the filmmaker "maintains a skeptical distance from seemingly authoritative visible evidence."[18] Obomsawin does avoid the strident tone that reduces some political filmmaking to the level of rude polemic, but this is the same filmmaker who often talks about "our people" in her voice-over narration. If she does not use that particular phrase in *Kanehsatake*, she tips her hand in another way, choosing to place herself in shot next to her Native interview subjects, something she does not do with whites.[19]

I suspect that Obomsawin is more of an old-fashioned positivist than Marks realizes. Rather than letting the evidence pile up in any direction that suits the audience, she uses her thematic emphases, camera work, editing, and music to illuminate a single path of plausibility through her material—if other interpretations always remain possible (as is always the case with cinematic texts), she seems to suggest that the facts on display come with a strongly preferred reading, which is her own. Even if she is less overtly demonstrative about her beliefs than some political artists, and if she seems relatively even-handed as a result, she still does not maintain a "skeptical distance" toward anything Native in her films—her passionate commitment requires intimacy and faith in relation to the Mohawk position. She depends on us overcoming our skeptical distance toward her images of circling military helicopters, rumbling tanks, and atrocities such as blackjack beatings of Mohawk men. She depends on us seeing them as she does: as unmistakable symbols of brutal neocolonialism, racism, and disregard for Native rights. She is a partisan, if relatively subtle in her allegiances, and she expresses neither skepticism nor distance toward her footage of Native mistreatment.

Yet, much to its credit, *Kanehsatake* is a partisan film that does not indulge simplistic pieties of oppression and resistance. In it Obomsawin shows how the warriors do not stand in opposition to an unbroken white monolith. Official documents, meetings, and press conferences appear on-screen, but she highlights the conflicts between official versions—some ministers are openly sympathetic to the Mohawks, while others express bellicosity. (Local whites get the same balanced treatment—some are shown responding with contempt toward Native people, while others share their heartfelt critiques of the raid.) Obomsawin often relies on the principle of ironic juxtaposition to undercut the official version of events. For example, government officials tell the media that "no restrictions" are being placed on the delivery of food across the barricades, but then several Mohawks and one Red Cross worker reveal the opposite to be true. Official rhetoric takes a beating in the next scene as well, which revises one of the stereotypical tableaux of Native-white relations. Early on, when white officials meet with Mohawk leaders to formulate a truce in order to avoid sending the army onto Native land, we see Ellen Gabriel giving an eloquent speech about the problems facing Mohawk people, then several government officials promising to remedy the situation. Obomsawin cuts to Federal Indian Affairs Minister Tom Siddon, a wealthy looking white man, making his pledge about this "place of tranquility" being respected, although most Canadian viewers would know that these words would soon be betrayed, adding even greater poignancy to the next statement. A middle-aged Mohawk man stands up, looks at the table where the government officials are seated, and addresses the crowd: "As far back as I can remember, there has always been a struggle," he says. "I hope that the creator will give you the

FIGURE 19. Across the razor wire in *Kanehsatake: 270 Years of Resistance* (1993). Photograph by: Shaney Komulainen. Used with the permission of the photographer.

integrity to fulfill these things." The camera pans toward Siddon and the other officials smiling awkwardly. The scene evokes the European paintings of treaty signings from the eighteenth century, except now the Natives are talking back, speaking for themselves, putting the federal officials on the spot rather than posing mute on the canvas.

As this scene might suggest, the filmmaker emphasizes the importance of Native self-determination, historical awareness, and pan-tribal solidarity in *Kanehsatake* as she does throughout her oeuvre. At a large rally for aboriginal rights near Oka, her camera pans across the crowd, while her microphone captures the energetic drum circles and the various speakers. "It is us who can determine what is best for us," says Chief Bill Traverse, drums pulsating in the background. "History can teach you many things, but you have got to listen," another speaker says. Later Obomsawin cuts to a huge banner over the barricade that asks, "ARE YOU AWARE THAT THIS IS MOHAWK LAND?" in both English and French, seeming to echo the famous statement in the title of the 1969 NFB Challenge for Change film *You Are on Indian Land*. And at several points in the film she shows Native people coming from South Dakota, British Columbia, and even Mexico in support of the warriors. "Even if we are not recognized as a nation [because of the standoff], it's brought all Indian nations together," says Ronnie Cross, also known as "Lasagna" for his Italian and Mohawk heritage. While Cross talks, Obomsawin cuts to a sign posted in the woods with the words "LASAGNA DEAD MEAT" scrawled on it by the soldiers.

Lasagna is not the only one at risk. The tension is palpable in *Kanehsatake* from the opening scenes to the closing moments, in part because we do not know quite how it will turn out for Obomsawin herself. In watching the filmmaker in danger behind the barricades, the viewer might be reminded of classic war documentaries like John Huston's *The Battle of San Pietro* (1945), which offer one of the unique pleasures of documentary, as described by the Hungarian screenwriter Béla Bálazs in his 1945 *The Theory of Film*. Bálazs suggested that nonfiction cinema was different from all other art forms because "the reality being presented is not yet completed," that we do not even know whether the filmmaker will survive what she is shooting at, say, Oka, and that "it is this tangible being-present that gives the documentary the peculiar tension no other art can produce."[20] Even if the viewer infers Obomsawin's safety from the fact of the completed film now running, it is not self-evident that she (or the other principals) will emerge unscathed.

Violence permeates the air at Kanehsatake, although most of it seems to blow across the barricades from where the soldiers and their white supporters are waiting for the Mohawks to make a reckless move. In this manner the film offers a biting critique of white violence, with nasty scenes of rioting French Canadians hurling garbage at heavily shielded police to protest the bridge closure and even nastier images of state violence against Mohawk people. When the army replaces the SQ at the barricades, Obomsawin lets her camera linger on a vast line of tanks, armored personnel carriers, military helicopters, and soldiers with shoulder-mounted bazookas as well as on individual acts of aggression on the part of members of the Canadian Forces—never has the Canadian state seemed so malevolent in cinema. Yet *Kanehsatake* is not a simplistic partisan film: it depicts violence on all sides. In one scene we see a large Native man punching and kicking a police officer. In another an ominous-looking Mohawk teenager calling himself "Freddy Krueger," after the serial-killer protagonist of the *Nightmare on Elm Street* movies, appears on-screen in full body camouflage and bandana-covered face, saying: "Hopefully I'll come out of this alive." If the film does not offer much explicit critique of the macho posturing that some male warriors adopted, Obomsawin's inclusion of this material does encourage such critical readings.

"The film is about the struggle," one Canadian writer has noted, "not about 'victims' or 'politics.' The people who were characterized in much of the media and by the military as criminals and extremists are instead painted as courageous and creative in Obomsawin's careful reconstruction of the events."[21] Yet, if Obomsawin chooses not to offer a simple glorification of Native resistance, it is, I believe, because she does not want to estrange potential viewers who are not already converted to the cause of Native rights. Accepting an honorary doctorate from Trent University in 2003, she told the graduating students "to keep an open circle so that you don't alienate anyone," and *Kanehsatake* seems a clear product of this lifelong philosophy. Writing in *Maclean's* in 1994, the journalist Barry Came observed that Obomsawin's version of Oka is constructed without obvious heroes and villains, at least not those of the cartoonish sort. Even when the scheming mayor of Oka, Jean Ouellette, seems to present himself as a "leading contender" for what Came dubs the role of villain, the filmmaker is quick to shift attention to the larger context of the golf-course controversy that includes, as the subtitle of the film has it, "270 years of resistance."[22]

Sketching out these 270 years in the next section of the film, Obomsawin gives a clear but awkward historical overview of Mohawk dispossession beginning in the seventeenth century—generally, she is more skilled at working with living human beings than at manipulating static images like historic paintings and maps, although the information is clear and shows the duplicity that the Mohawks have faced, especially with regard to the Sulpician order of the Catholic Church, which abused its crown-appointed control over their land. Always seeking balance even if her scales tip toward the Native side, Obomsawin follows the ominous footage of the church with a brief positive image of Christianity in Oka: a Native minister clutching a

Bible overhead while soldiers prevent him from crossing the barricade. "In the name of Jesus," he pleads to no avail as the soldiers stand firm.

After this brief historical overview, the film returns to the present day. Drums are beating on the sound track, and tanks are rolling into position on Mohawk hills. Unarmed Mohawk men and women are stopping soldiers with M-16s, demanding to know what they are doing on their land. A warrior talks about police brutality endured during an arrest, and a shaken father describes a soldier shooting into the ground near his son, the mud kicking onto their faces from the ricochet. After a Native man complains about the Catholic Church's abuse of Native rights, a traditional Mohawk "false face" mask appears stuck in the ground as an ominous sign, one that is confirmed when a young Mohawk woman named Chicky promises: "You're going to see a 'death feast.' . . . That's what they want." Chicky then talks about the need to stand up and fight back, as Obomsawin's protagonists often do. "No more compassion. I've had it," Chicky swears. "I'll never bow down to them because they'll just step on your hands."

The next image provides a jarring microcosm of the film overall. Shot from the ground with a beautiful blue sky in the background, the camera captures a masked warrior named "Psycho" warning a army colonel: "From here on in, we're going to be burying each other." The response from the colonel is just as threatening: "No Canadian military soldier will fire one shot . . . first." The last word is freighted with meaning: retaliation will be fierce. In case the viewer suspects this exchange is mere rhetoric, Obomsawin cuts to a French Canadian mob attacking a convoy of Mohawk elders, women, and children leaving the reserve in fear of escalating violence between the army and the warriors—softball-sized rocks shatter windows and land inside their cars, with one hitting a seventy-seven-year-old man (this exodus will become the subject of the later *Rocks at Whisky Trench*). Somewhat balancing her coverage with a quick nod in the opposite direction (where lesser sins are found, according to the film), Obomsawin then describes how two warriors vandalized a nearby house, although she is quick to mention that "the community"—a phrase that for her signifies the Mohawks and their supporters—was opposed to such criminal acts. It is clear that she wants the Mohawk warriors to appear as "soldiers of the Mohawk nation" engaged in legitimate resistance rather than as thugs and criminals, as Canadian officials, including Prime Minister Brian Mulroney, would have it. (Mulroney and other government officials used the word *terrorists* at the time, if not with the frequency it might been deployed in the post-9/11 media.)

When the warriors fall back into the treatment center to make their last stand, the film falls into darkness, with silhouettes moving in front of military krieg lights and Mohawk campfires. The images seem straight out of news coverage of a distant conflict, perhaps Guatemala in the 1980s or Angola in the 1970s. There are even echoes of 1960s Vietnam with a chopper roaring overhead in the darkness, an indigenous female voice singing on the sound track, and a square-jawed army officer, haughty in his black beret for the sake of the news cameras, looking fierce and mad like the young Kurtz in the photographs shown to Captain Willard in Francis Ford Coppola's *Apocalypse Now* (1979).

As much as it evokes war images from the nightly news and Hollywood, *Kanehsatake* is also about the phenomenon of media warfare, about using the camera as a weapon in both defensive and offensive capacities. We see an unarmed Mohawk defying a line of tanks in a scene right out of Tiananmen Square, seeming to play to the cameras in a way that evokes the famous footage from the previous summer. We also see the warriors watching their own television coverage while behind the barricades, appearing frustrated by the distortions of the non-Native media. Through these and many other images, Obomsawin emphasizes how the mainstream reporters have a partial view at best, with soldiers keeping most of them behind a cordon that literally separates them from the crucial events. At one point she includes footage of white reporters clamoring for the proper spelling of an officer's name in a way that implies an obsequious, spoon-fed relationship to the military. Then, in a particularly revealing shot, she shows a soldier taking surveillance photographs of the warriors with a telephoto lens, prompting the warriors to hang a massive canvas curtain to obstruct the army's view into the treatment center. While this action causes enormous frustration in the army ranks, Obomsawin is able to continue filming behind the curtain and create a scene that provides a potent metaphor for the warriors' actions at Oka as well as for Obomsawin's media activism: the curtain is an attempt to control the angle of vision on their lives and histories as Native peoples, an attempt to stop the destructive gaze of the Canadian government and commercial interests on their land, an attempt to privilege the Native angle of vision in understanding the significance of the pines.

Obomsawin continues to highlight the significance of vision in the scenes ahead. "We're your eyes," a sympathetic white photojournalist says after crawling under razor wire to join the warriors, much to the irritation of the army. "They're trying to blind us by getting us out of here," he says. "I'm not going to be blinded. I want you to see; I want the people to see what's going to happen." Obomsawin transitions to a night scene in which the army is harassing the warriors with searchlights before deciding to tear down the curtain. "We can't see," an annoyed officer yells in the darkness. "The only reason they are doing this [tearing down the curtain] is that they cannot see," Mad Jap explains to his comrades as the soldiers swirl through the darkness toward the curtain. "Get that fucking light off me!" Mad Jap yells at them, before the warriors return the favor with a bright light of their own. "You should be real proud," Mad Jap taunts one of the soldiers, illuminated in the bushes like the proverbial deer in the headlights. "They're gonna have your pictures in the papers . . . as *cowards*," he shouts. "Fuck off," the soldier says in response, looking straight at the camera with cold disgust.

Mad Jap's comment has an unintended significance for what Obomsawin is doing with her media work. The power to place someone's picture in the paper (or in a film) is an essential one in her universe, where political power comes from controlling the process of witnessing, documenting, and disseminating what is happening on the ground in moments of political and social turmoil. (Obomsawin often acts as a witness with her camera crew, which may account for the great reliance on actuality footage in her films, in which we seem to see events as they are happening, almost as if seeing through her eyes, rather than watching a never-ending stream of talking-head interviews or enduring a pedantic "voice-of-God" narration over a slide show of historic photographs.) At one point in *Kanehsatake* we catch a glimpse of Obomsawin behind the barricades as soldiers intercept rolls of film thrown from photojournalists to their editors, an obvious example of the state protecting the official version from democratic tampering. The battle to control the flow of visual evidence continues during tense negotiations over the razor wire, even over absurd issues such as whether the warriors did, in fact, pelt a tank with eggs. When asked whether he can prove that an egg hit the giant tank, the soldier replies, "Give me the camera, and I'll tape it for you," prompting a scoff from the filmmaker, who knows that she would never see the camera again.

As much as Obomsawin serves as an indigenous witness to state violence, she also testifies to the merits of the Mohawk cause. Throughout *Kanehsatake* she makes a concerted effort to humanize the tough-looking, code-named, masked warriors of the Mohawk nation, often through an emphasis on Native children. Warriors are said to be "family men," not desperadoes with long police records, as the authorities would maintain again and again in press conferences and interviews. When the army cuts the telephone lines to isolate the Mohawk resistance, the filmmaker shares a poignant scene of one warrior on a cell phone, talking in a gentle voice to his small children at home, with army helicopters roaring overhead in the night sky. She shares the sight of two young warriors making plans to marry, as if life goes on, even under siege. She shares her long-standing concern for the welfare of Native mothers, focusing on their efforts to feed their children with limited supplies in something approaching a war zone. In one telling instance of official pettiness, the camera reveals how a military bayonet has pierced each package of flour and corn allowed across the barricade, supposedly to keep contraband from making its way across.

In addition to the sympathetic look at warrior families, *Kanehsatake* shows the impact of state violence on individual Native bodies. In the most graphic footage in the film, Obomsawin brings the violence to a human level when she introduces Randy "Spudwrench" Horne, a Mohawk steelworker turned warrior whom the soldiers beat beyond recognition, apparently using a blackjack, among other instruments. Even as Horne lies unconscious, his head ballooning with blood, we see the reluctance of the army to grant him access to medical attention, except on their own restrictive terms. It seems to take hours to negotiate his safe passage across the barricade to a waiting ambulance, and, in this sequence, without making an overt editorial comment, Obomsawin has spoken volumes about state violence. In another example designed to show the absurdity of the army's actions, Obomsawin shows soldiers lacing the shallow waters around the treatment center with razor wire to keep small boats from landing with food or other supplies. "What other reservations are they going to surround?" asks a distraught Mohawk woman.

After seventy-eight days, the warriors announced their plan to surrender. Having left on the previous day, Obomsawin found herself in an ideal position to capture what happened next, and she builds a brutal and chaotic scene on the innovative editing of Yurij Luhovy: still photographs flash on-screen, punctuating the sixteen-millimeter footage of soldiers throwing warriors to the ground, children being separated from their parents, dozens of people being taken into custody, a scramble of frightened voices echoing on the sound track. It is a terrifying scene that marks the end of the standoff, but not the film. To prevent the audience from concluding that, with their humiliating capture, the warriors had lost their fight, Obomsawin adds a postscript that flashes forward one year. Now smiling Native people are marching together through the sunny streets of Oka. In voice-over, the filmmaker explains that all but three warriors were acquitted of the charges against them and that the total cost of the siege to the federal government was the astronomical sum of $155 million dollars. Yet the sense of hope and even triumph is mitigated in her next breath, when she notes that Mayor Ouellette, the politician who had proposed the golf-course development in the first place, has been reelected in Oka and that the status of the pines remains unresolved. The Mohawks may have won the battle, the film suggests, but the war goes on.

Kanehsatake maintains this sense of bittersweet triumph through the credits, with a final scene of the SQ taking shackled warriors into police headquarters while Mohawk women shout encouragement from the street. As the credits roll to reveal the vast number of people who worked on the film (ten camera operators, seven sound recordists, seven sound assistants, etc.), Obomsawin finishes just as she began, with Ellen Gabriel and Kahentiiosta talking about the virtues of the Mohawk people. These may be the final images, but they are not the most indelible. For me the lingering image of the film will always be an army helicopter droning overhead: it is an emblem of the Canadian state that stands in stark contrast to the mythologies of tolerance sustaining official political discourse. If anything, in the documentary vision of Alanis Obomsawin, Canada looks more like its brutal southern neighbor than it ever cared to admit.

In capturing the confusion and dismay of ordinary people engaged in armed resistance, Obomsawin's film reaches the level of insight that I admire in Barbara Kopple's *Harlan County U.S.A.* (1976), a similar film now regarded as a modern classic. Yet, because Obomsawin is a Native woman working in Canada, which seems to represent three strikes in the United States, audiences in the lower forty-eight have not seen *Kanehsatake* (or her other films) outside elite film festivals and the occasional college classroom. Still, the film was not relegated to the back shelf in the NFB warehouse, waiting for remote school districts to place their order—far from it. Like all her work, *Kanehsatake* made its way into the world through the NFB's extensive channels of distribution, meaning that it would be widely available across Canada and receive far more attention than the average nonfiction release in the United States. If reaching libraries, high schools, and nonprofit institutions has never lent cachet to a filmmaker, it has always been a worthy goal in Obomsawin's mind because it gives her another chance to shape the curriculum from a Native perspective, something her performances and educational kits had done in the 1960s. "All of my work—whether singing or storytelling or filmmaking—has been a fight for inclusion of our history in the educational system in our country," she has said, no doubt remembering her own childhood experiences with schoolhouse racism. "I wanted schools to be a better place for our children so that they can be honored for who they are and feel good about themselves."[23]

Kanehsatake also had an extraordinary life outside the NFB's normal distribution network among educational and cultural institutions. The film did well on British and Japanese television, won eighteen awards around the globe, and held the spotlight at major festivals such as Sundance. Among the three hundred films at the 1993 Festival of Festivals in Toronto, it was one of the few to garner cheers and even a standing ovation on its way to winning the festival's prize for best Canadian feature film of the year. Even with such accolades, the film was not aired on U.S. television, not even on public broadcasting stations with significant Native viewerships, and even Canadian television tried the same approach at first. When the film was released in 1993, the CBC continued its long-standing neglect of Obomsawin's work, in this case arguing that she needed to slice thirty minutes from the two-hour film to make room for commercial breaks. In a reflection of the considerable degree of autonomy that the NFB then possessed within the Canadian mediascape, Colin Neale, the executive producer who worked with Obomsawin on the film, rebuffed the network's demand. "We were not prepared to cut it down to someone else's specifications," he told *Maclean's*. Neale also said that the head of CBC documentaries, Mark Starowicz, "was not impressed with the film," although Starowicz claimed that his reservations about *Kanehsatake* involved only its length. [24]

Obomsawin did have an important ally at the CBC—the chairman, Patrick Watson, who admired *Kanehsatake* enough to host a party in the filmmaker's honor at his home during the Toronto festival. As an administrator reluctant to weigh in on programming decisions, Watson must have felt some frustration about the situation, especially as he listened to Obomsawin make her case for airing the film uncut and unaltered. "'Alanis is understandably angry,' Watson said about his network's stonewalling," *Maclean's* reported. [25]

Eventually, public interest in *Kanehsatake* overpowered the CBC's bureaucratic reluctance, and the network aired it on January 31, 1994. According to one Canadian writer, *Kanehsatake* gave "one dispossessed group a clear voice that echoes across this country." The same writer praised Obomsawin for her balance and passion, noting that the filmmaker "was able to contribute a depth of understanding and a dedication to the cause of the people behind the barricade so that they could tell their story to the world in their own way, clearly, calmly, without blind anger, but with the determination that the struggle will continue."[26]

Not all commentary on *Kanehsatake* was entirely positive. The articulate Mohawk spokesperson Ellen Gabriel, who later administered the First Peoples' house at McGill University, said after her appearance in the documentary: "I was hoping she would have shown more of the community members, because the people she interviewed were more the people from the Treatment Centre, who were not people from the community [some of the Mohawk warriors were not locals]. But overall, I think it's a very powerful film." Although the filmmaker was not willing to show the full extent of internecine strife that existed among Mohawks at the time, Gabriel was appreciative of what Obomsawin had done. "You would never be able to even describe—or people wouldn't believe—that this happened unless a documentary like Alanis' had come out. She helps to get the word out to places that otherwise wouldn't probably hear of these situations. I think she's done a more than excellent job of trying to help her people show their struggles and their humanity, and show to the future generations what their ancestors were doing in the late 1900s and beyond."[27]

Aftershocks

What happened at Oka continued to divide Canadian public opinion long after the release of *Kanehsatake*. In 1995, a provincial coroner's report blamed the SQ for most of the violence and needless chaos in the seventy-eight-day standoff but assigned responsibility for the sole fatality to the warriors. Although the report did not provide the name of the killer, it indicated, as we have seen, that a single bullet from the Mohawk position had killed Marcel Lemay.[28] The report did little to settle the frayed nerves of Oka participants and observers, Obomsawin included, and she continued to work through her experiences at Oka for the next decade, creating three more films out of what she had witnessed in the pines. Although they might seem dwarfed by the magnitude of the drama captured in *Kanehsatake*, these subsequent documentaries—*My Name Is Kahentiiosta*,

Spudwrench— Kahnawake Man, and *Rocks at Whiskey Trench*—are more than footnotes to the initial film.

Unlike *Kanehsatake*, *My Name Is Kahentiiosta* (1995) is a memoir rather than a history of the standoff, with one Mohawk woman providing a microcosm of the event and its aftermath. In traditional Mohawk fashion, Kahentiiosta begins the twenty-nine-minute film with a recounting of her birth and family history, before emphasizing the impact of the Oka crisis on her children. Hearing her voice-over rather than the filmmaker's, we learn about the feeling of "being invaded" and the sense of traditional Mohawk territory slipping away. "In my lifetime, we just see a big pile of steel going by," she complains about the St. Lawrence Seaway, where vast tankers have pushed out local fishermen. In addition to a thematic emphasis on changes forced on the land and rivers in the name of progress, the film highlights the importance of fighting back in self-defense when pushed, always a subtext in Obomsawin's work. Bringing together the two themes in one breath, Kahentiiosta says: "We were all ready to die—might as well go with the land." Obomsawin presents her protagonist both as a tough-talking *macha* warrior who rides behind the barricades on an ATV smoking Che cigars and as a more conventional thirty-something woman in a flower-print dress, seated in a pasture, talking about her connection to the trees. *Kahentiiosta* gives Obomsawin an opportunity to use more of her vast store of Oka footage, this time with an even greater focus on the contribution of Native women, and once again to frame the standoff as a Mohawk triumph. "We didn't lose," Kahentiiosta says, pointing out that the golf-course plan was halted and that the pines are still standing.

Of the four Oka films, *Kahentiiosta* is the smallest in scale and not quite as compelling as *Spudwrench: Kahnawake Man* (1997). This fifty-nine-minute film explores the life of the Mohawk steelworker Randy "Spudwrench" Horne before and after his gruesome beating in the woods around Oka. D. B. Jones, one of the historians of the NFB, has described *Spudwrench* as the "most rounded" of Obomsawin's follow-up films to *Kahensatake*. Making the often-expressed observations that her interviewing voice is "soft and lilting" and that "the film's gentle pace is a stylistic analogue to its mood of serenity," Jones

FIGURE 20. *My Name is Kahentiiosta* (1995). Directed by Alanis Obomsawin. Produced by Alanis Obomsawin. Photograph taken from the production. © 1995 National Film Board of Canada. All rights reserved. Photograph used with the permission of the National Film Board of Canada.

FIGURE 21. Randy "Spudwrench" Horne in *Spudwrench—Kahnawake Man* (1997). Directed by Alanis Obomsawin. Produced by Alanis Obomsawin. Photograph by: John Kenney. © 1997 National Film Board of Canada. All rights reserved. Photograph used with the permission of the National Film Board of Canada.

also makes some uncommon points about her use of "seemingly off-the-point cutaway shots [to] reinforce the mood: the girl on the porch swing, a man harvesting potatoes from his garden." He also suggests that the most remarkable thing about Obomsawin's version of the confrontation at Oka is that, in spite of the eruptions of violence and anger, "neither side really wants to hurt the other."[29]

Certainly, Spudwrench comes across as peaceful and hardworking, which suits the film's emphasis on the importance of Native labor to the wider economy of North America. In depicting scenes such as Spudwrench's long commute from Canada to New York City to toil on half-constructed skyscrapers, Obomsawin creates an insightful portrait of Native men as a neglected part of the working-class culture of North America, and her film reads almost like a First Nations companion to the labor-oriented textbook *Who Built America?* Soon after the release of the film, Obomsawin told one interviewer that she "wanted to show the contribution these [Mohawk] people have made for so many generations in terms of building bridges and buildings all around the world. It really is an important thing."[30] In addition to depicting the work ethic of Mohawk men, the film contains further attempts, as in *Kanehsatake*, to humanize the warriors with a sympathetic glance at their home lives, with wives and children given ample time to address the camera.

The final film on Oka (thus far) appeared in 2000 under the title *Rocks at Whisky Trench*. This well-shot 105-minute documentary recounts the trauma inflicted on Mohawk families, mostly women, children, and elders, who fled from their homes on August 28, 1990, when the Canadian Army descended on Oka. Forming a convoy to drive across the Mercier Bridge toward Montreal, seventy-five Mohawk cars passed through a narrow gap called Whiskey Trench, where angry whites were waiting for them with rocks, bottles, and racial taunts. Windows were shattered, faces were bloodied, yet the SQ made no arrests (although the police did prevent whites from storming at least one car). In interviews that Obomsawin conducted almost a decade after the event, the victims make clear the lingering effects of the experience and decry the white racism that fueled the violence. Perhaps more than any of her other films, *Rocks at Whiskey Trench*

FIGURE 22. Mohawk families running a gauntlet of rocks, bottles, and racist epithets in *Rocks at Whiskey Trench* (2000). Directed by Alanis Obomsawin. Produced by Alanis Obomsawin. © 2000 National Film Board of Canada. All rights reserved. Photograph used with the permission of the National Film Board of Canada.

provides a scathing indictment of white Canadian racism, including the racism of the mainstream media. "Many reporters covering the situation in Montreal had anti-Mohawk views," Obomsawin has said. "When they announced that the cars were on the bridge, they told people to get down there and stop them [the Mohawks] from escaping."[31] A passionate and compelling film, *Rocks at Whisky Trench* represented yet another attempt to depict the crisis from a Native point of view, although the passage of years had given Obomsawin an additional sense of urgency. "I felt very bad that a lot of people had died since the experience," she said, before explaining her rationale behind the four documentaries dedicated to showing the world what had happened at Oka. "It's for other generations to have an idea of what happened."[32]

If the Oka films are for the future, they are also for the other side, those who did not support the Mohawk cause—but even when Obomsawin challenges white attitudes toward Native peoples, she

FIGURE 23. Native activists confront armed soldiers in *Rocks at Whiskey Trench* (2000). Directed by Alanis Obomsawin. Produced by Alanis Obomsawin. © 2000 National Film Board of Canada. All rights reserved. Photograph used with the permission of the National Film Board of Canada.

does so without the rancor of an unskilled polemicist. Instead, she demonstrates an uncommon ability to combine passionate advocacy and a gentle, inclusive tone (often conveyed through her calm voice-over narration) and to come across as fair *and* committed. As a result, she has, I suspect, been able to avoid shutting down less sympathetic viewers, something that is not always true of political films set in Indian country.

At the same time that *Kanehsatake* was being trumpeted as a great accomplishment of the NFB, another Canadian film on Oka was not so fortunate in its public reception. Alex MacLeod's *Acts of Defiance*, a 1993 NFB film on Oka, was attacked in some quarters of the press as one-sided propaganda. One reporter claimed that only the soldiers appeared armed and dangerous in MacLeod's film while the Mohawks came across as heroic resisters—a phony posture, he argued, because the warriors were just cloaking their bid for power in what he called the "myth of the wounded Indian." Complaining about the $250,000 in taxpayers' money used to finance the film, the writer blasted *Acts of Defiance* as an example of gross revisionism for distorting what really happened. "Though it's only three years since Canadians were treated to nightly images of masked, rifle-toting Mohawks patrolling their barricades, almost every minute of *Acts of Defiance* includes shots of armed police officers, soldiers, helicopters or tanks," he writes in an article with the revealing title "Thugs of the World Unite." "Viewers are led to conclude that the backbone of the native resistance was teenagers, old people and women carrying babies, all engaged in a righteous revolution against Canada." When he notes that the NFB press release appeared to endorse the film's position, the reviewer brings in a conservative "expert" to dismiss the liberal interpretation of Oka in favor of this assessment: "What we have here is a socialist mindset that wants to read popular revolution and people all united against oppression into the situation." Rather than seeing Oka as a populist uprising, the "expert" suggests that Canadians need to reject misleading films like *Acts of Defiance* and appreciate the real model for the actions of the warriors at Oka: the Chicago gangster Al Capone and his henchmen.[33]

How were Obomsawin's Oka films—indeed, all her films—able to avoid this sort of knee-jerk condemnation?[34] The answer lies, I think, in a rhetorical strategy that her film career seems to embody: an attempt to use documentary film as a "middle ground" between Native and white Canadians, something that I explore in the final section of this chapter.

Documentary Film on the Middle Ground

In the past fifteen years, two interrelated concepts have taken root and blossomed in the work of historians and anthropologists, in particular those working on the tangled histories of Native and non-Native North America. The first concept is that of the *middle ground*, made popular by the historian Richard White. For White, writing about the eighteenth-century *pays d'en haut* region around the Great Lakes, the phrase applies to the "place in between: in between cultures, people, and in between empires and the nonstate world of villages." It was a zone of creative communication across borders, a "realm of constant invention" where cross-cultural sensitivity was an art form designed to resolve conflicts without violence. Those skilled in this art were usually doing their fast-talking with their own people in mind, but they had to convince the other side that their cause was reasonable, that "some mutual action was fair and legitimate," and that there were "congruencies" of interest between the Native and white positions.[35]

The second concept of interest is that of the *cultural broker*, the silver-tongued artist of the middle ground who has "breached language barriers, clarified diplomatic understandings, softened potential conflicts, and awakened the commonality of spirit shared by the human race."[36] Both these metaphors—those of the middle ground and the cultural broker—are flexible enough, I believe, to transpose usefully into film studies, where they could have particular relevance in describing documentaries intended to transcend cultural barriers. In this sense I propose that Obomsawin functions as a cultural broker for the electronic age, working on the middle ground of cultural production, and negotiating between parties with the complex language of nonfiction cinema.

Like the cultural brokers of the past, Obomsawin has moved across borders with the hope of preventing violence. In the case of *Kanehsatake*, she literally crossed the barricades between the government forces and the Native resisters, convinced that her presence would not only bring international attention to the story but also discourage even greater outbreaks of violence. "I don't like to give myself that kind of power," she says, but, as noted earlier, she was told many times that her presence had a restraining effect. She believed that the authorities were more circumspect in the presence of a camera, especially one in the hands of a well-known Native woman, and the warriors went so far as to say that "the best times were when the cameras were there."[37] This mitigating effect is possible only in the realm of nonfiction production. Because it purports to capture "reality" and "visual evidence" rather than a subjective vision of pure imagination, documentary provides an ideal middle ground for Native people hoping to stake their claims in the age of television.

To date, the literature on indigenous media has not focused in depth on its intercultural function, at least not in the explicit terms that I am suggesting. Although scholars have noted how visual arts "have become one of the main forms of intercultural communication between Native Americans and the non-native world" and painters such as Pablita Velarde have been described as "cultural brokers," this language has not been drawn into discussions of documentary film in general or indigenous media in particular.[38] Yet Obomsawin is engaged in the very same sort of effort: trying to get the other side to consider the plausibility of a Native position on a controversial subject such as Oka. Even before academics started using terms such as *middle ground* and *cultural broker*, Obomsawin seemed to think of her work along these lines, calling her films a "bridge" or "place" where Native people could enter into a dialogue with the mainstream of Canadian public opinion.[39]

The role of the cultural broker is a difficult one for an artist, and the challenge of working in two worlds has taken its toll on more than one who attempted to fill it. Pablita Velarde, for example, one of the best-known Native women painters of the twentieth century, suffered from being "an outsider and insider in two worlds," according to one scholar.[40] Yet somehow Obomsawin has found a degree of equilibrium between her two worlds, Native and white, perhaps because she started her creative life with the constant balancing act of bringing Abenaki songs and stories to all manner of audiences across Canada. "It was very hard at the beginning," she recalls, before describing her eventual ease on the middle ground. "I have developed my own way of standing on my two feet no matter where I am and being part of our culture and carrying it with me. I think I bring it to other people who meet me—I bring them something."[41] In her songs, stories, and films, she has brought a great deal to Canadians of all backgrounds, always hoping to pierce the veil of misunderstanding that covers many Canadian eyes, cameras, and televisions whenever Native people are involved. Still, her frustration flares up at times, as does the anger that once made her lash out at racist classmates as a child, and she seems sickened that many Canadians have not shaken their traditional ignorance of Native peoples. "They know nothing," she fumed in 2002, after nearly half a century of trying to educate them. Recent survey data suggest that her frustration is more than anecdotal. In 2003, almost half of all Canadians reported their disbelief in the legitimacy of Native land claims, while 42 percent supported the notion that Native treaty rights should be abolished altogether, prompting a spokesperson for the Assembly of First Nations to complain: "It really does point to a need for greater public education, more dialogue between First Nations and non-aboriginal people."[42]

Even in the face of such discouraging news and her own private moments of despair, Obomsawin has never stopped walking optimistically into the middle ground of cinema, hoping to connect Native and non-Native perspectives through the lives that she documents on-screen. "You need the relation and the learning places," she says, and, for her, documentary is a learning place that can include anyone willing to listen and watch for an hour or two. With an abiding faith in the power of nonfiction cinema to make sense across various lines of demarcation, she has said: "I think this is where documentary filmmaking becomes such an important way of preserving and teaching and making sure people have a place to speak. It changes society. It brings knowledge about the others that you always call the 'others.' And all of a sudden you realize that they feel like you, and they have stories that are similar, and they need you, and you need them. And I think the documentary world does that very well."[43]

Obomsawin's attempt to connect people across lines of difference is not just intellectual, historical, or logical in its appeal, and her films are more than dry recitations of salient information, in which visual "facts" are marshaled like evidence in a courtroom of public opinion. She seems very aware that more visceral forms of persuasion must occur on the intercultural middle ground, where sentiment is as important as data. For this reason, she is just as interested in emotional persuasion, in shaping an audience's feelings about Native histories and identities, although doing so without gross manipulation. When documentary reaches the heart of its audience without descending into base demagoguery, it is said to possess the intangible quality of passion, something that Obomsawin seems to offer in abundance to her viewers. Even as her work makes a strong case to the "rational mind," the place of facts and analysis that is "the official mind of science, industry and government," as Wendell Berry puts it, her strongest appeal is to what Berry calls the "sympathetic mind," the place where we formulate compassion and understanding when someone evokes a sense of shared humanity.[44]

Obomsawin has chosen an ideal medium for her intercultural messages of compassion, understanding, and toleration, the place where the sympathetic mind lives most naturally in our postmodern mediascape being, I believe, within the documentary form, with its great tradition of listening to outsider voices, pulling for the underdog, and pushing for social change. In the past decade or so a specious brand of commercial nonfiction, including the crass reality programs that top the Nielsen ratings, has begun to overshadow this humane tradition where filmmakers like Obomsawin have toiled. Her *other* visions provide a healthy corrective to the fundamental sadism and voyeurism of *Joe Millionaire, Cops,* and *Survivor,* not to mention the dull pieties of PBS series like *The American Experience.* Her work creates a space that, as Zuzana Pick points out, "promotes the circulation of affect between protagonist and viewer."[45] Or, to put it another way, Obomsawin shows us why we should care about people we might never meet. In the chapter ahead, I will attempt to show how her desire to forge this connection makes her reliance on documentary more than coincidental.

5

Why Documentary?

The restitution of things to their real place and meaning
is an eminently subversive fact.

FERNANDO SOLANAS and
OCTAVIO GETINO

Alanis Obomsawin has, as we have seen, known success as a storyteller, singer, activist, education consultant, and documentarian, yet
it is the last role that has occupied most of her creative life. What is it
about the documentary impulse that she finds so necessary and irre-
sistible? *Why documentary?* Certainly, she is not alone in her reliance
on nonfiction to achieve her creative and political goals—over the
past three decades, often with her leadership, documentary cinema
has become a preferred mode of expression for Native mediamakers.
"Documentary film is the one place that our people can speak for
themselves," Obomsawin has said. "I feel that the documentaries that
I've been working on have been very valuable for the people, for our
people to look at ourselves . . . and through that being able to make
changes that really count for the future of our children to come."[1] In
this chapter I want to explore the deeper nature of her documentary
expression, asking how it came to be the vehicle of choice for her complex artistic visions. As well as looking at the continuing "allure of the
real" for indigenous filmmakers like Obomsawin, I want to explore

documentary's function in the larger mediascapes of North America, using Obomsawin as a jumping-off point to reach some fundamental issues about "representing reality" in contemporary film and video. First, however, let me make some attempt to prove the assertion, often made but never quite demonstrated, that documentary has been the dominant mode in Native media.

The Dominance of Documentary

In 1991, a Native media producer told a film-festival audience in Minneapolis that Native people watch "white TV" and learn about "white culture" but never have the chance to turn the tables and share their own cultures. He argued that Native people needed to find a way to bring their own realities to the screen, even if the learning process was tentative and awkward. "We may not be able to do it right," he said modestly, "because we lack the funding, we lack the resources, we lack equipment—but we can put together images. We can put together stories. . . . We have that ability. We have that power and knowledge to put things together and explain ourselves to many non-Indian people."[2] In rapidly increasing numbers in the years since (and to some extent before), Natives have been doing just what this speaker suggested: making films and videos that bring Native perspectives to Native and non-Native alike. As a result of this desire to inscribe Native histories on various national imaginaries as well as of various personal motivations, the filmography of Native productions now comprises, according to one estimate, over a thousand titles.[3] That number might surprise readers who have not seen more than a handful of Native films in their university collections or distributor's catalogs, and it might even prompt them to wonder, What *are* all these projects?

Two things are clear: most of them are documentaries, and most of them are hard to find. In appendix B is provided a list of significant nonfiction titles with Native production, direction, or other substantial forms of creative control, not just those with a lone Native actor, writer, or cameraperson. Still, while the list is suggestive, even representative, it is far from comprehensive. The latter would be a worthwhile goal—but almost impossible given the dozens of projects whose existence is unknown outside a tribal complex in Alaska or Arizona. Sometimes this localism is by design, such as when a tribe documents an issue of cultural sensitivity that it does not want broadcast to the world; more often, however, it is by default, owing to cultural prejudices, funding shortfalls, or inadequate access to media outlets—any of these factors can keep a good project from wider circulation or a promising one from reaching its potential. While Obomsawin has been fortunate to work under the auspices of the National Film Board (NFB), which promotes her titles and keeps them in wide circulation for decades after their initial release, most Native filmmakers have endured far more frustrating circumstances in trying to get their films made and disseminated. As a consequence, even a fair number of the most important Native-produced titles are difficult to track down.[4] Yet, in spite of the structural pressures weighing against their success, Native filmmakers have created an impressive body of nonfiction work in the past three decades.

The first wave of Native-produced documentaries appeared in the 1970s with Obomsawin's early films as well as multipart television series such as George Burdeau's *The Real People* (1976) and Phil Lucas's *Images of Indian* (1979–81). More Native productions appeared in the 1980s, including George Horse Capture, Larry Littlebird, and Larry Cesspooch's *I'd Rather Be Powwowing* (1983), Chris Spotted Eagle's *The Great Spirit within the Hole* (1983) and *Our Sacred Land* (1984), Rick Tailfeathers's *Powwow Fever* (1984), Victor Masayesva's *Itam Hakim Hopiit* (1985) and *Ritual Clowns* (1988), Arlene Bowman's *Navajo Talking Picture* (1986), Sandra Day Osawa's *In the Heart of Big Mountain* (1988), Mona Smith's *Her Giveaway: A Spiritual Journey with AIDS* (1988), and Zacharias Kunuk's *Qaqqiq/Gathering Place* (1989), the last one of fifty nonfiction videos that Kunuk would produce about Native life along the Arctic Circle. Many of these directors continued making films in the 1990s and beyond, when they were joined by newcomers such as Roy Bigcrane, Dean Bearclaw, Loretta Todd, Allen Jamieson, Ava Hamilton, Ruby Sooktis, Derron Twohatchet, Beverly R. Singer, Harriet Sky, Christine Welsh, Barb Cranmer, Daniel Prouty, Paul Rickard, Lena and Aaron Carr, Carol Geddes, Puhipau, David H. Kalama Jr., Gary Farmer, G. Peter Jemison, Annie Frazier-Henry, and James Fortier. As even a very partial filmography might suggest, the list of Native-produced documentaries has become quite impressive.

Yet, when we turn to fiction film, the situation is quite different. Here we find the first surviving Native film, James Young Deer's *White Fawn's Devotion* (1910), whose early appearance is somewhat misleading given that a Native person did not return to the director's chair for the next seven decades.[5] If sympathetic Native portraits started to seep into the mainstream in the late 1960s with the release of films like Arthur Penn's *Little Big Man* (1969), real Native productions did not begin stirring again until the 1980s with two satirical works, Bob Hicks's *Return of the Country* (1983) and Gerald Vizenor's trickster fable, *Harold of Orange* (1984). Then, a few years later, Shelly Niro released *It Starts with a Whisper* (1993) and *Honey Moccasin* (1998), both of which were well regarded but little noticed. In a more commercial vein, Valerie Red Horse produced the feature *Naturally Native* (1997) with investment from the Mashantucket Pequot Tribal Nation, although it, too, failed to attain anything more than limited distribution.[6]

The real breakthrough came in 1998 with Chris Eyre's *Smoke Signals*, a solid, if unremarkable, buddy movie laced with wry Indian humor that seemed to astonish white audiences into smiling submission. For those who somehow slept through the *Smoke Signals* phenomenon, Zacharias Kunuk's Inuit epic *Atanarjuat: The Fast Runner* (2002) underscored the point that Native feature filmmaking had arrived as a cultural force. *Atanarjuat* even attracted the attention of Jacques Chirac, the president of France, who gushed about it being "ce film magnifique," while the *New York Times* called it a "masterpiece."[7] With the smaller-scale release of several other Native productions in the same time period, including Shirley Cheechoo's *Backroads* (2000), Randy Redroad's *The Doe Boy* (2001), and Sherman Alexie's *The Business of Fancydancing* (2002), Native fiction film seemed to have reached a new prominence in the first moments of the new millennium.

Two observations might undercut the satisfaction that one could take from this development. First, the main figures behind the recent explosion of interest in Native fiction film are mostly male: Chris Eyre, Zacharias Kunuk, Randy Redroad, and Sherman Alexie. Second, the flowering of Native cinema began long before the fuss over *Smoke Signals*: it happened in the less visible and less commercial realm of documentary and in the less celebrated hands of women like Alanis Obomsawin, Sandra Osawa, Arlene Bowman, Loretta Todd, Carol Geddes, Lena Carr, and others. As appendix B makes clear, these Native women have been telling stories on film for almost three decades, although too often their work has been left stranded at the crossroads of race and gender.

What I am writing in this book reflects my belief that nonfiction cinema deserves better—and not just in the case of prolific artists like Obomsawin. In the past decade documentary has begun to shed its image as the unloved stepchild of cinema studies. With the phenomenal success of softheaded "reality programs" on TV and the entrance of harder-edged documentaries like *The Fog of War* (Errol Morris, 2003), *Fahrenheit 9/11* (Michael Moore, 2004), and *Capturing the Friedmans* (Andrew Jarecki, 2003) into the American cineplex, scholars, students, and general audiences have begun looking at nonfiction cinema with a new intensity and interest. On the academic side of the spectrum, Bill Nichols, Trinh T. Minh-ha, Thomas Waugh, Michael Renov, Patricia Zimmermann, Barry Keith Grant, Richard Barsam, and other prominent scholars have launched a small renaissance in documentary studies. These writers have all taken the exploration of nonfiction discourse to an unprecedented depth, asking epistemological, ideological, and methodological questions that were often taken for granted in the past. With their careful investigations of representing reality as my model, I hope to treat Native nonfiction with the seriousness and care that it deserves and look at the underlying reasons why Obomsawin and so many other Native filmmakers have been drawn to it. For Obomsawin in particular, the answer to the question, Why documentary? could be summed up in two words: *John Grierson*. Without doubt, the great Scottish documentarian illuminated a general path toward nonfiction that Obomsawin seemed to follow, but, in the section ahead, I will suggest how such an answer might obscure more than it reveals.

Griersonian Documentary

Any attempt to understand Obomsawin's documentary project must come to terms with her relationship to the paterfamilias of the NFB, indeed, one of the key figures in the history of nonfiction cinema. Because Grierson founded the NFB and set the institutional tone for decades well beyond his own administration (1939–45), and perhaps because he had expressed his own peculiar admiration for Obomsawin, some scholars have seen her as following in the footsteps of the pioneering documentarian. Jerry White, for example, has argued that her work embodies "the very essence of a Griersonian ethic of filmmaking," something that "should not be downplayed simply because Grierson has fallen out of favor."[8] Although I respect White's attempt to redeem the Scotsman's legacy by showing his relevance to an important Native filmmaker, the flip side is, I believe, even more rewarding for us to consider, namely, the fundamental ways in which Obomsawin diverged from her putative mentor.

No one could dispute that Grierson's influence cut a wide swath through the NFB ever since its inception, just as it has wherever thoughtful and civic-minded people have picked up cameras and wondered how best to depict reality in a way that might change the world. One part Zeus and two parts Columbus in his own voluble rhetoric about the origins of nonfiction cinema, Grierson was, in fact, there at the beginning, one of the prime movers of social documentary, surveying "a whole world undiscovered, a whole area of cinematic possibility undiscovered," as he proclaimed in the last interview before his death in 1972. "All we did in documentary was we occupied Oklahoma," he said, choosing a rancid colonialist metaphor that suggests more about his ideological perspective that he ever intended. "I saw here was a territory completely unoccupied," he explained about the "empty" continent of nonfiction that lay before him in the 1920s and 1930s.[9]

In the brave new world of nonfiction that he imagined, Grierson wanted to sweep past the indigenous subjects who would galvanize Obomsawin's attention and attend to something much closer to home, much closer to his cultural roots in Scotland. Promoting a tough-minded, "realist" approach to documentary over so-called romantic visions that included works such as Robert Flaherty's *Nanook of the North* (1922), Grierson waxed poetic about the nonfiction film-maker's "social responsibility" to the dimly lit slums of the white working class, the kind of urban spaces he knew well from work-ing in factories along the Clyde, spending his free time around "the soapboxes of Glasgow Green," where he first heard the rhetoric of pro-gressive politics in the early 1920s. That is where the camera should be pointed, he argued, believing that to look elsewhere was the task of the foolhardy romantic and would serve no social good. Unlike the realist, the romantics had it easy—"easy in the sense that the noble savage is already a figure of romance. . . . Their essential virtues have been declared and can more easily be declared again, and no one will deny them." According to Grierson, the real challenge was to bring the nonfiction camera into the "streets and cities and slums and markets and exchanges and factories," to his own people, more or less, whose "essential virtues," he believed, were not so easily declared.[10]

It seems obvious that Obomsawin would agree with Grierson's most general principles, such as a desire to use nonfiction film for so-cial amelioration, to show structural forms of subjugation in place of individual failings, and to celebrate common labor and working-class grit. She recalled with admiration how Grierson "felt that poor peo-ple, common people, should be able to see themselves on the screen," which would "make a better life for them and for people at large in terms of understanding and feeling right about who they were."[11] Yet how unusual are such desires in nonfiction circles? Few well-known documentarians have eschewed these broad progressive tendencies, which strike me as too general to account for Obomsawin's unique voice and vision. I suspect that a closer look might reveal funda-mental contradictions between the Scottish propagandist for empire and the dissident First Nations media activist, that is, might reveal that Obomsawin represents not an indigenous reclamation of the Griersonian project, but its outright rejection.

Consider these crucial differences: Grierson believed that portrai-ture was what the NFB did best, while Obomsawin avoided biopics in favor of exploring a subject across geography (*Mother of Many Chil-dren*) or an event unfolding across time (*Incident at Restigouche*).[12]

Grierson was willing to stage scenes in a way that hardly seems documentary today, while Obomsawin relied on "actuality footage" (uncontrolled footage of events unfolding) far more than most NFB filmmakers. Grierson inadvertently gave birth to the hand-wringing "tradition of the victim" that has plagued nonfiction cinema ever since, while Obomsawin focused on the resistance, endurance, and creativity of the oppressed.[13] This last point is worth exploring in detail because it represents the deepest level of divergence between the two filmmakers.

For more than three decades, Obomsawin's work has run counter to the characteristic Griersonian emphasis on downtrodden victims in need of liberal salvation. Unlike soot-faced Griersonian subjects who languish in squalor until middle-class voters are roused into political action, Obomsawin's Native people are agents of their own fate who reject a dependent relationship with the state. On occasions when it is necessary to seek assistance from outside families and local communities, her Native subjects do not turn to federal or provincial governments for help. Instead, Obomsawin suggests, their personal and collective struggles are best addressed within a First Nations context, one that requires little from the outside world except the removal of its foot from their neck. That is quite different than the Griersonian model, where the problem is the *inattention* of the state, which can best be remedied through an empathetic chain reaction: public-spirited filmmaker presents social problem to middle-class audiences, who then press their political representatives in Ottawa (or London) to fix the situation with "expertly" crafted policies. In Obomsawin's world, of course, the problem is the *attention* of the state and its white middle-class supporters, whose deleterious policies and attitudes present the gravest danger facing Native cultures. When it comes to state intervention in the lives of Native people, the implication of Obomsawin's films is clear: *benign* neglect would be a blessing. Barring that unlikely situation, Obomsawin fights to mitigate the damaging effects of the state and to enlighten the general public as much as is possible, seeming to argue that Native people need nothing more than the space to extricate themselves from the colonialist gaze—ironically, the very gaze that Grierson perfected on film.

The reason for his cinematic colonialism is simple: at heart Grierson was literally a salesman for empire. Before coming to North America to launch the NFB, he worked at the Empire Marketing Board in London, producing documentary films to polish the tarnished image of British colonialism around the world. As he conceded, his well-crafted propaganda for the Empire Marketing Board was designed to "change the connotation of the word 'Empire'" in the minds of the colonized; after all, their numerical majority in places such as India was beginning to require a larger dose of persuasion to accompany the old stand-by of military coercion.[14] It is no surprise that, when Grierson arrived in Ottawa in the late 1930s (the NFB moved to Montreal only in the 1950s), he articulated a dominant cultural perspective with little regard for minority claims of the sort that Obomsawin would document in all her films. Thoughtful scholars like Jerry White might wish to expand Grierson's conservative nationalism to include Obomsawin's dissenting, multicultural vision, but it seems to me that the two perspectives are in fundamental opposition unless we engage in considerable interpretive back-flipping.

We can see their contrasting positions even when Obomsawin and Grierson crossed paths in the mid-1960s. They met when Grierson returned to the NFB after an absence of two decades, serving in a consulting role like a father meeting his now-grown children and offering advice on the proper way in which to conduct their affairs. Ever mindful of the political exigencies on which his institution rested, the elder statesman often reminded his NFB heirs that they were neither muckraking cine-journalists nor visionary artists: at root, they were *public servants* whose most important relationship was with Ottawa, the Canadian capital. But how could this make sense to Obomsawin? Her most important relationship was with First Nations people across North America.[15] Her work was (and is) for them, not for the crown.

This was not the only area in which Grierson's underlying conservatism might have placed him at odds with the Abenaki filmmaker, who seems too gracious to make this point herself. When the Challenge for Change initiative brought a few Native faces into the NFB filmmaking process for the first time on *You Are on Indian Land* (Mort Ransen, 1969) and other projects, Obomsawin thought that it was "wonderful" and part of a "very special time at the film board."[16] *You Are on Indian Land* created a remarkable opening for Native filmmakers that, as Faye Ginsburg has written, "signaled a crucial shift in assumptions about who should be behind the documentary camera, one that has had a lasting effect on First Nations film and video production in Canada."[17] The legendary filmmaker George Stoney, then the executive producer of Challenge for Change (and the force behind *You Are on Indian Land*), wanted the program "to be more than a public relations gimmick to make the establishment seem more in tune with the times." He wanted the NFB to fulfill its promise to "promote citizen participation in the solution of social problems," even if he had to rattle some cages in the process.[18]

As a new spirit of activism emerged in the Canadian mediascape, Grierson had a much different reaction than Obomsawin. Sitting on the sidelines in his consulting role at the NFB, Grierson shook his head in dismay at what he saw happening. Rather than supporting the spirit of grassroots agitation taking root in the media and other aspects of Canadian life in the 1960s, Grierson encouraged Canadians to stop whining about their nation's shortcomings and instead take quiet pride in their collective triumphs. Canada's great problem was, he maintained, not its government's failed policies; rather, it was the sour attitude of media professionals more interested in causing trouble than appreciating the accomplishments of the status quo.[19]

Grierson died in 1972, but, had he lived to see Obomsawin's tough-minded political films of the 1980s and beyond, he would, I expect, have dismissed them as divisive and negative because she was willing to expose the bitterest conflicts within Canadian society and to rebuke the Canadian state for its failures. In the films she made after his death, Obomsawin would often take controversial, even subversive positions with regard to the Canadian state. Films like *Incident at Restigouche* and especially later work like *Kanehsatake* and *Is the Crown at War with Us?* would have infuriated the NFB founder, whose chief interest in times of crisis was the preservation of national unity. Although Grierson may have espoused the rhetoric of social uplift to justify the intrusive documentary gaze, he always "stopped short of describing reality when it became politically uncomfortable," as the Canadian journalist Robert Fulford has pointed out, noting that, when the Second World War erupted, Grierson steered his filmmakers around the controversial issue of conscription in Quebec. "To have exposed tension in Confederation would have been, in the Griersonian view, irresponsible," Fulford writes. "Better to fill the movie screens of the nation with legions of happy war workers, doing their bit for democracy, and leave Quebec's grievances for later."[20]

Throughout his career Grierson folded under political pressure in a way that Obomsawin could never countenance—for evidence, see the earlier account of her refusal to listen to NFB superiors who told her not to interview government officials for *Incident at Restigouche*. "When faced with real people caught up in real difficulties," writes Brian Winston, "the Griersonian social activist and public educator tended to be replaced by a dispassionate and distant journalist."[21] This inability to stand firm in its challenges to the status quo has led Robert Fulford to question Grierson's legacy to Canada filmmaking: "He left behind a film culture that was simultaneously focused on 'realism' and terrified of being so realistic that it might disturb someone."[22] Obomsawin would have no such qualms when it came to showing the failures of the Canadian government.

I do not dispute the closeness of the filmmakers on a personal level. One NFB producer recalls that Grierson was "absolutely spellbound by this woman. . . . I think he was a drum carrier on one adventure to a reserve. He carried her drums for her. And they became very good friends." Near the end of his life, Grierson was even asked to serve as godfather for the filmmaker's daughter, Kisos.[23] Yet underneath these warm personal relations were incompatible goals for Canadian documentary cinema, and, if Obomsawin's activism behind the camera has earned her the generic label *Griersonian*, we should remember that she was anything but Griersonian in the particulars. Long before she joined the NFB, Obomsawin realized that the Canadian national imaginary was not a welcoming place for Native stories, and she looked for new forms of indigenous cultural activism that could challenge this situation. If Grierson had dreamed of "a

national use of cinema" that would allow Canadians to see themselves whole, Obomsawin would borrow his nationalistic fervor for
the benefit of First Nations and reveal the disturbing aspects of the
white Canadian project.[24] If Grierson invented an NFB where cele-
brating the benevolence and unity of the Canadian state was more
important than unflinching attention to the "creative depiction of
actuality," to use his famous phrase, then Obomsawin would develop
a documentary counterdiscourse that stared straight into the heart
of state violence—and just how willing she was to insert herself into
dangerous and controversial situations was apparent in the making
of *Kanehsatake*. Grierson may have convinced her (and many other
Canadians) of the social power of documentary through his rhetoric
and his work at the NFB, but he seems to have had little influence
on her work after this initial moment of inspiration, which is why I
think that her lifelong commitment to documentary has been more
than a function of intersecting biographies. In the next section I want
to consider the pragmatic forces as well as the larger representational
impulses that have drawn Native media activists like Obomsawin
toward nonfiction expression in recent decades. Only then can we
make sense of the question, Why documentary?

Allure of the Real

Part of the answer is obvious to those who know something about film
production: it's cheaper. Fiction films often require higher production values, greater length, expensive actors, equipment, and sets, and
more frequent hassles with investors who have too much money at
stake to wait quietly in the wings. Documentarians—not all, but many
of them—live in a different world, a down-market terrain where activist motivations might be relevant, financial stakes are lower, sets are
inexpensive or even free, high-end cameras and lights are not always
needed, and the cast is whoever wanders into a shot and agrees to
sign a release. I exaggerate for effect, but the gist of what I am saying
is true—although it does not explain why Obomsawin has remained
devoted to the nonfiction form.

   If some Native filmmakers have turned to nonfiction out of relative
poverty, Obomsawin has been something of an exception. Because of

her enviable role at the NFB, she has not had to worry about financing as much as independent producers, whose more limited resources and keen competition for an ever-diminishing pile of grant money might give them no other option than low-budget video documentary. Although Obomsawin has sometimes needed to hustle to find coproduction funds outside the NFB, she has been able to make all the projects she has envisioned in the past thirty years, something that puts her in rare company among nonfiction filmmakers—perhaps only Ken Burns or Frederick Wiseman in the United States could say the same.[25] Her budgets may not have approached the approximately $13,000,000 that Burns spent on *Jazz* (2001), but the sums involved were not insignificant. In the 1990s, the NFB estimated that it spent, on average, over C$500,000 per on-screen hour, putting a two-hour film like *Kanehsatake* in the million-dollar range.[26]

So if Obomsawin was not making nonfiction simply out of financial necessity, what other motivations were at work? One explanation is that documentary made particular sense for her context, both institutional and national. As most readers are aware, the NFB has been steeped in documentary filmmaking for almost three-quarters of a century, and any filmmaker in its ranks, whether Native or non-Native, must feel the gravitational pull toward nonfiction that emanates from its Montreal offices—it is simply what the NFB does best. And the reason the NFB has been so invested in nonfiction has to do with national context: documentary has special significance in Canada, where the Griersonian project took root more deeply than anywhere else in the world. For white Canadians in particular, documentary has long been an essential mechanism for cultural nationalism, prompting, according to David Hogarth, the Canadian Television Fund to dub it "a profoundly Canadian form" in 1999. Documentary television in particular has been heralded as Canada's "most distinguished contribution to televisual form, and television's most substantial contribution of a Canadian sense of place," as Hogarth puts it. In short, documentary has been a key site for the production of Canadian identity, for generating a unique sense of (white) Canadian peoplehood, which, in the eyes of some critics, has made it a "hegemonic cultural apparatus *par excellence*."

Because it has assumed such a "heavy rhetorical burden in Canadian cultural discourse," as Hogarth claims, it makes sense for oppositional artist/activists such as Obomsawin to be drawn to it—where else could she get such a sober hearing for Native points of view? If documentary was at the heart of the Canadian public sphere, she was going straight there to make her appeal.[27]

Yet, as one factor bleeds into another, it becomes clear to me that the answer to the question, Why Documentary? involves more than economic determinism or even the particular institutional or national cultures in which Obomsawin has worked. Rather, her reliance— indeed, the general Native reliance—on nonfiction also stems, I think, from documentary's unique role in the contemporary mediascape of North America. Offering a mode of address that seems *almost* as "serious" as official reports or social scientific research, documentary has evolved into the most accessible of the *discourses of sobriety*, a loose category that includes economics, education, foreign policy, science, and other "vehicles of domination and conscience, power and knowledge, desire and will," as Bill Nichols puts it. Within the documentary arena, claims about the social are given more credence than with other forms of creative expression such as fiction film, poetry, or painting. Unlike these other media, nonfiction film *appears* to bear the indelible imprint of the real, the apparent one-to-one link between event and evocation that scholars describe as *indexicality*. Much of the power of documentary comes from its ability to trade in potent fragments of authenticity known as *indexical images*, which can spark the "you are there" sense one gets when looking at a Robert Capa photograph of a soldier dying on a Spanish battlefield—it is a gut feeling that this image is utterly real and unfakeable (even if digital technology has changed all that forever). As Nichols has suggested, indexical images have a stickiness that binds them to the particular, the historical, the real, and gives them additional social weight, far beyond what is warranted. What Nichols calls the *documentary effect* pushes the viewer "back toward the historical dimension and the challenge of praxis with a forcefulness born of the text's almost tangible bond to that which it . . . represents."[28] Because of this representational force in the imagination of many viewers, documentary has become a critical site for making arguments about the world, albeit one whose power is easily abused.

Although documentary is in many ways as artificial as its fictional counterpart, viewers are often willing to accept it as an unproblematic form of realist expression, which, as more than one government agency has noticed, makes it very well suited to political persuasion. Homi Bhabha, Patricia Zimmermann, and other scholars have pointed out that nations depend heavily on their ability to "narrate themselves" and have relied on documentary as an important resource in this self-defining process, with the most obvious result being propagandistic films like *The Triumph of the Will* (Leni Riefenstalh, 1935) or *Why We Fight* (Frank Capra, 1943–45). (Less obvious, but no less pernicious, is how the corporate media have proved a welcoming home for official versions of reality.) Obomsawin and other dissenting artists have also recognized the power of documentary, which they have used for opposite ends: to unravel the homogenizing fictions of the nation and replace them with *other* visions that have been ignored, repressed, shunted to the side in the past. The result is the great tradition of activist documentary that tends to build on (and feed) the work of existing reform movements—for example, antiwar films often developed out of antiwar movements that can support and disseminate them. Native nonfiction, at least as Obomsawin practices it, is yet another aspect of this long tradition of documentary expression as cultural activism, one that is predicated on the perceived power of nonfiction discourse to change the world.

Some academic observers might raise an eyebrow at this continuing faith in documentary's power, the nature of which has been closely questioned in the past decade. In summarizing some of the main debates in contemporary documentary studies, David Hogarth notes three potential problems for those who might put their media hopes in nonfiction projects. First, in an image-saturated world in which no one visual text is taken seriously as an object of contemplation, documentary will inevitably lose its power to persuade. Second, as the stylistic lines between documentary and fiction continue to blur, viewers will lose sight of the real in the ever-expanding haze of blurred boundaries.[29] Third, digital technologies will undermine the indexical status of the photographic image in a way that makes *seeing is believing* an ever more ludicrous proposition. Yet so far none of these have poisoned the allure of the real for the average viewer. As Hogarth points out, audiences remain largely immune to these intellectual quandaries and continue putting stock in nonfiction discourse in a manner that prompts CNN and other media giants to increase their investment in the form.[30] Somehow, even today, documentary retains much of its traditional power to inspire and inform, and its privileged status among visual media remains largely intact. This persistent allure of the real comes, I believe, from the illusion that shrouds nonfiction discourse—the dubious principle *seeing is believing*.

Many viewers believe that *nonfiction* means "nonfiction," that the prefix *non-* does, in fact, negate the subjectivities of the text.[31] The resulting hermeneutic of gullibility, in which authenticity is taken for granted whenever a text is properly framed as "sober" nonfiction, has become the bane of media scholars everywhere, who assume, quite rightly, that it opens viewers up to crude ideological persuasion. Such blind faith in the televisual may be fading somewhat in light of cynical reality programming, in which the producer's motivations and manipulations are often too obvious to hide, but, in the meantime, the perceived authenticity of documentary has a silver lining. As long as viewers tend to regard documentary as a more serious, more credible, more authentic reflection of the world, then we can do a world of good if this faith is handled with appropriate care. Native activists with camcorders can use documentary as an ideological solvent to strip away the illusions of the dominant culture and reveal the underlying order of things—in effect, to create a cinema of decolonization, or even what I will later describe as a *cinema of sovereignty*. This is why, as Stephen Leuthold has suggested, Native people often regard documentary as "a form of historical truth speaking . . . a way of accurately recording and presenting both history and contemporary lives in contrast to the fictitious world portrayed in popular imagery [like Hollywood movies]."[32]

This decolonizing impulse has obvious appeal—and urgency— for indigenous peoples, who have often turned to documentary as part of a larger, and quite sensible, media strategy. According to two Latin American filmmakers, Fernando Solanas and Octavio Getino, a realist approach is a wise first step toward developing a cinema of decolonization in any context. "Imperialism and capitalism, whether in the consumer society or in the neocolonialized country, veil everything behind a screen of images and appearances," they write. "The restitution of things to their real place and meaning is an eminently subversive fact."[33] As a discourse of sobriety, at least in its more credible manifestations (Obomsawin, Claude Lanzmann, de Antonio, Marcel Ophuls, Kopple, Wiseman, Morris, etc.), documentary has been a useful weapon in the culture wars of the West, in those Gramscian battles of position to determine which ideas will flourish at the center of the national imaginary and which are exiled to the margins. Getting one's perspective taken seriously at the very center of things is crucial to activist filmmakers like Obomsawin; this desire is what makes her a cultural broker between Native and white and what makes her an artist at war with the remnants of colonialism. She wants to speak truth to power in the Chomskyan sense, and documentary provides her with an ideal means of amplifying her voice to an audience well beyond her own community.

Yet, again, this is just one of her motivations. When asked why documentary is so important to her, Obomsawin explained: "Because it's the life and history of all people. This is why documentary is important for all—not just us [Native people]." Her belief is that Native people cannot function effectively in the present without a profound sense of their past: how can someone thrive in contemporary society, she asks, if they are not allowed to know their traditions, where they come from, what the world of their parents and grandparents and great-grandparents was like? In answering such questions, she says: "I think this is where documentary filmmaking becomes such an important way of preserving and teaching and making sure people have a place to speak. It changes society. It brings knowledge [about] the others that you always call the others. And all of a sudden you realize that they feel like you, and they have stories that are similar, and they need you, and you need them. And I think the documentary world does that very well."[34]

In this statement as elsewhere, Obomsawin's rationale for doing documentary breaks down into at least three parts: documentary's historiographic ability to convey repressed knowledge about the past; its perceived ability to effect social change; and its ability to convey her own ethos of humane universalism across parochial divisions such as those of race and culture. I cover these three points in some detail as I see them as fundamental to Obomsawin's documentary practice.

Documentary/History

The first point, about the intersection of documentary and history, is essential. Not only is Obomsawin connected to the indigenous present, but she is also connected to its past in ways that most filmmakers would never contemplate. I have already written about the storyteller aesthetic that she brings from Abenaki culture and how documentary cinema became an extension of what her tribal elders taught her in the oral tradition. Even when she was first struggling to learn how to make movies in the late 1960s, she never had any doubt about her work's significance to her tribal past "I felt I was pleasing my ancestors," she said, "and I don't mean just my village but where I came from as an aboriginal woman."[35]

Through her documentaries, Obomsawin attempts to inscribe the historical onto the contemporary, reminding us that the past has special relevance for Natives, that it remains alive in ways that are politically and socially significant. Obomsawin is not alone in her reliance on documentary to connect viewers to the neglected histories of Natives. Steven Leuthold has noted that indigenous documentaries such as *Kanehsatake* "often tie the past to the present," emphasizing the linkage between historical events and contemporary concerns. He points out that Native documentary cinema arose in the 1970s, around the same time as "distinctly native still photography" and for many of the same reasons.[36] He does not list the reasons, but I assume that they include a newly emerging sensitivity to Native cultures on the part of nonprofit and government agencies that might support media activism, a growing sense of empowerment among Native peoples in the wake of the Red Power movement, and greater access to sophisticated representational technologies in places like Montreal, Seattle, and Los Angeles as well as in remote locations across Canada and the United States.

Leuthold suggests that, for Native filmmakers and audiences alike, the documentary, with its familiar reliance on storytelling, offered a compelling mechanism for preserving and publicizing Native histories, even to some extent pushing aside traditional oral histories as "a way of creating familial continuity and cohesion."[37] One scholar has described Obomsawin's work as the cinematic equivalent of "Amerindian autohistory," a term coined by Georges E. Sioui (Wyandot) to describe an approach to the past in which disparate forms of Native recollection (oral, written, and artistic traditions) are given the same weight as official processes of memorialization, mainstream academic discourse, and other non-Native forms of interpreting the past.[38] By revealing the moments of convergence between Native and non-Native perspectives, "autohistories" can suggest the validity of Native accounts even to skeptical outsiders.

In Obomsawin's case, her cinematic autohistories are very much at odds with what is taught in the schools of Quebec, Calgary, Vancouver, Los Angeles, Atlanta, or Boston. After all, the United States and Canada, the two great imperial civilizing projects of North America, have covered their tracks with the dust of myth since the moment of their birth, leaving what really transpired on this continent unknown to most citizens of both countries. At every turn in our education, and underneath vast swaths of our public culture, we are given a triumphal march of progress, a stirring drama called the *conquest of the West*, with starring roles afforded to stock characters such as individualism, materialism, capitalism, modernism, reason, progress, and democracy. As the anthropologist Kathleen Stewart points out, when we think about the settler-states on North America, we are so inundated with the myths of nationhood that "an exegetical list of traits comes to us as if from a news brief from Washington or from the memory of a fourth-grade textbook on American Civilization," and I'm sure that a slightly altered version of that sentiment would apply above the Forty-ninth Parallel. In her research, Stewart looks for alternative narratives in what she calls a *space on the side of the road*, where the Other can talk back to the mainstream mythos and open up a gap in the "order of myth itself—the grand order of summarizing traits that claim to capture the 'gist' of 'things' " where we live.[39] This spatial metaphor goes to the heart of Obomsawin's project: for thirty years, she has been creating a space for herself and other Native people at the side of the road of the Canadian mass media, trying, not always in vain, to get oppositional visions of the past taken seriously.

Documentary/Social Change

The second point about Obomsawin's motivations—that documentary can be an engine for change—is more controversial. Scholars, filmmakers, and other onlookers have never agreed about the real-world impact of cinema in general, let alone one as confusingly rooted in reality as documentary. Some skeptics have even suggested that documentaries have no discernible impact on the world whatsoever and that their real value lies only in the fleeting, individual stimulation of the interested viewer—or, even worse, only the filmmaker.

The legendary documentarian Frederick Wiseman fits into this cynical camp. "Documentaries are thought to have the same relation to social change as penicillin to syphilis," he says acidly. "The importance of documentaries as political instruments for change is stubbornly clung to, despite the total absence of any supporting evidence." Wiseman even refuses to distinguish between documentaries and obvious works of fiction such as plays, poems, or novels, as if there were no effective difference between *Cats, The Night before Christmas, Beyond the Valley of the Dolls*, and documentaries like *Shoah* (Claude Lanzmann, 1985), *In the Year of the Pig* (Emile de Antonio, 1969), *American Dream* (Barbara Kopple, 1991), or *Kanehsatake*—all are simply "fictional in form and have no measurable social utility," he says.[40]

Wiseman's point of view does not convince me, and I am not even sure how he can make such an argument when his first film, *Titicut Follies* (1967), caused such a political and legal uproar with its depiction of gruesome conditions in a Massachusetts state mental institution. Unlike Wiseman, I believe that documentary filmmakers such as Obomsawin do more than satiate our idle craving for interesting information, for what Bill Nichols describes as wanton *epistephilia*—learning about the world just for the heck of it. If such epistephilic desire often leads nowhere other than our own couches and VCRs, I still believe that a powerful argument can rouse us to action in a way that Wiseman thinks impossible. On these rare occasions, at the very least, documentary cinema has the power to move the viewer to "confront a topic, issue, situation, or event that bears the mark of the historically real," as Nichols puts it. [41]

Obomsawin shows how this confrontation can knock us off the couch and spill into the streets in meaningful ways—indeed, much of what I have already said about her career suggests that documentary can get results, even clear and immediate results (if not entirely "measurable" in the sense that the lawyerly Wiseman might prefer). Leading a camera crew behind the barricades at Oka to shoot what would become *Kanehsatake*, Obomsawin was told repeatedly that her presence made a difference, that a Native person with a camera had a restraining effect on the military. Screening *Incident at Restigouche* in the town where it was filmed, Obomsawin created a communal experience that seemed to provide the Mi'kmaq viewers with a greater understanding of what had happened and even, in some cases, a sense of personal dignity. In making *No Address*, the filmmaker encouraged some small but concrete changes in welfare administration, such as allowing people to use homeless shelters as their address for receiving government aid, which had not been allowed before. "This is why I make these films," she has said: "to go for changes." [42]

Perhaps the best example is *Richard Cardinal*, whose real-world impact I mentioned earlier in passing. "One time I was in Edmonton," Obomsawin remembers, "and a man who had been the provincial ombudsman presented me with two reports, saying that the Richard Cardinal film had helped force new policies and laws in Alberta." When the ombudsman said as much to an audience, someone demanded to know why the government needed Obomsawin's film to rouse it from its bureaucratic slumbers? "Sometimes this is what it takes," he replied, matter-of-factly. "Sometimes the general public must put pressure on government for there to be a change." [43] In addition, the viewing of *Richard Cardinal* became a permanent addition to the training of social workers in Alberta after the provincial government bought the rights to use the film for this purpose. "Many social workers in different departments see it now," Obomsawin has said with satisfaction.[44] Given these concrete results from her documentary practice, it is hard to understand the position that Wiseman articulates. At least in a best-case scenario, such as Obomsawin's thoughtful, well-researched, and institutionally supported work, documentary does matter to the world at large.

Documentary/Universalism

This third point concerns Obomsawin's ethos of humane universalism, her passionate belief in extending dignity and basic rights to all aspects of Canadian society, most especially those who have been pushed to the margins—Native children in foster care, small bands of resisters against the encroachment of the state, the homeless, and the addicted. Believing that all human beings deserve respect, self-determination, and a fair hearing, Obomsawin has applied her personal doctrine of universal human rights to Native people in particular, who have, she believes, been subject to a disturbing degree of abuse, intolerance, and ignorance. Her means of combating this situation is through listening to those marginalized voices. "For me, every human story, every life matters," she says. "I'm interested in everyone's life—what they've gone through, how they live, how they feel, how their spirits are."[45]

Such sentiments have long been associated with the documentary form. At least in its more admirable aspects, documentary cinema has always been a place for expressions of cross-cultural empathy, invocations of human connection, and hopes for social amelioration—all qualities that are fundamental to Obomsawin as a person and a political artist. Given her political goals as an artist and activist as well as her personal background, the humanizing discourse of documentary suits her perfectly. Obomsawin comes from a humble background little different from that of her Native subjects, which means that she is more than another privileged observer engaged in *studying down*, as the social scientists once put it.[46] In her documentary efforts, she extends her hand in solidarity to the kindred spirits around her and does so in a way that sets her apart from many documentarians. As a result, she never seems wracked with the debilitating self-consciousness that afflicted, for example, James Agee, that great poet of human particularity, in his collaboration with the photographer Walker Evans, *Let Us Now Praise Famous Men*. For Agee, ever the pensive Christian, fear and mystery were at the center of his foray into the unenviable lives of Depression-era sharecroppers, about whom he transmitted a few relevant bits of rural discomfort to better-heeled readers in New York and San Francisco. As anyone who has read the first chapters of Agee's book will recall, he constantly threw up his hands in dismay at the presumption, the impropriety, the impossibility of the documentary task he had undertaken at the behest of *Fortune* magazine, whose simple assignment led, eventually, to an idiosyncratic work of genius that has cast a long shadow over all subsequent nonfiction.

Yet somehow Obomsawin stands outside its shadow. Because she comes from such a different place than the famous Harvard/Exeter/ *Fortune* magazine writer of midcentury—a different place, really, than most of those who have attempted to document reality—she expresses none of the bourgeois self-flagellation that Agee employed, quite artfully, to excuse his privileged presence in an illiterate hollow of Alabama sharecroppers. So often a cultural insider among the people she is filming, Obomsawin has a far different relationship to her subjects than most mainstream documentarians, for whom Agee could be said to speak. If Agee was tortured by his sense of being the outsider among the oppressed, Obomsawin seems to feel a deep and gratifying bond of shared experience with her subjects, making her as close to an insider as she could be without coming from the specific village in question. "I don't want to be the outside eye looking in," she says emphatically.[47] Always striving to honor the connections between Native people, she has made lifelong commitments to the communities she depicts on film, which gives her work, as Robert Appleford has suggested, "a vital depth that is missing in many of the films made by those unfamiliar with native life."[48]

Her desire to look at indigenous issues "from within" has informed all aspects of her documentary practice, creating a spirit of solidarity with her indigenous subjects that follows her through the filmmaking process. While Obomsawin was working on the final touches of *Incident at Restigouche*, Mi'kmaq people from Restigouche drove to Montreal to visit her in her editing suite. Her sense of connection prompted her to hold the premiere for the film where it was shot, rather than at a distant film festival. Such acts of reciprocity between filmmaker and subject are essential to her view of documentary, and she delights in how such moments bring the community together, sometimes in a manner that is transformative. On the night of the first screening in a Restigouche church hall, Mi'kmaq children were running around until the film began and the marching boots of the Sûreté du Québec boomed from the speakers—suddenly, the children were silent and still, watching the film recount the traumatic events that most of them had experienced firsthand. The power of the moment extended beyond the children in the room, Obomsawin believes. "The film gave people dignity," she says, remembering: "There's one man who was badly beaten, and pulled by the hair, and paraded through the reserve—we see him on screen. And he told me that his son had seen him being arrested and had heard what people were saying. I guess the young boy was humiliated and embarrassed about his father. The man said, 'After the film, my son kept hanging around and then told me he finally understood what had happened.' I brought dignity to his father, and so from feeling ashamed, the boy's feelings switched."[49]

Unlike the author of *Let Us Now Praise Famous Men*, Obomsawin has no reason to doubt her connection—personal, historical, tribal— to her interviewees, and for this reason she does not swim in the Ageean sea of guilt over the act of representation. Where she is coming from is miles apart from the average documentarian (read: white/male/middle class), and, while James Agee might well have been from another planet for all he had in common with sharecropper wives like Sadie Rickets and Annie Mae Gudger, Obomsawin is usually toiling in her own backyard, figuratively speaking, as an Abenaki woman exploring the lives of Mohawks and Mi'kmaqs, those neighboring tribes to the east and west of her own people to whom she has devoted at least seven of her more than twenty films. All her work is a result of her profound sense of social responsibility to her indigenous neighbors, a responsibility best fulfilled, she believes, through documentary.

Obomsawin is not the only filmmaker with this contention. The British director Ken Loach told *Positif* in the early 1990s that filmmakers with the means to address the general public must "expose the lies and hypocrisy of politicians and the interests they represent." Documentary muckraking of this sort is a "responsibility," Loach claimed, because it has far more value than "a hundred self-absorbed movies, however prettily shot."[50] Obomsawin seems to embody this position, having decided that documentary is the best vehicle that she can imagine for her particular cinema of duty, one that compels her to stand with other Native people—indeed, with all oppressed people of decency—in opposition to the injustices of the world.

Vargas Llosa's Question

Earlier I mentioned the renaissance of documentary studies, a laudable development that seems to be trickling back and forth between film studies and adjacent fields such as English, sociology, American studies, and anthropology. At that time I mentioned the enduring power of documentary and suggested why it was useful to an activist filmmaker like Obomsawin. But I do not want to paint too rosy a picture about documentary today. All too often (and despite the breakthrough success of a few recent titles by Michael Moore and others), the thoughtful regard for nonfiction exists in academic isolation, while the general public lets out a gaping yawn in the face of nonfiction that seems the least bit challenging or serious. Documentary might be a significant discourse of sobriety that warrants our attention as scholars, students, and filmmakers, but, frankly, it's not reaching every demographic: a good portion of the general public is simply uninterested in what it has to say. To them—and their numbers are legion—serious documentary is just plain old change-the-channel boring, in part because its sobriety is so very much at odds with the vast sea of infotainment and pseudorealities elsewhere on the tube.

In a larger culture resistant to artistic seriousness of all kinds, some hoary cultural prejudices still linger to keep documentary a few steps beneath other art forms in the grand pecking order of creative expression. Consider, for example, the recent question posed by the novelist Mario Vargas Llosa: "Why literature?" In a widely quoted essay of that title in the *Atlantic Monthly*, Vargas Llosa answers his rhetorical question in a number of ways that he considers unique to the written word. Yet his paean to the sagging shelf of literary classics strikes me as too narrow, too parochial, and not just because it comes from a celebrated novelist who is invested in the word in every way imaginable. It is because much of what he says about literature could be said of documentary cinema as well, at least as it is appears from the imagination of someone like Alanis Obomsawin. Let me trace some of the similarities that might prompt another question—Why not documentary?—when looking to ordain one form of expression as having particular value to the world.

In his essay Vargas Llosa sounds the alarm about the declining interest in the world of literature, arguing that a society without literature is "condemned to become spiritually barbaric, and even to jeopardize its freedom." En route to a rather defensive celebration of the word and its supposedly unique properties, he shoots past the reality of what other mediums (such as nonfiction film) can offer. Consider how what he says about one could apply to the other. Just like literature, documentary film can offer a space for powerful evocations of the real (or what might be real) pulled from the recesses of the human imagination. Just like literature, documentary has the ability to serve as what Vargas Llosa calls a "common denominator of human experience," where disparate individuals can transcend the accidents of race, class, and gender that plow through our identities and mangle our sense of common cause. Just like literature, documentary can allow us to "understand each other across space and time," perhaps saving us from the sectarian sins of race and nation. And, quite unlike literature, documentary often brings us into physical proximity with other human beings, in a theater or a living room or a church hall in a Mi'kmaq fishing village. One point for documentary.[51]

Not that Vargas Llosa would notice: "Nothing teaches us better than literature to see, in ethnic and cultural differences, the richness of human patrimony, and to prize those differences as a manifestation of humanity's multi-faceted creativity."[52] Ironically, he elevates one of those creative facets above the rest in his rush to assert the singular glories of the word. Yet I wonder: would a fine novel about Oka surpass what Obomsawin has accomplished there? I'm not sure it would. As a writer of both fiction and nonfiction, I can appreciate the word fetish that goes into Vargas Llosa's pronouncements (which may reflect the wider cultural prejudice against the image that has its roots, according to Mitchell Stephens, in the Protestant Reformation).[53] But, in the age of literature's great waning in terms of popular appeal, I wonder if we should put aside our literary lamentations to practice speaking across borders in the new lingua franca, in the images and sounds that propel the most seductive cultural engines of the new millennium—cinema, television, and the Internet, the last of which is struggling out of its textual shackles with every small expansion of bandwidth. When Vargas Llosa frets that a "totalizing and living knowledge of a human being may be found only in literature," that an "integrating vision," a "universalizing discourse" exists nowhere else, he is little more than an aesthetic reactionary.[54]

I have a more optimistic view, one in which visual culture has room for something more than infomercials and *Big Brother*. Perhaps nonfiction film and video can be understood—*and nurtured*—as another forum for the literary impulse, rather than its looming replacement, and documentary artists such as Obomsawin, who comb poetry and provocation out of social facts, can be appreciated as literary artists working in a new medium, as televisual Zolas. Tom Wolfe once asked where the new Zolas would be found, now that postmodern gamesmanship, as he saw it in the late 1980s, had killed off the great novels of social change. Young novelists elbowed one another aside to counter Wolfe's charge, but few thought to look at videotape, that inelegant sandwich of plastic and magnetism that holds the creative life of people like Obomsawin. Certainly, no one thought to look at the far end of the shelf reserved, somewhat begrudgingly, for independent documentaries—those little films with little audiences, yet still larger than the readership of many prizewinning novels.

We do not need to degrade the image to exalt the word, yet Vargas Llosa does just this in his influential essay, claiming that film and video cannot teach us "the extraordinarily rich possibilities that language encompasses" because "the audiovisual media tend to relegate words to a secondary level with respect to images."⁵⁵ Here he is just wrong, and what he asserts must be the product of a busy writer's inattention to the more complex shadows on walls of cinema. As mentioned in a previous chapter, Obomsawin begins her projects by listening carefully to the spoken word, then recording stories in multiple languages on plain audiotape, before even thinking about images. Vargas Llosa is simply ill informed about the case of polyglot filmmakers such as Obomsawin: documentary is not deaf to the nuance of language and can be invested with the richness of the human voice.

I love the celebration of literature as much as I love literature itself, yet I would ask Vargas Llosa and his logocentric companions to make room on their shelves of leather-bound classics for some migrants from another genre of creative expression, one that has literary qualities all its own. Although documentary filmmaking is a young art form compared to most, it may have more in common with literature than we realize. Perhaps in a few hundred years, when *Kanehsatake* is as venerable as *Don Quixote* seems now, when the documentary tradition has been nurtured, tortured, and creatively hijacked as much as the art of fiction, then we can put the two side by side and better recognize the family resemblance. Not just the sainted novel but also the documentary film is among what Vargas Llosa describes as the "ways that we have invented to divest ourselves of the wrongs and the impositions of this unjust life."⁵⁶

Redemption?

I focus on Obomsawin because I think that her work has uncommon power—perhaps even enough to convince people of the merits of documentary in its sanest and most compassionate form. In *Beautiful Losers*, Obomsawin's friend Leonard Cohen asks the question, "What is a saint?" In a novel that one critic has described as the "sometimes perverse search for modern sainthood," one of the characters provides us with an answer: "A saint is someone who has achieved a remote human possibility."⁵⁷ In her efforts to bring recognition to the repressed and endangered aspects of First Nations' life, Obomsawin has become a kind of alternative media saint, at least in Canada, where she has received accolades and admiration from many quarters. She has been awarded the prestigious Order of Canada as well as honorary doctorates from York, Concordia, Trent, Carleton, and other universities. She has won dozens of prizes and achievement awards for her filmmaking career, including the Canadian Native Arts Foundation National Aboriginal Achievement Award. She has served in leadership positions at the Native Women's Shelter of Montreal, the Canada Council's First Peoples Advisory Board, the Aboriginal Peoples Television, and the Public Broadcasting Association of Quebec. Without question she has been the most influential Native media figure in North America, and her films, as Zuzana Pick has claimed, "have fundamentally altered the way in which the cause of First Peoples have been communicated to non-Native Canadians," as I noted in the first pages of the book.[58] Even Kateri Tekakwitha, the mute object of Cohen's fetishistic reveries about Native sanctity, could not have done more for Native people.

I suspect that James Agee would have been skeptical of such success, having once fretted: "Official acceptance is the one unmistakable symptom that salvation is beaten again, and is the one surest sign of fatal misunderstanding, and is the kiss of Judas."[59] Yet somehow Obomsawin has avoided the pitfall of co-optation, instead seeming to grow bolder and more autonomous with every passing year. Rather than caving in to the pressures of success, she has carved out a niche that might be called the *radical center*, where an artist, once well enough established, can forge some independence even inside a state institution like the NFB. It is, once again, a middle ground of sorts, a slender place between power and truth, that she occupies along with a select few artists. Although her place may be at the symbolic center of the Canadian mediascape, she still continues to draw her strength from her experiences and interactions at the margins.

As Obomsawin and other creative people make quite clear, the cultural margins are not lifeless places that artists must flee in desperation to find appreciative audiences for their work—far from it. Ecologists have long suggested that the edge of the forest, where the trees give way to pastures, can be the most rewarding destination for foraging animals. Liminality and fecundity are not opposed to one another in nature, nor are they, I hope, in the cultural life of a nation. It almost goes without saying that some of the most interesting perspectives and developments exist around the bend from normative cultural discourse and that isolation from the mainstream can be a creative blessing. The great challenge, of course, is ensuring that art on the edge is not associated with life on the edge, that creative and economic marginalization do not go hand in hand, as so often is the case. This double whammy against the creative impulse is a blow to public life as well as to the life of the mind, and it deprives us of whatever ideological redemption that political art can offer.

Yes, I have used the words *redemption* and *saint* in reference to Obomsawin's documentary project in the preceding pages, suggesting either that I have not outgrown my Catholic school training or (more likely) that I have been up too long in the perversely religioliterary imagination of Leonard Cohen. Let me be clear about what I mean by these words because I am quite certain that my definitions would disappoint the black-cassocked Christian Brothers who wandered the halls of my old New Jersey high school. One of Canada's brightest native sons, the literary critic Hugh Kenner, once commented in his book *The Pound Era* (1971): "Whoever can give his people better stories than the ones they live in is like the priest in whose hands common bread and wine become capable of feeding the very soul."[60] Aside from the gender of the pronouns, that is what I am talking about. Perhaps *saint* is too strong a word, even in the limited manner in which I am using it here, but I want to suggest a deeper role for art in general and nonfiction cinema in particular—and suggest that certain documentarians have embraced what might pass for a sacred task in a secular age, namely, that of preaching parables of the real to the politically unconverted who want for "better stories" (sometimes without even knowing it). It is in the nature of art, at least where it intersects with an activist's intelligence, to dream of remaking the world.

Perhaps I am being naive; perhaps it is too much to expect redemption of any kind from the ephemeral world of art, even from projects as embedded in the real as Obomsawin's. After all, the ideological sins of nationhood in North America, where long-simmering anti-Indianism and crudely masculinist visions of history have taken hold for centuries, are not so easily cleansed from view. If so, I deserve a trip to the theoretical woodshed for suggesting that a Native artist could effect some small redemption within the national imaginary, that her work might do something more than flicker past on-screen and be gone—and I can think of at least one scholar who might be inclined to doubt my words.

In her stunning book of nonfiction theorizing called *States of Emergency*, Patricia Zimmermann even appears to strike preemptively against my sort of musings. In her polemical engagement with our current media culture, Zimmermann disparages the "religious conception of documentary redeeming the nation and the spectator through good works and good intentions, like a missionary to the masses of the uninformed." Lamenting the overdependence on texts that will "activate" our politics, she seems to scorn the Griersonian state of affairs in which we need films like *Richard Cardinal* to get us riled about Native foster care in Canada. Zimmermann argues that this is what documentary tried in the past, and her implication is, I think, that it was not enough. Instead, we need something edgier, more challenging, something that ruptures the formal orthodoxies to which political documentary has often been stuck. It is a powerful critique, yet, in her "non-negotiable imperative" to reformulate independent documentary for the new millennium, she seems a little too quick to dismiss the lessons of older nonfiction filmmaking as out-of-date and theoretically retrograde.[61] No doubt, she is right that we need new strategies for telling stories about the real world and its most urgent problems, but I suspect that the best of these innovations will be built on groundwork laid by Obomsawin and other women whose documentary counterdiscourse is more subtle in its subversions, more palatable to ordinary viewers, than supposedly avant-gardist projects that make a show of pushing the envelope for the benefit of six like-minded souls.

Still, I appreciate Zimmermann's basic desire to rattle the status quo and explore new forms of political mediamaking. Without question, it is a shame that dull orthodoxies have turned *documentary* into a sleep-inducing word for many people. As Louis Marcorelles once wrote: "Thousands of bunglers have made the word [*documentary*] come to mean a deadly, routine form of film-making, the kind an alienated consumer society might appear to deserve—the art of talking a great deal during a film, with a commentary imposed from the outside, in order to say nothing, and to show nothing."[62] Yet, in a time of excess information, indeed, a grotesque surplus of damaging stimuli, well-crafted documentaries like *Incident at Restigouche* or *Spudwrench*—uncontroversial in format, oppositional in content— can focus public attention and move at least some people to reassess their beliefs. Even if redemption for the nation at large is too much to expect from any kind of creative act like cinema, individual salvation is quite possible for those whose minds are not terminally closed. We need to have hope in this possibility.

Why? What do I mean by this? In a sense I am talking about faith after all. Zimmermann chides those who adopt a "religious conception" of documentary's power, but what is wrong with a taste of that dubious fruit if it inspires us to keep hacking at the web of mythologies in which we are forced to live? After all, we do not want to zap the creative metaphysic that propels good work into being, that productively deludes the artist (or perhaps not) into thinking that his or her work will strike home with more than a few friends and critics. If Vargas Llosa and so many others can find quasi-religious transcendence in the literary act, then why not in documentary cinema as well? After all, where else in the realm of expressive culture are we supposed to turn for illumination? We need a redemptive force based on the intellect in our systems of information; we need powerful antidotes to the seductive mythologies of nation and capital; and we need them in the realm of new media (cinema, television, the Internet) as much as in the old (books, songs, sculptures). We need it more than we realize.

This is not the time to debunk documentary for its epistemological shortcomings, just as Native people are beginning to gain a foothold in its production. We have taken the critique of representation far enough in recent decades, whether it is the poststructuralist turn in the academy since the 1970s or the reflexive documentaries beginning with Jean Rouch and Edgar Morin's *Chronicle of a Summer* (1961). Today we no longer have a pressing need to reveal the "constructedness" of nonfiction to the point of demolishing its semiotic authority, given that documentary is the one place within our electronic media that allows some complexity and contemplation, not to mention some oppositional edge. Instead, this is the time for muckraking documentary projects, which are built, inevitably, on the precepts of realism and positivism—on perceived facts and our faith in them. Without utterly losing our heads in the slipperiness of representation, we must *critically* reinvest our faith in a seemingly factual mode of communication where the reality of someone like Alanis Obomsawin can challenge the greater national imaginary and perhaps bring human beings together across tiresome lines of division. Surely, there is some secular sanctity in the most passionate representations of the world around us, in particular human visions that flagellate the national body and gesture toward political salvation. If we honor these *other* visions, perhaps, as Tiziana Terranova has suggested, media activists like Obomsawin might be able to "inject the media landscape with enough impetus to collect the scattered postmodern subjectivities into something that would be closer to the mass explosions of the previous decades."[63] It is a hopeful thought in these dark days for observers of the mass media and its perverse political economy.

Today, we are witnessing the trashing of the real, the willful distortion of actuality in the service of ideology and profit, and the dissipation of truth in the black hole of commercial mass media. What I am proposing as a form of resistance is a "return to the real" that allows us to put stock in the *other* visions of Obomsawin and other alternative media figures as something more than subjective idiosyncrasies. Those who care about such things have long realized that documentary is not real, but that it's real enough to matter, and that it matters very much right now.[64] To a degree that was unthinkable in the past, "life experience," as Todd Gitlin has pointed out, "has become an experience in the presence of media," one that is essentially seamless in nature. "Even as we click around, something feels uniform—a relentless pace, a pattern of interruption, a pressure toward unseriousness, a readiness for sensation, an anticipation of the next new thing."[65]

Documentary as Obomsawin practices it can rupture this seamless torrent of image and ideology. Instead of joining the torrent, it can offer slow, serious, and even subversive points of view. I know that I have learned—and felt—all sorts of things from documentaries. When I was in college, Emile de Antonio's *Millhouse* (1971) provided me with my first visceral sense of the duplicity of American power during the cold war, Ira Wohl's *Best Boy* (1979) made me wonder anew about the fragility of the human condition, and the Maysles brothers' *Salesman* (1969) revealed the Lomanesque futility propping up the great engines of capital. Documentary even schooled me in its own limitations. Trinh T. Minh-ha unveiled the manipulations of the Western gaze in her *Reassemblage* (1982), while *How the Myth Was Made* (1976), George Stoney's critique of Robert Flaherty's legendary work in Ireland, revealed the elasticity of the visual record in a way that I had hardly imagined. So years later, when I saw *Kanehsatake*, I was not surprised by its impact on my own thinking. The film gave me a glimpse of First Nations histories through the lens of a landmark event I had barely registered before, enough of a glimpse that I wanted to overcome the provincialism of American studies (and Americans generally) to look north and learn something about what was going on in places like Oka. I think that I have completed that cycle—viewing and then doing—enough times in my own life to know that nonfiction is more than a solipsistic exercise, that Wiseman is wrong, that Obomsawin is right to keep making films, and that hers is a model to which we might aspire. How this might be the case for indigenous people in particular is the subject of the next chapter.

6

Cinema of Sovereignty

As the start of the new millennium came and went, Alanis Obomsawin followed the path of more than one well-regarded artist: having
reached a certain stage in a storied career, she turned her gaze ever
closer to home. Nearing and then surpassing seventy years of age, the
filmmaker did not slow down in the slightest but instead returned her
cinematic energies to the Wabanaki people, the cultural grouping of
Algonquin speakers composed of her Abenaki kin as well as Mi'kmaq,
Malicite, Passamaquoddy, and Penobscot neighbors across the far
northeast. Once again it was the Mi'kmaq in particular who drew
her attention. Intending to document yet another encroachment of
state authority on Native rights, she went back to the Mi'kmaq fishing village of Restigouche fifteen years after her original visit as well
as to the communities of Burnt Church and Estigouche. As in her
1984 documentary *Incident at Restigouche*, the problem was once
again related to the water, where a bitter dispute with government
authorities was brewing over Mi'kmaq fishing rights. Over a span
of several years between 1998 and 2002, the filmmaker visited the
impoverished fishing communities, carefully documenting the conflict and its aftermath. Having grown accustomed to working on a
grand scale with her sprawling series of Oka films, Obomsawin did
not limit herself to a single glance at the Mi'kmaq situation, instead
preferring to release an ambitious pair of ninety-minute documen-

taries called *Is the Crown at War with Us?* (2002) and *Our Nationhood* (2003).

Even the titles of these films are unusually revealing about the film-maker's point of view, now marked by growing impatience and frustration over the disregard of Native rights. "It was kind of a shock that in the year 2000 we are seeing this thing happen again," Obomsawin said.[1] Perhaps more clearly than ever, her latest work illustrates her response to such situations, namely, the development of a bold media strategy that we might call an indigenous *cinema of sovereignty*. Before explaining this concept through an examination of Obomsawin's two most recent documentaries, I want to provide some background on the conflict itself and explain how fishing rights became so central to contemporary Native politics, especially for coastal tribes such as the Mi'kmaq. Like Obomsawin's Abenaki relations, her Mi'kmaq neighbors are little known and often misunderstood even within their own province, let alone in the broader sweep of North American politics.[2] As does Obomsawin herself, their story deserves, I believe, greater currency in the United States and Canada, both of which have fought hard against the tribe's survival as a sovereign nation.

Background to the Conflict

That the great crisis of the Mi'kmaq people would flow from the water in their midst—indeed, that water would once again symbolize their lifeblood as a sovereign people—must have come as no surprise to tribal citizens who had been schooled in the ways of Glous'gap, the indomitable Mi'kmaq cultural hero from their mythic past. As an embodiment of the Great Spirit, this legendary "elder brother" had guided the Mi'kmaq into existence in the first chapters of their tribal cosmology. Ever since, Mi'kmaq children who listened to tales of his adventures would have learned about him creating the wide waterways and beautiful land all around them; battling Gitji' Kwa'bit, the Great Beaver, to prevent him from reshaping the world; and fighting to free Mrs. Bear when a sorcerer kidnapped his forest friend. They would also have learned about how the first Mi'kmaq village swelled in numbers under his protection, as he taught their ancestors to catch salmon, sew clothing, and build shelter alongside the icy stream he had chosen for their benefit. "All was going well, just as Glous'gap had intended," says one contemporary Mi'kmaq storyteller on whose work I am drawing here, "until, that is, the water ceased flowing."[3] In a tale called "Glous'gap and the Water Monster," Mi'kmaq children would have learned what happened next.

For several anxious months, their ancestors waited in vain for the water to return. At long last, the village elders decided to send one of their young men north along the streambed, now littered with dry leaves and dead fish. After an arduous journey, the young man discovered the source of the stream and the problem itself. Somehow a new village had sprung up, populated by a strange race of people— not quite people, really, at least not by Mi'kmaq standards, for they seemed selfish, cold, and unwelcoming. The young man noticed that they lacked the hearts of real human beings and even polluted the water with their own toxins. Pleading for a small cup of this foul water to slake his thirst, the young man was denied even a drop, with the explanation that all the water was the exclusive province of their great chief.

After asking how to find this great chief, the young man soon encountered a warty, yellow-eyed beast the size of a mountain. He approached cautiously and told the beast about the Mi'kmaq dilemma downstream, but it gruffly replied that it did not care in the least. The rapacious beast had already swallowed bears, trees, moose, and even entire villages and now made motions to engulf the young man, who, wisely, ran back to his village.

Glous'gap soon heard what happened and prepared himself for battle: he grew to a height of twelve feet and shook the earth with his stomping feet. Moving quickly through the woods, he located the beast far upstream and demanded a return to the natural order of things, but the response was the same: "All the waters are mine! Go away! Go away! Or I'll kill you today!" Not one to take no for an answer, Glous'gap attacked the great beast and slit open its enormous gut, spilling out a vast quantity of water that quickly refilled the stream as far as the Mi'kmaq village and well beyond. The story ended with Glous'gap punishing the beast for its greed by squeezing it between his palms until it was shrunk into a humble, croaking creature now known as a frog, which he then tossed into the swamp.

I tell this story not just because it a wonderful example of the Wabanaki oral tradition in which Obomsawin herself was steeped or because it establishes the centrality of water to the Mi'kmaq worldview. I also share it because it provides a rich metaphor for the situation that Obomsawin would document off the shores of Restigouche and Burnt Church. No better allegory could be imagined for the Mi'kmaq struggle to protect their ancient water rights against the "imperial monster" of the modern state, that encapsulating and polluting power that sought to ignore treaty obligations, choke off the Mi'kmaq lifeblood, and hoard the sea's natural resources for itself and its non-Native constituents. And, even if one doubts that the symbolic roots of the contemporary fishing disputes touch the core of tribal mythology, there is little doubt that they weave throughout hundreds of years of Mi'kmaq history, especially after contact with Europeans.

Like the Abenakis and other tribes of the eastern seaboard, the Mi'kmaq had the historical misfortune of discovering Europeans in their midst not long after Columbus first set sail. In 1504, a "floating island" (a ship) crawling with "bears" (strangely attired sailors) dropped anchor off the coast of Nova Scotia where the Mi'kmaq lived, ending their age-old belief that they were the easternmost people on the earth.[4] Within decades, these "floating islands" were a common sight, as the Europeans established a permanent presence among the Mi'kmaq and their neighbors. The European motivation was in the sea itself, in particular, the abundant fisheries that had allowed the Mi'kmaq to depend on the ocean for 90 percent of their diet.[5] By the seventeenth century, Europeans were operating a booming fishing trade that was even more profitable than the legendary fur trade of North America, and each year their ships were bringing millions of fish to markets in Paris and elsewhere across Europe. Prosperous as the Europeans were, it was a difficult time for the tribe. Although the Mi'kmaq were not often at war with these new arrivals from France and elsewhere on the European continent, the tribe suffered a serious population decline because of disease, falling from a high of perhaps fifteen thousand at contact to just thirty-five hundred by the early eighteenth century.[6]

The situation grew worse over the course of the eighteenth century with the arrival of English power in the Maritimes. The title of Obomsawin's *Is the Crown at War with Us?* comes from a Mi'kmaq fisherman who asked a rhetorical question with a long and painful history of his Abenaki interviewer. Blessed and cursed with enviable natural resources and a location of strategic importance, the Mi'kmaq soon found themselves engaged in centuries of enervating conflict with the English crown and its Canadian successor. If the tribe had sometimes been able to work out a satisfactory relationship with the French, the Anglophone authorities seemed mostly interested in eliminating the Native presence in their midst and did all they could to hasten the precipitous decline of the Mi'kmaq population well into the nineteenth century. Disease, alcohol, the encroachment of white hunters, and other factors contributed to this demographic decline, as did the genocidal policies of the government and its white supporters. As one historian has noted, the eighteenth-century English colonials served poisoned food to Mi'kmaq guests, issued bounties for Mi'kmaq scalps irrespective of victims' sex or age, and intentionally distributed disease-ridden cloth, resulting in the deaths of three hundred Mi'kmaqs. The Mi'kmaq were even unlucky enough to experience the wrath of the infamous Major Rogers himself, the nemesis of the Abenakis who, as we have seen, had burned the homes of Obomsawin's ancestors. In 1759, the same year he attacked the Abenakis, the major led a raid on a Mi'kmaq encampment in Nova Scotia during which he followed the same gruesome protocol that marked his appearance at Odanak.[7]

Outright war with the crown devolved into various forms of internal colonialism in the nineteenth century. As white settlers kept arriving on Mi'kmaq land in disturbing numbers, government authorities pushed assimilationist policies that would shift the tribe from "savagery" to "civilization," as they saw it.[8] Much was lost from the Mi'kmaq world over these decades, yet something essential was preserved, in part because in 1853 the tribe secured a small but important portion of its traditional land base as a reserve. Despite the

limited refuge that the reserve offered, cruel tests of domestic de-
pendency marked the Mi'kmaqs' lives in the late nineteenth century
and continued into the twentieth, as the Mi'kmaq people and their
children, including the future poet Rita Joe, were jerked between
modes of assimilation and resistance. The poet recalls being filled
with bittersweet fascination for the regal power of the metropole
in the 1940s and how easily that feeling was punctured by the drab
reality of colonial life. Describing an event from her time in an Indian
boarding school in Nova Scotia, she captured an emblematic moment
in her poetry: "I am happy / The King and Queen will pass by on a
train, they say / All the boys and girls on the reservation / Will receive
pants, skirts and sailor blouses." When the day is over, somehow the
royals have failed to appear, and she has lost her chance to wear the
new clothing. Disappointed, the child in the poem responds: "Gone,
my longing to see the King and the Queen."[9]

Later, as a teenager going to school in Halifax, Rita Joe experienced
the common alienation of Mi'kmaq children growing up far from
home, looking for their place in a modern white nation whose young
men yelled "squaw" at her on the streets of the small city (echoing
the treatment that Obomsawin received a few hours east in Three
Rivers). Joe remembers the scene in her verse:

> Your buildings, tall, alien,
> Cover the land;
> Unfeeling concrete smothers, windows glint
> Like water to the sun.
> No breezes blow
> Through standing trees;
> No scent of pine lightens my burden.

By the 1970s, Rita Joe was on a poetic parallel to Obomsawin's career.
She was finding her voice as a Mi'kmaq poet and directing it, often,
at the white Canadians who did not seem to understand her people.
"Your history tells our children / what you want them to learn," she
complained, and she asked her imaginary listeners for a moment of
empathy in place of smug certitude: "Let us trade places just this once

/ And you listen while I go on about my culture / Important just like yours / But almost dead."[10]

Until quite recently, most academics would have accepted this last line at face value, pointing to the fact that 99 percent of Mi'kmaq land had been lost since contact with Europeans. Yet the tribe was far from "dead" in the twentieth century—its language was very much alive, along with much of its cultural heritage, even if outsiders tended to overlook these facts.[11] One of the by-products of the Mi'kmaq's long history of contact was a perception, quite common by the twentieth century, that they were no longer "real Indians" (Abenakis have encountered the same bias). White scholars and other onlookers assumed that five centuries of cultural exchange, intermarriage, and assimilation had pushed Mi'kmaq identity to the breaking point. By 1958, one Canadian archaeologist had even declared: "The Mi'kmaq is faced with the unenviable choice of going out into the white man's world where he may find a future but must lose his past, or of remaining in the reserve where he may keep his past but have no future." Lamenting this situation in the kind of terms often associated with the myth of "the vanishing Indian," the archaeologist added: "Could we not have spared a little dignity to their sunset?"[12]

Throughout the twentieth century this was the dominant perspective among white Canadians, who grew up learning little about Mi'kmaq history and culture except its supposed disappearance. Given this ignorance, it is no wonder that few Canadians would understand why contemporary Mi'kmaq people would reassert centuries-old treaty rights as their own. From such an inherently imperial vantage, white Canadians might have been tempted to think that an authentic Mi'kmaq nation was nothing more than a rhetorical conceit, one that had evolved in the wake of 1960s liberation movements into a desperate legal strategy to secure natural resources. Few outsiders knew the truth as Obomsawin did. In preparing to make a film about her northeastern neighbors, she was walking into a black hole of public awareness—with few exceptions, the Mi'kmaq had not been the subject of significant media attention.[13] Once again her desire was to present the silenced voices, tell the neglected stories, and show that the vital relation between the Mi'kmaq and the sea was more than a nostalgic stereotype, that it was a legitimate and legally binding attribute of their sovereign nationhood.

Is the Crown at War with Us?

> Without fish they would have to endure evil days.
>
> SEVENTEENTH-CENTURY FRENCH
> JESUIT DESCRIBING THE MI'KMAQ

Water between trees, water shimmering with sun, water as far as the horizon. With each cut, a wider slice of the Mi'kmaq world appears on-screen, and the images flow in this manner for nine of the first ten shots, none of them on-screen for more than a brief moment. Sophisticated folk music on the sound track adds a note of languid melancholy to the images, some well crafted, others more amateurish, in an odd mix of video and sixteen-millimeter that has never marked Obomsawin's work before. (The video appears simultaneously crisp and shallow in comparison to the richer film image.)

In addition to a poetic litany of water imagery, Obomsawin touches on her usual preoccupations in the first moments of Is the Crown at War with Us?—the vulnerability and resilience of Native children, the rich and calming natural resources of Native land, the prominence of Native women in tribal life. She even combines all three elements in one quick sequence: Mi'kmaq children descend a staircase, then the camera seems to gaze appreciatively up the trunk of a tree, all while a Native woman's voice is heard talking about the pain of what happened to her people on the waters in the year before.

Cut to the distant past—a Catholic church, the voice of a priest, snapshots of Mi'kmaq children after their first communion, the 1940s, the 1970s, the 1990s. Even in the first minutes of the film, Obomsawin moves several times between past and present, intertwining the two in the way that has become customary for her. The temporal shuttling continues into the next scene: a man in traditional garb addresses the camera in his traditional language, before a young woman dances in matching clothes as an off-screen voice explains in the language of contemporary higher education how his world, the Mi'kmaq world, is interwoven in deeper ways than social science or state bureaucrats can understand.

We return to the water. An eloquent young Mi'kmaq man, wide like a linebacker, pilots his small craft a mile from shore, while on the sound track a voice explains: "We played and lived our whole life around that water; it revolves around that water. It is integral to our culture and our people and our livelihood." Cut to the linebacker gently explaining how the Canadian government has robbed his children of their right to fish. Cut to another fisherman, more hardscrabble in aspect, calmly stressing his willingness to resist the efforts of the government.

Even in the first moments of this documentary, most Canadian viewers would realize that Obomsawin is going against the grain of mainstream press coverage. Across Canada during the late 1990s, the headlines in local, provincial, and national newspapers were filled with language tipped in favor of the government's position, with loaded words including *illegal traps, warriors, extreme militancy, intransigence,* and *warpath.*[14] "Polite Canada sits on its hands as Native militants flout the law and demand the moon," cried a headline in the Alberta-based *Report Newsmagazine.*[15] One academic observer named Paul Fitzgerald claimed: "The Canadian public were denied extensive exposure to the views of the other side, that of the small First Nations community directly affected."[16] According to Fitzgerald's analysis, mainstream media went on a "vast fishing expedition" for "quick and easily digested stories" about Burnt Church, leaving the Canadian public in the dark about the deeper histories at work. While Fitzgerald argued that too often the point of view that made its way into the press was nothing more than a hastily digested version of official press releases, another writer complained that the words of government spokesmen were being elevated "to the status of objective truth."[17]

Certainly, few outside observers would have known that Burnt Church had an unemployment rate that was more than double the provincial average for New Brunswick (35.6 vs. 15.5 percent) or that Mi'kmaq fishermen were dropping less than 0.5 percent of the 950,000 traps in the local waters, the rest being the property of non-

Natives, who reaped as much as C$100,000 a year for a few months' work.[18] Nor would most viewers watching, say, CBC newscasts in their living rooms have understood the underpinnings of the Mi'kmaq case, which was formidable on both legal and moral grounds. After all, the Supreme Court of Canada had supported most of the Mi'kmaq treaty-based fishing claims in the 1999 Marshall decision, and problems arose only when the federal Department of Fisheries and Oceans (DFO) took a position that ran counter to the highest court's decision. Obomsawin's documentary attempts to correct this perceptual imbalance between what was right as she saw it and what was widely understood about the Marshall ruling and its impact on the Mi'kmaqs' sovereign rights to the seas.

Not even ten minutes into *Is the Crown at War with Us?* Obomsawin reviews the legal situation of Donald Marshall and the landmark case that bears his name.[19] According to the filmmaker, the Canadian Supreme Court decided that the Mi'kmaq retained particular fishing rights, rights that were based on eighteenth-century treaties whose validity the government had tried to undermine.[20] Obomsawin lets a stuffy English voice read from the old treaty while black-and-white archival images move past—this film has the best use of still photographs in her career. Next, she shows the joyous response in the streets of Burnt Church when the court decision affirmed the Mi'kmaqs' right to the waters, at least to the extent of making a "moderate livelihood." The film points out that a "moderate livelihood" involves just four traps per Native person during a few weeks each fall, which represents a small fraction of the total number of traps in the waters and certainly far less than what non-Native commercial operations were using.

In celebration of the decision, the Mi'kmaq take to the ocean in their various boats, with Mi'kmaq women in the lead. "It took the women of our community to make it happen," says a Native man in voice-over, making a characteristic Obomsawin point. But the film shows how non-Native fishermen fought back almost right away, with the result being that soon the communities were "at war," as Obomsawin puts it. A flotilla of non-Native fishing boats, some 150 vessels, crowds into Mi'kmaq waters, and burly fishermen begin storming

FIGURE 24. Mi'kmaq women with their lobster traps in *Is the Crown at War with Us?* (2002). Directed by Alanis Obomsawin. Produced by Alanis Obomsawin. Mi'gmaq fishermen Karen Somerville (*left*) and Miigema'gan. Photograph by: Pamela Mitchell. © 2002 National Film Board of Canada. All rights reserved. Photograph used with the permission of the National Film Board of Canada.

into one another's faces: the Mi'kmaq curse at the men trying to keep them from fishing, while whites throw out racial slurs, shoot bullets in the direction of Native boats, and vandalize dozens of Native traps.

Even worse is the official response, in which the DFO seems to disregard the Marshall decision and instead clamp down on Mi'kmaq fishing with a variety of bureaucratic pretexts. Claiming that the decision gave them the obligation "to limit treaty rights in the interests of conservation and fairness," the DFO adopts an aggressive posture toward the Mi'kmaq fishermen. In the film we see a sympathetic white lawyer who explains to the camera that the state "brought its full force to bear with helicopters, patrol boats, guns, dozens of [Royal Canadian Mounted Police] cars, on the people of Estigouche." In grim echoes of Oka, Obomsawin shows armed police officers arriving in powerful boats to harass the small Native skiffs that remain near the shoreline. Between such raw, dramatic footage, Obomsawin cuts away to show the state trying to defend its position, which, in the context of her film, seems untenable. In a televised press conference, Robert

Nault, the minister of Indian affairs, explains, "We no longer have an extinguishment policy" with regard to Native rights, but his words do not seem persuasive when juxtaposed with the DFO's actions on the water.

As in many of Obomsawin's earlier films, the voice of the state seems at odds with the voice of the people, at least that of the Native people, who come across as both earnest and reasonable. In one of the film's best interviews, Obomsawin sits down with James Ward, a muscular, self-defined Mi'kmaq "warrior." With a martial bearing acquired during years of U.S. military service and a sophisticated understanding of the issues at stake that he honed in graduate studies on the subject of aboriginal self-determination, Ward is both a powerful physical presence and a highly articulate spokesperson for the Mi'kmaq cause. As he describes the situation at length, Obomsawin cuts away to archival photographs that connect him with warriors of the Mi'kmaq past, thereby casting an aura of historical legitimacy on his position.

The heart of the film is in the section after that in which we are able to witness violent confrontations between government officials and small Native fishing boats. Water splashes on the lens as we follow the Royal Canadian Mounted Police (RCMP) and DFO efforts to shut down what they call *unlicensed* Native fishing, even at the small-scale subsistence level that the tribe insists is its sovereign right, an insistence based on the Marshall decision and other historical reasons. Using shaky amateur video footage that captures the Mi'kmaq point of view, Obomsawin does a remarkable job of showing the tensions on the water. Shouts and threats echo from both sides as government agents ram into small Native fishing boats, capsizing several of them, and even turning around to run over half-sunken vessels. Native mothers watch from the shore, praying for their sons to make it through the danger, while the RCMP shoots tear-gas canisters and seems to act like "modern-day Indian fighters," as one Native interviewee puts it.

For anyone vaguely familiar with recent Canadian history, the shadow of Oka must linger over these events, a fact that one Native spokesman makes explicit when he warns government ministers about repeating what happened at Kanehsatake. Another Native fisherman shakes his head sadly and asks the eponymous question: "Is the crown at war with us?" As if to suggest an affirmative answer, Obomsawin cuts to the DFO's capture of several Native fishermen, including several who had been knocked out of their boats and into the churning sea. The men seem overwhelmed and exhausted when pulled from the water, yet we learn from a Mi'kmaq interviewee that the RCMP charged them with "assault with a deadly weapon" for brandishing a wooden paddle.

Obomsawin makes no secret that she is recording these events from a Native point of view, and, even within the film itself, she hints at the galvanizing power of what she is doing with her cameras. "I didn't see how bad it was until I saw the tape of what happened," says one Mi'kmaq fisherman who had been on the waters during the clash. "That was when it was really scary," he tells Obomsawin, who cuts away to slow-motion images of the man's boat being rammed. "Because I almost died out there," he continues, "and I don't want to leave my kids yet. It's hard to believe we have to fight this hard for something that's ours already." Throughout *Is the Crown at War with Us?* Obomsawin makes her activist position even more explicit than it is in past films. "Hey, come closer, I want to talk to you," she yells at government officials from the stern of a Mi'kmaq boat, but the officials seem wary of the camera and speed off. In a later scene a Mi'kmaq elder asks her if the government position seems "crazy," and she says "yes" with a laugh. By choosing to leave such moments in the film, it is clearer than ever that she includes herself in the first-person plural that appears in the titles of her two newest films.

Is the Crown at War with Us? "is a gritty film [that is] not as aesthetically complex as some of [Obomsawin's] other films," Liz Czach, a programmer for Perspective Canada at the Toronto International Film Festival, has said. "It speaks of a certain urgency."[21] Czach is probably right, although the film succeeds, I believe, on other fronts. Not only does it provide a gripping account of a particular Mi'kmaq crisis, but it also captures Obomsawin's ongoing concerns about Native people. As do her earlier films, *Is the Crown at War with Us?* documents the oppressive nature of the encapsulating state, the creativity and tenacity of Native resistance, the strategic importance of pan-tribal solidarity, the political prominence of Native women in contemporary First Nations, and the occasional willingness of progressive white supporters to cross racial lines to offer crucial support. The film ends with an August 2002 agreement that affirms some aspects of Mi'kmaq sovereignty, although the real victories are apparent only in the sequel, *Our Nationhood*.

Our Nationhood

Our Nationhood begins in much the same way as its predecessor, although from the first moments it seems rougher in construction and more militant in tone. In the opening scenes, we see camouflaged Mi'kmaq men setting up a barricade across a highway—it is not quite clear what is happening at first, although it soon becomes evident that the men are asserting their rights to ancestral woodlands. In wobbly amateur video, we see these Mi'kmaq loggers working to establish their own claims to their traditional forests, while the Canadian government articulates other designs for the land. In the first half hour, the film does a good job of depicting the negotiation process between the parties, showing how the tribal leaders keep framing the issue as a question of sovereignty, much to the government's chagrin and/or incomprehension.

As usual, Obomsawin moves quickly to a historical overview of Mi'kmaq history, one that emphasizes Native traditions of environmental conservation in both logging and fishing. "It was nature that taught them how to live," Obomsawin says in a gentle voice-over that seems a little too didactic in places. "Their territories and resources were taken away from them," she says, "and the fight continues to this day." Executing a very effective cut from historical maps of the nineteenth century to contemporary video footage of Mi'kmaq men in the woods, she suggests the continuity—and legitimacy—of the struggle.

In the next section of *Our Nationhood*, Obomsawin moves between logging and fishing, the woods and the sea, the two great natural assets of the Mi'kmaq people, and draws comparisons between the fishing crises at Restigouche in the early 1980s and the current logging

FIGURE 25. Mi'kmaq roadblock in *Our Nationhood* (2003). Directed by Alanis Obomsawin. Produced by Alanis Obomsawin. Photograph taken from the production. © 2003 National Film Board of Canada. All rights reserved. Photograph used with the permission of the National Film Board of Canada.

dispute. Both situations were, she suggests, the result of government infringement on Native sovereignty. To underscore the point, she uses several minutes of footage from her classic documentary *Incident at Restigouche*, before cutting to the traditional chief, Gary Metallic, speaking in Mi'kmaq to a crowd of locals in the late 1990s (the chief is traditional in the sense that his influence comes from lineage rather than elections, which are invested with the authority of the state). The chief refers to the events from the 1980s as if they are still very much alive for his Mi'kmaq listeners and cites the historic precedent of Restigouche to support his strategy of continuing civil disobedience and unyielding resistance to the crown. His point of view appears to have carried the day because the next sequence shows the tribe setting up the giant barricade that appeared, with little context, in the opening scenes. Massive front-end loaders dump upended cars across the highway to stop traffic until Mi'kmaq demands are met. Not surprisingly, protestors from neighboring white communities are soon in the streets. "I don't believe it's their ancestral rights," one young female protestor complains to the camera in French. "Every year they have new ones," she adds in disgust, adding another characteristically Obomsawin moment to the film.

Unsympathetic whites are not the only obstacle that the Mi'kmaq encounter in *Our Nationhood*. As Obomsawin often does, she pays careful attention to the inner workings of the mainstream media, showing how white journalists were running amuck on the normally quiet reserve, pointing cameras and microphones in every direction. Seeing their backstage confusion is illuminating, to say the least, about the construction of mainstream news coverage of important events like the ones we see unfolding here. Yet uncomprehending journalists are but a small obstacle compared to the Canadian government itself, whose ministers display a surprising level of intransigence toward the Mi'kmaq in general and especially toward Chief Gary Metallic, a former steelworker who comes across as both telegenic and truculent in his on-screen defiance of both the government bureaucracy and the elected band leaders of the Listuguj First Nation, whom he sees as insufficiently autonomous from the state. In one press conference a high official talks about the absolute need to respect the democratic process, but, when the Mi'kmaq community votes against one of his proposals, he then belittles them as small group of "dissidents" with whom he cannot negotiate. In the end, however, he must negotiate with the tribe, which we see making a thoughtful, collective decision to accept a partial victory regarding the logging woods. As Obomsawin shows the Mi'kmaq beginning the peaceful removal of the highway barricade, Chief Metallic and other leaders describe the importance of such incremental steps in restoring tribal sovereignty. "The land was taken illegally," Metallic says to Obomsawin's camera, before explaining that his tribe will regain their ancient territories "sooner than people think."

The film might have ended with this comment somewhere near the hour mark, but it is fortunate that it does not. *Our Nationhood* gains considerable force in its last section, the final half hour of the film. After a title announces "Part II: Three Years Later," Obomsawin explains that "changes did occur." Creating a much more upbeat tone than she did in part 1, Obomsawin shows a joyous Mi'kmaq community gathered around a traditional drum, then a vast celebratory march through the streets of the reserve, and finally a dedication ceremony for an official Mi'kmaq fishing fleet and wharf. Leaving behind the logging crisis almost entirely, part 2 focuses explicitly on fishing and provides a sort of coda to *Is the Crown at War with Us?* In several moving interviews, Obomsawin revisits the men injured at Restigouche in the early 1980s. "From '81 to now, it's a giant change," says one, and Obomsawin takes pains to show how much the tribe has transformed its own situation. By 2002, the Mi'kmaq had assumed control of their waters without federal interference and had even launched a commercial training program for young Mi'kmaq fishermen and -women. "Now we decide on how we are going to fish and how everything is going to work," says a Mi'kmaq man with his temples going gray. "And, like I said, twenty years ago we didn't have that."

In the highlight of the film, Obomsawin then dissolves to an image from *Incident at Restigouche* of the same man as a teenager, standing alongside the same water, with the same body language, lamenting the original 1981 raid. This sort of diachronic analysis in the final third of *Our Nationhood* is the most valuable aspect of the film because it shows the fruits of a long-term process, a process that Obomsawin has been documenting all along. The film soon comes to a close on a positive note. "Instead of the white man controlling us, we can control ourselves," explains a fisherman who had been maimed in the 1981 raid. "The Mi'kmaq people are like a sleeping giant," says another, in the final words the film, "and the giant is finally waking up."

Despite the power of its final scenes, *Our Nationhood* does not have the impact of its companion piece, *Is the Crown at War with Us?* The camera and sound are sometimes uneven, and the unfolding events are not quite as dramatic. Also to its detriment, the film focuses on a few male figures rather than showing the broader Native community, especially the women, who usually provide Obomsawin with her ensemble cast. For all these reasons I can appreciate the assessment of the *Variety* reviewer who decided that *Our Nationhood* "doesn't come close to the power of [*Kanehsatake*]."[22] Other reviewers have been more generous, one claiming that the film represents "a work of great craft and art . . . [and] further proof of Obomsawin's place as a respected elder of Canadian documentary."[23] Whatever its shortcomings, *Our Nationhood*, along with *Is the Crown at War with Us?* provides an essential document of the changing Native situation in Canada in the twenty-first century. "History is not going to look kindly on how natives were treated in this episode," one local observer said about the fishing disputes in particular, and this is undoubtedly true if Obomsawin's work makes its way into the historical record.[24]

For me, the importance of Obomsawin's latest Mi'kmaq films, aside from providing what at some point might become a historiographic corrective, is in how they exemplify the powerful media strategy that she has developed to support First Nations sovereignty. In the sections ahead, I try to explain the broader significance of her work to Native sovereignty across Canada and the United States, with lessons that might apply to indigenous people around the globe. But, to begin, I share some background on the representational exploitation that has dogged Native people from the earlier clicks of the camera, before positing a mode of resistance that I draw from Obomsawin's work—a cinema of sovereignty.

The Politics of Indigenous Representation

Philosophers tell us that it doesn't matter what the world thinks of us, that nothing matters but what we really are. But philosophers don't understand anything. As long as we live with other people, we are only what other people consider us to be. Thinking about how others see us and trying to make our image as attractive as possible is considered a kind of dissembling or cheating. But does there exist another kind of direct contact between my self and their selves except through the mediation of the eyes?

MILAN KUNDERA, *Immortality*

Although the sad history of Native depiction in photography and cinema might suggest otherwise, ruthless photographic exploitation was not an inevitable by-product of a Western technology set loose on an unsuspecting people. Quite the contrary. At the very beginning of photographic history, Native people exercised a surprising amount of control over their own images. In *Print the Legend*, Martha A. Sandweiss describes the case of Keokuk, the Sauk and Fox chief, who visited the office of a St. Louis daguerreotypist in 1847. As the first Native American to have his picture taken inside a portrait studio, Keokuk might have seemed vulnerable to whatever unscrupulous practices the photographer could dream up, such as coaxing the chief into a degrading pose, hawking his image as a penny postcard, or even turning over the photograph to government authorities to exploit its propaganda value. All manner of mischief was possible, but, as Sandweiss points out, "nothing embedded in the very concept of photography itself dictated such a use of the pictures."[25] Indeed, she shows how, for a brief moment in the 1840s, Native people could seek out a camera to document their lives for their own (often unstated) reasons, without fearing that their images would disappear into the outside world for reasons unknown except to commercial artists or government agents. The daguerreotype was just too difficult to reproduce for such unseemly endeavors, making it much simpler for photographers to respect the wishes of their Native sitters and let them decide the fate of their own portraits.

All this changed in the 1850s with the advent of the glass-plate negative process. As Sandweiss argues, the new technology changed the business of photographing Natives and, indeed, made it a true business for the first time. Now that hundreds of copies of one image could be created at low cost, white photographers began to conjure up lucrative new possibilities for their prints, and their pecuniary impulses transformed what their cameras were willing to "capture." No longer would Native people such as Keokuk have the ultimate authority over the creation and dissemination of their own images. Instead, portrait photographers began taking shots that prioritized their own needs for salable images, deciding what was salable on the basis less of indigenous realities than of hegemonic narratives about Native people as an exotic or vanishing people. Not only did this change the nature of the image itself, as photographers contorted their sitters to fit white cultural expectations, but it changed the subsequent use of that image. Keokuk might have controlled his solitary daguerreotype image until his death, but, once his likeness was transformed into a copy negative, he had no say in its illicit proliferation—which is how it ended up in an 1877 government catalog that described him as a "magnificent savage."[26] Losing control of the physical object meant losing control of how it was presented—and, more generally, that Native images were now ripe for commercial and ideological exploitation. Thus, in the middle of the nineteenth century, the photographic representation of Native people had begun its long descent into exploitation and misrepresentation. It is a story too obvious, too well-known, to warrant retelling here. Suffice it to say that the camera would rarely serve the self-defined interests of Native people in the century ahead.

Today, we have come full circle in at least some promising contexts, and, as one scholar notes, "the modern communications technology that threatens indigenous peoples also provides them with the means to bargain for their cultural survival."[27] With Obomsawin in the fore, Natives have entered the mass media on their own terms, attempting to do what Keokuk could not: have authorship and ultimate authority over their own image. As independent producers working with tribal governments, commercial television outlets, state institutions such as the National Film Board (NFB), and nonprofits like the Native American Public Broadcasting Consortium, Native people have created hundreds of titles, a fact to which I alluded in the previous chapter. If there is a general tendency in this incredible surge of indigenous media, it has been toward the reestablishment of *representational sovereignty*, by which I mean the right, as well as the ability, for a group of people to depict themselves with their own ambitions at heart. Is there a role for non-Native people in this quest for representational sovereignty? Yes, but not without serious qualification.

No matter how well intentioned non-Native documentarians, ethnographic filmmakers, or Hollywood filmmakers might seem, their work cannot speak for Native people in the same way that that of cultural insiders can. I am not saying that only Native filmmakers can produce good work on Native subjects—documentaries such as Jay Rosenstein's *In Whose Honor?* (1997) clearly suggest otherwise.[28]

However, as a general rule, I suspect that cultural insiders have a better vantage from which to tell their indigenous stories.

Let me be clear: I am not advocating a crude notion of biological insiderism, in which expertise on vast racial or ethnic landscapes is bequeathed to individuals by virtue of their genetic makeup. That position has always struck me as a little strange, at least on a personal level, because I realize how little I know of the Irishness to which I am heir. Beyond the superficialities, I have never studied the Celtic tradition with much care or interest and have not spent much time in communities where it was the defining characteristic. Because of this relative ignorance and isolation, I suspect that most Irish people would rightly cringe if I began pontificating about "the Irish condition" or advertising my blood-borne expertise on "the troubles" to television crews and book publishers.

Given this skepticism about equating identity with expertise, I am attempting to use *cultural insider* as something more than a racial position, as something that instead forefronts lived experience without suggesting that race is irrelevant: experience, not blood, must be the key factor, although I realize that the latter can shape the former in powerful ways.[29] The religious studies scholar Christopher Jocks (Mohawk) has put it this way: "One simply cannot gain an accurate understanding of what goes on in Indian Country without living in and around an Indian community for a long period of time. . . . In fact, one really needs not just to reside but to reside *as a relative*, since there are vast dimensions of meaning that are only acted out in this way."[30] Residing "as a relative" is a function of indigeneity, of having been embedded in some organic fashion within an aboriginal community over the long haul, and not the sort of experience that one can get from swooping into town with a film crew for several weeks or even from living as a participant-observer on the edges of a community for the length of a twelve- or eighteen-month grant. If this gives the upper hand to those who grew up in a particular community, I should note that it is not so simple—terms such as *relative* or *insider* are not without wrinkles.

When moving from the particular to the general, it is tempting to gloss over the contradictions on one's way to the proverbial big point.

I admit that there are complications that I cannot explore here. For instance, as more and more Native people take up camcorders and sound recorders, Native media producers might argue about which among them has the right to speak for a particular First Nation. Some might attempt to disqualify certain filmmakers from speaking on their behalf, arguing that the person in question is not sufficiently Native on any number of grounds (the Indian Arts and Crafts Act of 1990 resulted from the same controversies in other mediums).[31] Still others might direct their "sovereign gaze" in directions I cannot imagine, including, in some circumstances, against other groups of Native people. I leave such problems for Native communities to work out on their own terms. Here I suggest simply that what Alanis Obomsawin has done is worth considering as a model for a cinema of sovereignty that could benefit many indigenous peoples in North America and elsewhere. Given her success with both Native and non-Native audiences and what I see as the formal and ideological sophistication of her work, I believe that her career has lessons that extend beyond her own immediate interests. To put it simply, a film such as *Our Nationhood* is about much more than fishing; it is about what the title implies on a number of levels. However, before I make this argument in full, I need to pause for a brief note on the terminology involved.

Rethinking Sovereignty

Sovereignty is among the most potent and puzzling terms in Indian country today. Some scholars dislike it altogether, arguing that it represents a "cruel, mocking legalism" that has little weight in reality, given the lopsided power relations between Indian nations and their encapsulating states.[32] Some Native activists reject it as a term of European origin that does not have a place in their own intellectual history. For example, the Mohawk writer Taiaiake Alfred argues for a radical "de-thinking" of the concept, which he sees as incompatible with authentic Native politics. In his forceful *Peace, Power, Righteousness*, he claims that sovereignty as it is usually understood has "no relevance to indigenous values" and, thus, no place in "the language of liberation."[33]

Yet most observers, Native and non-Native alike, regard sovereignty as an "indispensable tool"[34] that cannot be tossed aside without tremendous risk, given that "nearly every issue that Native Americans face is overshadowed by it," as one editorialist has observed.[35] At least in the foreseeable future of Indian country, sovereignty is here to stay, and even its harshest critics seem open to the possibility of indigenizing the concept. Alfred himself has written: "We need to create a meaning for 'sovereignty' that respects the understanding of power in indigenous cultures, one that reflects more of the sense embodied in such Western notions as 'personal sovereignty' and 'popular sovereignty.'"[36] In the past decade, Alfred and other Native intellectuals have begun to do just what he proposes and have begun broadening the concept. Audra Simpson, a young Mohawk anthropologist, has described indigenous sovereignty as "simply about being," and, in a similar vein, the Mohawk political leader Atsenhaienton has talked about sovereignty as a "state of mind."[37] Whereas in the Western understanding sovereignty is often localized in the institutions of the state, Atsenhaienton argues that it defies such institutional containment and instead resides in the very people of First Nations. For these Native intellectuals, the implication is that sovereignty is much more than the province of the state in some legal or political sense; rather, it is a profoundly diffuse, deeply ingrained, almost holistic sense of governance that courses throughout tribal communities in elemental, and perhaps ineffable, ways.[38] If, as Atsenhaienton suggests, the essence of sovereignty is in the Native ability to use "our terminology to express our self-determination—how we will exist, how we relate to each other and to other people"—then a cinema of sovereignty must facilitate that process in the mass media in ways I will attempt to outline.[39]

"Access to the tools of creation and self-representation is the beginning of self-determination," Marjorie Beaucage, a Métis filmmaker, has said. "For too long our stories have been told by others and our dreams and visions misrepresented."[40] Some non-Native observers might have difficulty imagining such a situation. As I noted in the last chapter, white Canadians have long enjoyed their own sovereign visions in the state's use of documentary to create, refine, and promote a unique sense of Canadian peoplehood. At the same time to the south, Hollywood has promoted a more diffuse, yet still potent, sense of white American identity throughout much of the twentieth century, with the result being a profound streak of nationalism that surges through most Hollywood products. Obviously, as the story about Keokuk might suggest, First Nations have faced very different circumstances with regard to their own images. Denied access to the mass media for most of the last century, Native cultures in North America have not had the benefit of "imagining" their communities in the electronic public sphere, a crucial forum for political self-definition, one that can influence the views of cultural insiders and outsiders alike. Although this situation is changing even as I write, the origins of the process are several decades in the making, hidden in the generally unwritten history of indigenous media on this continent. [41]

Certainly, most of the credit for developing "sovereign forms" of indigenous media goes to Native figures such as Alanis Obomsawin, Sandra Day Osawa, Gerald Vizenor, Phil Lucas, George Burdeau, and others who began making films in the 1970s and 1980s. Their work has been part of an agonizingly slow process of wiping the war paint off the lens, as Beverley Singer puts it, and it has not occurred in a creative vacuum: sympathetic observers have played an important role, too. For example, non-Native media theorists like Eric Michaels began asking the right questions in the early 1980s as part of a larger academic trend in which autonomous indigenous voices were afforded a new level of respect outside their own communities. At the same time, ethnographic filmmakers such as David and Judith MacDougall (*Familiar Places*, 1980) began to work collaboratively with Native people in Australia, bringing them into the production process in ways that heralded a new humbleness on the part of white filmmakers who had long spoken on behalf of "their" Native objects of study. [42] Because Native participants often received valuable technical training in these collaborative projects, they have been useful stepping-stones to what I am calling a *cinema of sovereignty*.

What do I mean by this seductive phrase? Simply put, for people to have the opportunity to make films that tell their own stories, in their own way, to the world. It is more than this, of course, as I will soon enumerate, but the essence of the concept lies in the words of Mokuka, a Kayapo leader and videomaker from deep in the Brazilian Amazon, who addressed a crowd on the opening of the Centro de Trabalho Indigenista in São Paulo in 1991: "Right! All over the world people are looking at these videos we are making of ourselves. . . . These videos will be seen in all countries. Tell your children and grandchildren, don't be deaf to my words, this [work] is to support our future generations, all our people. This is what I say to you today. . . . I am Kayapo doing this work. All of you in all countries who see the pictures I make can thereby come to know our culture, my culture of which I tell you today."[43]

As my use of this quote might suggest, the cinema of sovereignty is about authority, autonomy, and accountability in the representational process. Like the work that Mokuka describes, it is the embodiment of an insider's perspective, one that is attuned to cultural subtleties in the process of imagemaking as well as in the final image itself. (This means that it does not pry into culturally prohibited areas like so many films about Native people.) Its essential question must be the same as the one that the Warlpiri people ask of their own indigenous media in the Australian outback: "Can video make our culture strong?"[44] It is another version of the question asked by Sam Yazzie, a tribal elder who was one of the Navajo participants in a famous 1960s experiment in indigenous filmmaking: "Will making movies do the sheep good?"[45]

Visual anthropologists and other scholars have debated the answer to such questions for several decades, with some coming to the disheartening conclusion that the Western technology called *cinema* is inevitably corrosive to Native cultures.[46] I am not so technophobic, nor do I see Native cultures as fixed entities that cannot adapt creatively to new technologies. Instead, I believe that, with some attention to the preconditions for representational sovereignty (which I will soon describe), the answer to the Walpiri and Navajo questions can be yes. I am not alone in my cautious optimism. In a general sense, a diverse group of scholars including Faye Ginsburg, Terence Turner, Steven Leuthold, Beverley Singer, and Jacquelyn Kilpatrick seems to share the belief that autonomous Native media has become a political and social necessity for indigenous people. Video can make a culture strong, at least as part of a larger, multifaceted effort. It can do the sheep some good—if we understand those animals in the way that I think Sam Yazzie intended, namely, as an elegant metonym for a traditional Native culture.

Let me concede up front, however, that *sovereignty* must be understood as a relative term in the realm of cultural production. Given the hybridized nature of neocolonial life for most indigenous people in the Americas, it is impossible to create a pure alternative to the chaotic, pulsating, omnivorous mainstream. Indeed, so difficult is it to free oneself from overlapping influences (of style, technique, etc.) that scholars have suggested that "the idea of a First World that is neatly distinct from a Third World no longer makes sense"—and vice versa.[47] This is especially true of a Native filmmaker like Obomsawin, who finds herself in the midst of a state institution like the NFB, in a cosmopolitan city like Montreal, in a polyglot nation like Canada. Yet, even if some cross-pollination is inevitable, a distinct cinema of sovereignty can, I believe, still thrive in the hands of Native people working on behalf of First Nations. Using Obomsawin as a touchstone in the pages ahead, I lay out the main principles of the potent media strategy that she has inspired.

Such bold principles might seem absurdly prescriptive and presumptuous coming from a cultural outsider such as myself. I plead guilty to this charge, offering only this defense: I merely drew these insights out of the work of someone who knows what works and what does not in the tricky realm of intercultural communication. As I noted in the preface, at least one scholar has claimed that Obomsawin is single-handedly responsible for changing the perception of Native people in modern Canada, and, for that alone, it seems reasonable to ferret out the broader applications of her work.[48] She must be doing something right, something pretty damn important, even if it has fallen under the radar of most film scholars and teachers.

Strategies of Representational Sovereignty

What are the attributes of a cinema of sovereignty that can be teased out of Obomsawin's long career for the benefit of other indigenous media producers? What qualities have allowed her to connect with audiences both in small Native communities and at elite film festivals?

The first is that her work is the product of a sovereign gaze, one that is imbued with the self-respect and unique ambitions of a self-defined sovereign people, even if this sovereignty carries with it a complex and contested legal status. Rejecting the encroachment of external media nationalisms, her cinematic vision reflects an indigenous sovereign gaze, a practice of looking that comes out of Native experience and shapes the nature of the film itself. The gaze is sovereign, I argue, when it is rooted in the particular ways of knowing and being that inform distinct nationhoods. It is sovereign when cultural insiders are the controlling intelligence behind the filmmaking process, no matter how much non-Natives might help in various capacities. It is sovereign when Native people have, as Atsenhaienton puts it, the ability to use "our terminology to express our self-determination—how we will exist, how we relate to each other and to other people." And it is sovereign when it works against what one scholar has dubbed the "'whiting out' of the Indigene—the projection of white concepts and anxieties about the primitive on to the Aboriginal Other—effected by the white camera eye" in Hollywood and Canadian feature films, mainstream documentaries, and traditional ethnographic cinema.[49] By focusing attention on that which has been overlooked, concealed, or distorted in the mainstream media, Obomsawin's cinema of sovereignty provides an ideological rebuke to dominant practices of looking at Nativeness and, in this sense, troubles the visual impulses of white settler cultures in the United States, Canada, Australia, New Zealand, and elsewhere.

Another lesson that we can glean from Obomsawin's work is that a cinema of sovereignty must speak in the language of equals, assuming a "nation-to-nation" relationship between historically unequal parties such as between the Mi'kmaq nation and Canada. Neither deferential nor hostile in this engagement with the citizens of another nation, the filmmaker chooses instead the traditional diplomatic route of mutually respectful dialogue, even when such rhetoric conceals mutually distasteful ambitions. As befitting this middle-ground approach, she refuses to indulge in the simplistic demonization of all things Western that, in the wake of 9/11, scholars have begun to call *Occidentalism*. Occidentalism reduces the West to an inhuman malignancy, thereby inverting Said's classic notion of Orientalism, in which Arab and Asian peoples were objectified and exoticized from afar.[50] So Obomsawin does not hate Canada or wish harm on its citizens—far from it. She has a deep and perhaps surprising fondness for the country in which she has lived for almost all her life. She merely wants Native polities, whether Mi'kmaq, Abenaki, or Cree, to be placed on an equal footing in the public imagination, the political process, and the law within Canada and the international community.[51]

To achieve this goal despite the contested nature of indigenous sovereignty, Obomsawin includes a strong pedagogical element in her documentaries. Like members of other minority groups, Native people have often shouldered the burden of educating the world about their own histories and aspirations, and Obomsawin has been no exception: for almost forty years her explicit goal has been to create a "learning place" in her cinema for Native and non-Native alike.[52] In this sense her work provides a space for pedagogical engagement that runs parallel to Linda Tuhiwai Smith's notion of *research* as a "significant site of struggle between the interests and ways of knowing of the west and the interests and ways of knowing of the other."[53] In a moment I will discuss "ways of knowing" in Obomsawin's work, but first I want to touch on her presentation of Native "interests."

As is apparent in all her films, Obomsawin believes that the economic, political, and social interests of First Nations have been neglected to the point of crisis, whether in James Bay, Restigouche, Oka, or elsewhere. In response, she strives to fulfill what Ward Churchill once called the *imperative task* of Native filmmaking, namely, to reveal "the real struggles of living native people to liberate themselves from the oppression which has beset them in the contemporary era."[54] Obomsawin has been an exemplar on this front since the early 1970s, having never flinched from the harsh realities of Native-white relations. As the film curator Bird Runningwater has pointed out, her major contribution in films like *Is the Crown at War with Us?* is her exposure of the continuing brutality of state violence against First Nations, a fact that most viewers would associate with the nineteenth century, not the twenty-first. "The Native person as a victim of attack is often described," Runningwater has said. "[Obomsawin] shows the images of these attacks happening in modern times."[55] Wisely, Obomsawin seems to aim her exposure of such issues at more than one audience, creating a cinema of sovereignty that is at once local, national, and global in orientation. Citing the examples of the Waiapi in Brazil and the Inuit in the Canadian Arctic, scholars have written about the many instances in which the empire "speaks back" as indigenous people use cultural products "to reaffirm ethnic and local values over the homogenizing forces of global media networks."[56] For politically minded Native filmmakers such as Obomsawin, the battle is inevitably fought on multiple levels and with multiple publics in mind. It is local because her work respects the tribal particularities at hand and seeks to assist in immediate, short-term efforts (such as the Mi'kmaq fishing crisis); it is national because it engages the national imaginaries of a particular First Nation as well as of the Canadian state; and it is global because it is part of a larger insistence on indigenous rights around the world that scholars have begun to call *international indigenism*.[57] At all levels her goal is to demonstrate the legitimacy of Native claims and to insert Native perspectives into global mediascapes.

Embedded in the notion of *Native perspectives* is a question of philosophy. I believe that Obomsawin's desire to reveal the legitimacy of Native claims rests on an unstated epistemological foundation, one that is essential to any indigenous cinema of sovereignty: a profound respect for Native ways of knowing and remembering. In each of her films since *Christmas at Moose Factory*, Obomsawin has adopted a posture of careful listening as she records Native voices and stories. This is in keeping with her general tendency, noted in chapter 5, to place Native oral traditions on the same level as non-Native forms of writing and remembering the past. In this regard her films might resemble the testimonial tradition in Latin America in working to sanction the claims of alterity and the manner through which these claims are voiced. Another analogue has emerged within recent Native American studies: her documentary project might serve as a cinematic equivalent of what Eva Garroutte calls *radical indigenism*, a "distinctly American Indian scholarship" that is radical, not in the Marxist sense, but in the etymological sense of taking us to the root (*radix*) of the "dominant culture's misunderstanding and subordination of indigenous knowledge." Garroutte argues that colonial legacies have deformed the academy and made it an unwelcome home to alternative ways of knowing: too often as scholars approach Native cultures, the exigencies of "rational inquiry" demand that they strip away the sacred and the perplexingly unfamiliar to create "legitimate" forms of intellectual knowledge. In opposition to this Eurocentric standard, radical indigenism invites scholars to *experience* "tribal philosophies" (rather than just *studying* them) and to discover legitimacy and rationality where social scientists have often presumed their absence. This experiential brand of scholarship also requires a level of personal investment that goes well beyond the ethnographic norm of "field work" to an even deeper intimacy and investment with "tribal relations" (what Jocks terms *residing as a relative*). Although this demanding ethos of radical indigenism would be open to Native and non-Native alike, Garroutte expects that it would resonate most deeply with Native scholars: "I believe it is their passion that can ignite the first flame—the flame that blazes up to illuminate a radically new vision of scholarship and new possibilities for Indian communities."[58]

I believe that Obomsawin's cinema of sovereignty transposes the humbling lessons of radical indigenism onto the sometimes arrogant art of filmmaking. In the spirit of what Garroutte describes, Obomsawin works from a position of unqualified faith in the merits of indigenous worldviews as well as from an enduring connection to the communities where those worldviews hold sway. Also in the mode of radical indigenism, Obomsawin respects what she hears in Native communities and puts it at the center of her filmmaking practice, instead of imposing the voice of academic experts, strikingly few of whom appear in her films, even to offer sympathetic pronouncements. Unlike documentarians who lean heavily on academic talking heads to validate the points of ordinary people, Obomsawin has created a cinema of sovereignty in which Native expertise is allowed to stand on its own, free from patronizing attempts to buttress it from the outside. She has always been critical of outside experts who mine Native communities for data without really knowing or respecting the world in which they are operating: "If you are going to a community and you are learning and you want to write a thesis about what you are learning, you have got to have some respect for the people you are working with. . . . [You can]not think that they are inferior to you because they did not go to university."[59]

Her willingness to accept Native communities on their own terms carries over into her presentation of Native individuality: Obomsawin refuses to homogenize Native subjectivities to create what one might sarcastically call the *universal, omni-purpose Indian*. For example, her latest films highlight the extraordinary diversity of Mi'kmaq people in terms of class, education, appearance, and attitude. Some of the men in *Is the Crown at War with Us?* and *Our Nationhood* seem to fulfill stereotypes of defiantly macho, camouflaged warriors, while others come across as soft-spoken, contemplative, and intellectual— and more than one fit into both camps. In acknowledging such complexity Obomsawin captures the diversity of Native experience in a way that confounds mass media stereotypes, replacing Native absence with an unexpected presence. Her work is a passionate response to the black hole in the mass media where the actual Native should be but where instead there is only a strange simulation that Gerald Vizenor calls an "*indian*."[60] Musing about the best-selling books in which faux *indians* provide a decorative New Age motif, Vizenor has suggested that "the tragic stories of an *indian* absence are worth more to publishers than a real sense of presence and survivance." In other words, most audiences expect fulfillment of their hoary stereotypes about Natives, and the "media simulation" of the *indian* serves this purpose, saturating popular culture in Canada and the United States despite lacking any real "native connection or constituency."[61] In the hands of someone like Obomsawin, a cinema of sovereignty can attempt to make this connection, to address this constituency, to fill in the hole where the *indian* has lived with something more than ersatz projections. It is about the creation of space for Native actuality.

Obomsawin's rejection of the mythic *indian* provides an important antidote to a problematic notion floating through recent anthropological discourse, the idea that films on indigenous people need to indulge the preconceptions of outsiders in order to have an impact. In making a documentary about the Mi'kmaq in the early 1980s, the anthropologist Harald Prins decided that "exotic imagery" is what gets Native faces on television, and that, without a dose of primitivism, a so-called cultural survival film would have little chance to appear before a mass audience. For this reason, he argued in the pages of *Visual Anthropology* in 1997 that such films must carefully pander to the Western fetish for romantic Native stereotypes, if only as part of a pragmatic media strategy that "promotes a people's general public appeal." Barring such indulgence, Native people will have lost a rare opportunity to engender much-needed sympathy among the dominant society, where a quiet yearning for an Edenic alternative has created an "ideological fund of goodwill towards indigenous peoples as 'victims of progress'" struggling to hang onto a more "harmonious," "natural," and "innocent" way of life.[62] Given these assumptions, Prins believed that a well-designed cultural survival film could tap into this fund of goodwill as the first step toward political mobilization around Native issues.

This is where the cinema of sovereignty must diverge from Prins's model of cultural survival filmmaking: it is not willing to accommodate itself to Western norms for the sake of being heard, at least not as Obomsawin has practiced it. Although Prins's model might have been a reasonable first step toward developing more autonomous forms of indigenous media when it was first articulated in print in the mid-1990s, even then it was based on some troubling notions. Who would have advised civil rights leaders in the 1960s to draw on the abundance of white goodwill reserved for African Americans who seemed to fit Sambo or Stepin Fetchit stereotypes? How different from that ugly scenario is the manipulation of Native primitivism for even the best political motivations? Moreover, such pragmatic pandering could have ill effects over the long haul, as Prins himself concedes when he notes that, while "exotic imagery" in the cultural survival film is politically potent, it could undermine the way of life that it seeks to dramatize. Quoting Edmund Carpenter, Prins concludes his article with these lines: "All this is good fun until one realizes that some day [indigenous peoples] will know their heritage through such films. . . . The power of film is such that they may someday accept this as a valid account of their ancestry."[63]

To me, Obomsawin's career seems to suggest that primitivism is not necessary for political impact or mass appeal, given that her work has had demonstrable political effects in several instances as well as significant audiences on television, in hundreds of schools and universities, and at dozens of film festivals in Canada and elsewhere. As far as I can tell, her cinema has never accommodated Western prejudices to make itself heard (even if it wisely avoids antagonizing its largest potential audiences with a strident tone or a unnecessarily militant posture). Rather than painting Native people as victims in need of Western salvation, her work makes its appeal on what Obomsawin seems to regard as a universal playing field of reason, compassion, and decency—not some phony metaphysical plane on which tree-hugging, spirit-questing, magical Indians are served up like an endangered species on the Discovery Channel. Her Natives are never languishing away in a far-off disappearing world that some white liberal viewers might like to preserve; instead, they are presented as citizens of an aggravated and increasingly organized sphere of difference in the very backyard of mainstream Canada. Rather than wielding Otherness as a tool to pry open a wellspring of Western empathy, Obomsawin's cinema of sovereignty instrumentalizes it along the lines that Dick Hebdige has traced (perhaps foreshadowing Garroutte's concept of radical indigenism). The great cultural studies scholar has talked about sites where the Western *we* is invited to learn from the Native *them* with neither cynicism nor sycophancy. According to Hebdige, Otherness is instrumentalized when it is imagined as a viable alternative, a living possibility, not as a colorful deadend on the byways of cultural diversity.[64] Obomsawin does just that, on-screen and off-. In her career the refusal to indulge primitivist expectations extends beyond the cinematic text to include the filmmaker herself, who—in her person as much as in her art—defies and transcends the puerile fascination with the Native filmmaker as a technological curiosity. In her public demeanor she is worlds apart from the exotic novelty act that, according to Rachel Moore, some have seen in the spectacle of a Native person with a movie camera.[65] As such, her work spurns rather than inspires neocolonial twitters and patronizing glances. It commands respect rather than curiosity.

Thus far, Obomsawin's career seems to offer ideal lessons in the creation of representational sovereignty, but things become somewhat messier when we turn from the symbolic to the pragmatic, to the realm of funding streams, mailing lists, and ticket prices. In an ideal world a cinema of sovereignty would be autonomous in production and responsible in distribution.[66] Obomsawin has a mixed, but instructive, record on this front. Like most indigenous media producers, she has had limited success in maintaining the "sovereign" aspect of making and showing her work.[67] For example, the Mi'kmaq nation neither produced nor disseminated the two documentaries that I discussed earlier in the chapter—indeed, few First Nations would have the resources to make this material commitment to Obomsawin's work. Nor did the Mi'kmaq have final say over her films in a way that would place representational sovereignty fully in their hands. Never willing to relinquish the ultimate authority for what appears on-screen, Obomsawin does not reach the Platonic ideal of egalitarian cooperation in the artistic process, although she comes reasonably close in some ways. When it comes to documenting the lives of other Native people, she might not open up the process to absolute democracy, but she is patient, she is respectful, she hires Native interns, she is culturally appropriate as only a cultural insider can be, and she zealously protects Native perspectives in everything she does at the NFB. Some might quibble with her decision to remain at the NFB, but I think that she has played her hand just right. Working within the NFB is a golden sacrifice that she makes to ensure stable funding and widespread distribution. Despite such a potentially problematic arrangement, she has not had to compromise her ideals in ways that I can detect, and I suspect that this is because of the uniquely privileged role that she has created for herself at the NFB. Some combination of her talent and the institution's symbolic economy (i.e., the political need to have a token Native person somewhere in its ranks at a time when she was an almost solitary presence) has protected her over the past three decades and counting.

What Obomsawin has created at the NFB under these conditions is quite remarkable: a semisovereign realm for First Nations' perspectives within the heart of the federal communications apparatus. Hers is an exceptional situation, one not easily replicated, and she has mined it for all it is worth, making all the projects that she has dreamed up, and ensuring that her work does more than sit on library shelves: she takes pains to secure "responsible distribution" of her work so that her films become more than hopeful messages in bottles thrown into the sea of the mass media. As much as is feasible, she follows her work into the world, arranging premieres of her films in Native villages like Restigouche and Burnt Church, and using these occasions as opportunities to talk with Native people whom she might not otherwise meet. Viewing her work as a prelude to conversation, Obomsawin allows her films to serve as an extended invitation to indigenous commentary, giving the Native subject an opportunity to respond to the Native image—and the Native imagemaker—in a way that is all too rare. As she sets up a conversation around her work, she helps create solidarity and insight within specific communities as well as building a "counternational" audience for her cinema of sovereignty.

The fruits of her approach are apparent in the comments of a Mi'kmaq woman named Miigam'agan, a mother of three who lives in Burnt Church. Remembering how she felt when Obomsawin arrived with her NFB crew to shoot *Is the Crown at War with Us?* as well as the happy moment when her community was able to see the finished film, Miigam'agan says:

> During the fishing crisis, we had a number of people that came and did stories, interviews, and documentaries. When she did call I wasn't open—I wasn't rude or anything, but I was already feeling a little bit overwhelmed with the media here. . . . So she came, and *then it was almost like we were interviewing her.* She was bringing her final work for us to look at. It was a history here in the community to see that many people in one room. People were laughing and crying. Even for me, I've lived here for so long, but to be

able to hear voices from other community members that I know normally would not talk as openly and comfortably in public forums—it was such an awareness. (emphasis added)

Obomsawin has similar memories of the premiere, which she held in a school gymnasium in Burnt Church. "It was just incredible," she recalls. "When you go to the communities it's always so special." She remembers how the audience, including many people who had taken part in the turmoil, watched the film with passion—crying, laughing, talking loudly.[68]

As this example suggests, a cinema of sovereignty should be based on the principle of reciprocity. I have already noted how the relationship between imagemaker and Native subject has often veered into rank exploitation. Only in recent decades have filmmakers and photographers striven for a more egalitarian relationship with the people in front of their lenses, and some have even hoped to become mere instruments of their subjects' will, thereby "facilitating their objectives in representing themselves," as Eric Michaels puts it. Yet, often, a patronizing element still undergirds this well-intentioned exchange because the Western imagemaker must instruct the Native subject in the pitfalls of the medium: Don't sit like that unless you want to look silly. . . . Are you sure you want to pose like that? . . . What is lacking, as Michaels points out, is instruction in the other direction—the establishment of a reciprocal relationship in which the photographer or filmmaker learns from the subject.[69]

Native filmmakers like Obomsawin are unusual in this regard because in many cases they already possess traditional knowledge as well as Western representational know-how yet they honor the potential for a reciprocal arrangement. In Obomsawin's case this takes the form of an unwavering attitude of respect and openness toward Native people. Obomsawin may have the ultimate authority over the filmmaking process, but she does everything possible to avoid setting herself up as *the expert*. Unlike the example of Keokuk cited above, her cinema of sovereignty is predicated on an enduring ethical relationship between media producer and subject. As Michaels once pointed out, "literally millions" of pictures have been taken of indigenous people, yet most have done little good for anyone except the photographer[70]—I think that this is because they were born out of what I might call *representational wedlock* (i.e., there was no lasting bond between the parties). For this reason, Obomsawin strives to maintain lifelong relationships with the people in her films, once again working in something akin to the spirit of radical indigenism.

There is one last point that I have learned from Obomsawin's work: a cinema of sovereignty is an art, not a screed—that is to say, its success in presenting an indigenous perspective depends on the degree to which it is compelling cinema. No doubt, what is compelling has a great deal of cultural specificity, but good art has a way of transcending such boundaries to resonate with diverse audiences. What I am stressing should be obvious, although it often gets buried at the chaotic intersection of art and politics: attention to cinematic artistry, however defined, is essential to getting one's message into the world. Only well-told stories will hold the attention of disparate audiences that might include Mi'kmaq children in Restigouche, Anglo-Canadian families in Alberta, Quebecois intellectuals in Montreal, and media professionals at Sundance (where *Is the Crown at War with Us?* had its U.S. premiere in 2003). This final point about the role of artistry is crucial—without artistry, none of the others will make a difference.

Conclusions

Somewhere in New Brunswick in the late eighteenth century, a loyalist officer wrote that the Mi'kmaq people "consider the English as having taken away from them their hunting and fishing grounds, which is their only means of support. They are not favourably disposed towards us, and have been only kept in order by terror."[71] Perhaps a cinema of sovereignty can provide an antidote to that terror, both in its corporeal and in its ideological manifestations. As I have tried to make clear throughout this book, the ability to control one's own image has bedeviled Native people such as the Mi'kmaq for hundreds of years. One historian has described how nineteenth-century British colonials rendered the Mi'kmaq powerless through the control of information as much as anything else: "The Mi'kmaq were relegated to the peripheries of colonial society, tethered by the manipulation of incoherent messages from the white community."[72] In taking her Native activism behind the lens, Obomsawin demonstrates that indigenous media can at the very least document, and perhaps even counteract, the coercive force of the state that people like the Mi'kmaq have faced for centuries.

What Obomsawin has endured and accomplished is fascinating enough for its own sake, but I believe that the most generalizable truths about her career are lurking in the last dozen or so pages, waiting for someone to pick them up and try them out on a digital camcorder and some Final Cut Pro software. Nowadays, it doesn't take much to implement grand cinematic principles—certainly, far less than it did when Obomsawin got her start. Of course, one could add any number of pragmatic considerations to the list—how to raise money, how to write grants, how to get low-cost gear, etc. But these are addressed elsewhere, ad nauseam, in the literature on independent filmmaking. What I am attempting here is advice of a different order, how-to at the quantum rather than the quotidian level.

But *caveat lectur*: the list of strategies is neither exhaustive nor exact. The conditions in which art is made are too variable for *precise* recipes to work on every occasion, and I do not expect the filmmaker/reader to respond like a weekend chef thumbing through a cookbook in search of a foolproof dish. As an occasionally reckless practitioner as well as a more cautious theorist, I am well aware how things can burn and fall, just as I am well aware that certain general insights about cooking are worth knowing in every kitchen. It is in this spirit that I have sought to deduce these various strategies for representational sovereignty with the hope that they might end up in the hands of indigenous mediamakers who can create something brilliant, radical, and true, something that extends what Obomsawin has been doing for more than three decades. What I have enumerated is merely suggestive, hopeful, and always open to other possibilities for counteracting the mind-numbing onslaught of various official and corporate visions of the world. Perhaps Obomsawin's moment has passed, although it would still deserve recognition in hindsight. Perhaps we need *other* visions that are more experimental and more confrontational in nature. Perhaps Obomsawin's insistence on realist nonfiction is too narrow, at least for the rich Vizenorian puns, ironies, and perplexities that seem to shape so much of Native life.[73]

It is possible . . . but I doubt it. After looking closely at Obomsawin's work for several years, I believe that there is something there, something to challenge the presumptions of empire that hang overhead for all of us—and, in the Mi'kmaq case, for the precisely five hundred years since they first spotted Europeans on "floating islands" in their harbors. What is that *something*? More than anything, it is a renewed understanding of the Native past and present. In the hands of Native filmmakers like Obomsawin, a cinema of sovereignty might lead to a broader appreciation of an essential truth that lines these woods and prairies and cities and suburbs of North America—that "Natives," as Gerald Vizenor says, "are the diverse visionary sovereigns of this continent." Native filmmakers such as Obomsawin are creating a cinema that gestures in the direction of that all-too-hidden reality.[74]

CONCLUSION

Today, Alanis Obomsawin has come full circle in her creative work to arrive at the very place where she started in the rural woods of Quebec and New Hampshire quite some time ago. In the process of beginning a new documentary on Abenaki culture, she will soon add her voice to the burgeoning "Abenaki renaissance" whose arrival she has been hastening through song, story, activism, and now film for most of her adult life. Once again her work will address the distortions in prevailing views of indigenous reality, in this case to reveal the vibrancy of contemporary Abenaki culture in Canada and the United States, something that might come as a surprise to the general public and even to scholars whose knowledge of the tribe is limited to academic readings. According to the historian Alice Nash, most writing on the Abenaki people has centered on the seventeenth and eighteenth centuries, to the exclusion of all else. The reason for this is unsettling: "[The] implicit (and sometimes explicit) assumption . . . has been that later generations of Abenaki people were too assimilated, too acculturated, or too intermarried to compete with the so-called 'authentic' Indians of the distant past." To refute the charge that the Abenakis are somehow inauthentic or have vanished from the continent, Nash has pointed to the work of the anthropologist A. Irving Hallowell, who visited Odanak in the 1920s to talk with Théophile Panadis and other Obomsawin family members. Even back then, in the decade just before Obomsawin's birth, it was necessary for Hallowell to argue against public perception with research showing that Abenaki culture was far from dead—that in fact it had proved itself remarkably resilient in the face of European American encroachment.[1]

Hallowell's lesson remains true today, perhaps more than at any time in the past two hundred years. After all, the fruits of the Abenaki renaissance are readily apparent to tribal scholars such as Frederick Matthew Wiseman, who notes that the new Wobanakik Heritage Center opened its doors in northern Vermont in 1998, new Abenaki bands have begun forming across New England, and new connections spanning the U.S.-Canadian border have begun to be made between Abenaki people. "The bear is awake, and Koluscap [Glous'gap] is returning," Wiseman says, firm in his belief that "the Anglo seats of power finally comprehend that the greater Abenaki Nation will realize its dreams of sovereignty."[2] The Abenaki have come a long way since racist depictions such as *Northwest Passage* marred Obomsawin's youth or even since the public school textbooks of the 1960s described her people as "very cold blooded and cruel" while noting that the power of the Abenakis was "gone forever" once Major Rogers attacked Odanak in 1759 and "killed most of the tribe."[3] Like the films that Obomsawin has made on behalf of her Mohawk and Mi'kmaq neighbors, her documentary on Abenaki culture and history should provide a useful corrective to this legacy of distortion and misrepresentation.

Now in her early seventies, Obomsawin continues to lead a professional life whose pace would tax a far younger person. In addition to her film projects, she has become involved with a number of Native media organizations in leadership roles that reflect her stature as a respected elder in her field. In recent years she has served on the boards of Studio One (the Native production unit of the National Film Board [NFB]), a radio venture called Aboriginal Voices, and the Aboriginal Peoples Television Network, which she views as an important new forum for Native stories. "It's a place for people to come and have their stories told," she says with high hopes. "We'll see

stories that we've never seen before. There [is] such a high potential
for learning for Aboriginal and non-Aboriginal people alike."[4]

For her service to such organizations as well as for her own creative
work, Obomsawin has continued to receive accolades in Canada and
abroad. In the new millennium, she has been chosen for Canada's
prestigious Governor General's Award in Visual and Media Arts as
well as the inaugural Dr. Bernard Chagnan Assiniwi Prize at the
Montreal First Peoples' Festival. She has been given several lifetime
achievement awards and honorary doctorates, and her work continues to garner prizes and enthusiastic showings at festivals around the
world, including in Toronto, Vancouver, San Francisco, Oakland, Los
Angeles, New Orleans, Oklahoma, Ohio, New York, New Zealand,
France, Hungary, Spain, and Estonia. Somewhat closer to home, the
Saskatchewan school system has even designated her "an official role
model" for Native youths, an honor she shares with such luminaries
as Sitting Bull, Pontiac, Maria Tallchief, and Leonard Cohen's favorite
saint, Kateri Tekakwitha.

Obomsawin has also been a great influence on Native filmmakers,
although it is difficult to calculate the impact of someone whose
career has lasted so many years and touched so many individuals—
at best I can share a few revealing anecdotes. Loretta Todd, one of
the leading practitioners and theorists of Native filmmaking in the
past decade, has talked about Obomsawin's importance to successive generations of filmmakers. "Alanis had been everyone's hero,"
Todd says. "She had been making films for a long time, and telling
very sensitive stories, and obviously was very accomplished."[5] Another tribute comes from Katerina Cizek, a Czech-born filmmaker
who was a young student journalist when she saw Obomsawin behind the barricades at Oka. "She was standing at the blockade with
her cameraman at her side, interviewing a Mohawk Warrior," Cizek
remembers. "She looked proud, her hands planted firmly on her
hips, obviously devoted to her documentary mission. With army helicopters and madness swirling all around, she was an apparition of
hope. I knew that, whatever might happen that afternoon, history
was being chronicled, and that a true story would one day emerge."
In observing Obomsawin at work, Cizek believed that she was "wit-

nessing the power of documentary firsthand." "For the next decade, it would be her images, her films, and her voice that would define the world's understanding of Kanehsatake, this decisive Mohawk stand for justice."[6]

Even after hearing these words of praise, the skeptical reader might wonder why I have been so taken with Obomsawin's work—I'm not Native, I don't live in Canada, and I was barely born when the NFB first hired her. Frankly, I cannot help but prize an independent filmmaker whose vision has held steady for thirty-five years of principled cultural critique, who stands for something more than herself, and who embodies the best media practices in the face of the worst. So, rather than fetishizing the swoops and pans of well-known fiction film auteurs, whose every pant and sigh seems to make it into print, I have sought to scrutinize one of these poets of the real whose work goes unnoticed in all but the most exceptional cases (i.e., Michael Moore); indeed, something strikes me as upside-down when our society's fantasies are recorded with more care and expense, and shared with more passion, than our realities. Consider this: the combined budget of Obomsawin's entire career plus those of all the documentaries made in North America in the past five years would hardly match the $200 million budget of a special-effects bonanza like Stephen Sommers's *Van Helsing* (2004), whose imaginary demons somehow generate more curiosity than depictions of the world in which we actually live. Although it is possible that the success of Moore's *Fahrenheit 9/11* will inspire both investors and imaginative people to look anew at the untapped potential of nonfiction cinema, serious documentaries have rarely received the financing, promotion, distribution, or appreciation that they deserve.

To put it bluntly, this is no way to run a visual culture, not with so much at stake. A vast transformation in our public sphere is taking place, one that puts images at the center of the understandings—or misunderstandings—that govern our beliefs and behaviors.[7] Words can flow for hundreds of pages, vividly well crafted, artfully chosen words, but it is not until the image appears in front of us that the event is seared in our imaginations forever—witness the sequence of events in the Iraqi prison scandal in spring 2004, in which the written reports were sloughed off until a few digital snapshots hit the Internet and astonished viewers around the world. The *pictorial turn* is what W. J. T. Mitchell has dubbed this shift from the word to the image, a shift in emphasis away from one kind of information toward another—perhaps the most profound reorientation of its kind since Gutenberg.[8] If this transformation has been rupturing the older ways of communication at least since the age of Chaplin, it has also intensified and accelerated in the days of twenty-four-hour news cycles, three-hundred-channel dish televisions, and broadband Internet access. One of the operating principles of this book comes in the wake of this transformation: the fact that visual culture has assumed an ever-expanding role in the shaping of human consciousness carries with it, I believe, a set of obligations for anyone interested in gazing beyond the superficial. For those of us with the sadly uncommon luxury of a moment's reflection, there is an obligation to swim against the prevailing flow of information and seek out new channels, new currents, and new outlets that might convey some neglected truths about the world. We cannot allow ourselves to be swallowed in the semiotic undertow of corporate media and government flacks, whose relatively unified way of seeing the world is fast inundating how we see for ourselves. As their Manichaean simplicities and ideological homogeneity become the nightly norm for viewers anchored in front of their televisions, *other* visions—such as Obomsawin's brand of personal, counternational, noncommercial art—have become a precious commodity.

The unfolding wars in Iraq and Afghanistan have added a note of urgency to this situation. Ten years ago, just after Operation Desert Storm, W. J. T. Mitchell wrote: "CNN has shown us that a supposedly alert, educated population (for instance, the America electorate) can witness the mass destruction of an Arab nation as little more than a spectacular television melodrama, complete with a simple narrative of good triumphing over evil and a rapid erasure of public memory."[9] If it is too soon to claim that history repeated itself in the year 2006, troubling echoes are not hard to find. Instead of weapons of mass destruction, we are given narratives of gross simplification, many rife with racist undertones, proliferating like wildfire since 9/11 and leaving very little room for nuanced dissent and informed analysis. Instead of offering hard questions and independent reporting, major news networks have served as platforms for the administration's "saturation bombing" of the public sphere, especially in the months leading up to war, and in the process have supplied some of the necessary ingredients for a Middle Eastern quagmire.

I think that Native filmmakers like Obomsawin work to reverse this sort of imperializing process, perhaps because many grew up with a painful awareness of how indigenous people, whether in Iraq or Kanehsatake, can fall victim to the deficiencies of the pictorial turn. Talking about the importance of indigenous media in 2003, Obomsawin said: "I learned that this is the most powerful place to be—because of the kind of culture we live in now, including our own people and our own children. [They] don't listen to just stories told by the old people anymore. They're watching TV. . . . So, it's very important to have a presence in the images that they look at. That's including education and certainly film. Now we have our own channel on television, the Aboriginal Peoples Television Network, that is constantly showing videos and films made by our own people or about them. . . . *That's where the power is right now.*[10] Such alternative media projects, including Obomsawin's own, offer the best sort of cultural critique: one that builds toward something, instead of merely stripping away what stands. As Bruno Latour has written, the best sort of critic is "not the one who debunks but the one who assembles, not the one who lifts the rugs from under the feet of the naïve believers [in whatever popular orthodoxy] but the one who offers arenas in which to gather."[11] I think that the gentle, inclusive critique of Obomsawin's work on the cinematic middle ground, whether literally in theaters or metaphorically in our minds, creates this sort of space for gathering and reviewing what we presume to know about the worlds of indigenous peoples. Obomsawin's goal has always been to illuminate rather than castigate, to connect rather than condemn, even in the turmoil of Oka. Despite the racism that she encountered there across the razor wire, Obomsawin told reporters: "There's also a lot of people who don't know us, yet really have a lot of compassion and interest. They want to find out more about the different nations here, and about the Mohawks. And they want to do something to help."[12] Rather than simply offering condemnation of the Canadian state or white racism, her work points in the direction where something better might be found, where understanding, tolerance, optimism, and social justice are interdependent.

Throughout this book I have taken aim at the hypocrisy and insensitivity of the Canadian state toward First Nations peoples—how can it be otherwise when one is writing about Burnt Church, Kanehsatake, or James Bay? However, I must follow Obomsawin's lead in making an important point in Canada's favor. In occupying the radical center with gravity and grace, Obomsawin has been a rare example of an artist/activist from the margins who has gained access to the capital of the center (i.e., the millions of state dollars that have gone into her films), and her hard-won presence at the heart of Canadian society reflects a nation whose multicultural ideas are *sometimes* more than hollow rhetoric. While her prominence says something quite striking about her own perseverance and talent, so too does it say something about the nature of Canadian society that over time has embraced her. "That is the incredible part of this country," Obomsawin recently said. "There is a freedom that doesn't exist everywhere else. . . . [I]t is a very healthy place to be."[13] By contrast, I fear that her maneuvers on the radical center, that small patch of relatively well-funded subversion, would have been next to impossible in the United States, where media corporations have shown no interest in indigenous points of view, and where right-wing politicians begin fuming whenever a trickle of state funds ends up in the hands of an artist smearing chocolate on her naked body or painting the Virgin Mary with daubs of elephant dung. To my mind Canada is a better place for having Obomsawin's powerful—and even redemptive—documentary discourse in its midst.

Obviously, Obomsawin strikes me as a special filmmaker, someone who is doing something worthy of attention and perhaps even emulation. Throughout this book, I have tried to recover her work from the semiobscurity of video libraries and film festivals and to use it as a lens onto the larger landscape of indigenous mediamaking and representation. In particular I tried to show how her filmmaking practice might be understood as a cinema of sovereignty with valuable lessons for other indigenous mediamakers. I tried to show how her Abenaki heritage, in particular her knowledge of its oral tradition, informed her cinematic project in unique ways, as did her gendered position as a Native woman. And I tried to show why the four films she fashioned out of the Oka crisis represent a major achievement in the history of nonfiction film. The risks she took, the passion of her storytelling, and the importance of the event being captured all combine to mark a special moment in the documentary tradition as I see it. Given her rare ability to combine an uncompromising political stance with an accessible mode of presentation that does more than preach to the converted, I have been hard-pressed to suggest a better model for cross-cultural communication in the age of electronic media.

Such claims may seem overheated, given the almost complete absence of her name from the standard histories of cinema, even those devoted to nonfiction (Ellis, Barnouw, Barsam) or Native cinema (Kilpatrick, Singer), but I hope what I have written will support a reassessment of Obomsawin's place in the documentary canon.[14] If a filmmaker of her stature does not appear somewhere in the grand sweep of nonfiction that seems to run from Robert Flaherty to Michael Moore, then the Native accomplishment in nonfiction film must be even less visible, and less appreciated, than it is in the world of literature, where Native writers have been cracking open the canon at least since N. Scott Momaday won the Pulitzer Prize in 1969 for *House Made of Dawn*. My only response to this neglect of thoughtful filmmaking is to write about it, to encourage others to use it in their classes, to ask students to watch it. Indeed, I keep writing about documentary in its most admirable aspects with the hope that I will not stultify the thing I love. The BBC's Nicholas Frasier once seemed to suggest as much, complaining: "Academic criticism is the death of the documentary impulse."[15] His lament is one that creative people have always made about armchair critics, and I retain some hope that exploration and desiccation are not conjoined at the hip.

So I hold up Obomsawin as a model of the documentary impulse, of alternative media production at its best, of representational sovereignty for indigenous people—if just one of many possibilities.

While she has excelled with films that are activist in origin, accessible in tone, state financed in execution, polyglot in language, and counterhegemonic in content, I know that others could suffocate under these conditions: I realize that every creative artist must find his or her own way. Someone else would have been stifled by the bureaucracy of the NFB, by her insistence on forefronting the political, by her willingness to privilege accessibility over experimentation, by her reliance on a gentle tone instead of a caustic one. That's fine. A thousand flowers can bloom in our documentary cinema as long as not all of them are the property of Mark Burnett (*Survivor; The Apprentice*) or Malcolm Barbour (*Cops*), as long as we agonize appropriately over how reality should be brought to the screen in the ways that Claude Lanzmann has suggested. For the French filmmaker of *Shoah*, everything about documentary poses a necessary conundrum: "How to transmit, how to instruct, how to interrogate, how to remain dispassionate while, as we each desperately strove to do, methodically unveiling a hell; how to remain calm in the face of grief and tears, without letting oneself be carried away by the emotion which would preclude all work, how to denounce in the truest manner injustice and crime?" His only answer was: "A thousand questions, a thousand paths!"[16]

Sadly, some paths are more comfortable than others, and the road to what Obomsawin is doing has always been quite narrow. Prolific, conscientious, independent documentarians like her are a rare—and, some would say, disappearing—sort, enough so that the myth of the vanishing Indian seems to have given way to the lament over the vanishing documentarian. Every few years we are reminded that documentary is in a terrible condition, that it is suffering from a hardening of the creative arteries, that it is in a dire state of emergency. The last phrase comes from the title of Patricia Zimmermann's recent book, where she shows how the battle between official/corporate visions of the nation and what I am calling "*other* visions" became such a noisy part of our cultural politics. Writing just before the unprecedented success of documentaries such as Moore's *Fahrenheit 9/11* (2004), Morgan Spurlock's *Supersize Me* (2004), and Andrew Jarecki's *Capturing the Friedmans* (2003), Zimmermann argued that for twenty years conservatives had launched successful attacks on public funding sources for independent documentary in Canada and the United States, while corporate media showed ever-decreasing interest in financing or broadcasting dissenting points of view, even as the proliferation of cable channels would seem to auger the reverse. As a result, independent voices had become what she called an *endangered species*.[17] Zimmermann was not alone in her concern. When the editors of *Imagining Reality* wrote to the great filmmaker Chris Marker to ask him about the future of the form, he begged off answering the question while wishing them the best in their endeavor. "Rarely has reality needed so much to be imagined," he observed.[18] Documentary has always had more than its fair share of Cassandras—and rightly so. It is a fragile business with little to support it except creative commitments, political hopes, and a keen sense of outrage. Like any art of substance, it is inevitably endangered, fragile, underappreciated.

All this is true, yet it goes on, and filmmakers like Obomsawin and her heirs keep pursuing their quiet democratization of the mass media. "For me," Obomsawin says, "documentary will always be needed because it's the voice of the people."[19] If this phrase sounds out of step with our times, it is more than a false echo of activist (or intellectual) longing—it is something real out there, something distinct from the synthetic voice of the corporation and the state, whose warped versions of reality suck us into *Real World*, MTV *Cribs*, *Temptation Island*, or *Fox's "Fair and Balanced" News*.

Shortly before he died in 2002, Pierre Bourdieu, the celebrated French sociologist, talked about the importance of developing alternatives to the corporate global media and their illusion of choice. Bourdieu argued for a more fundamental level of choice, one that allows us to select something other than Coke or Pepsi, Ford or Chevrolet, *Survivor* or *Sixty Minutes*. "If I say that culture is in danger today, if I say that it is threatened by the rule of money and commerce and by a mercenary spirit that takes many forms—audience ratings, market research, sales figures, the best-seller list—it will be said that I am exaggerating," he suggests. "If I recall now that the possibility of stopping this infernal machine in its tracks lies with all those who, having some power over cultural, artistic, and literary matters, can, each in their own place and their own fashion, and to however small an extent, throw their grain of sand into the well-oiled machinery of resigned complicities . . . [i]t will be said perhaps, for once, that I am being desperately optimistic."[20]

I do not think Bourdieu is asking too much from residents of the creative world: the power of what he is suggesting has long been exploited at the margins of cultural discourse as well as in the precarious radical center. Obomsawin, for one, has documented the world as she sees it from both vantages, as cultural and gender outsider pushing her positions into public view and, later, as an esteemed member of the media establishment with the rare power to speak her mind. With her uncommon commitment to documentary expression in its most passionate form and her ability to develop this commitment in the face of the insensate corporate juggernaut that reduces everything to measly product, Obomsawin continues to practice the art of documentary in a way that gives me, at least, some reason to share Bourdieu's unfashionable optimism.

With her thoughtful and poignant worldview, Obomsawin has made cinema into a productive middle ground where disparate people can recognize one another through whatever veils of prejudice might otherwise keep them apart. In projecting her eloquent, uncompromising vision onto the Canadian national imaginary without alienating those whom she has neither convinced nor converted, she has gently placed more than a few grains of sand into "the well-oiled machinery of resigned complicities" that works against the welfare of Native people in various quarters of North America. Indeed, in the chaos of modern Canadian life, where turbulent events such as Restigouche and Oka can take place, and children like Richard Cardinal can end their lives for the lack of understanding, Obomsawin has brought unheard voices and new perspectives to audiences struggling to understand the many paths of First Nations into the future of their shared continent.

FILMOGRAPHY

All Obomsawin's films are available for purchase on the Web site of the National Film Board (NFB). Go to http://cmm.onf.ca/E/recherche/index.epl and enter the film title (or Obomsawin's name) into the search engine to see the NFB's online catalog.

Christmas at Moose Factory
1971, 13 min., 7 sec.
DIRECTOR: Alanis Obomsawin
PRODUCER: Robert Verrall, Wolf Koenig
SCRIPT AND TEXT: Alanis Obomsawin
IMAGES: Ben Low, Raymond Dumas
MUSIC: Sinclair Cheecho, Jane Cheecho, Arthur Cheecho
SOUND: Jacques Drouin, Roger Lamoureux, Bill Graziadei
PRODUCERS: National Film Board of Canada

Mother of Many Children
1977, 57 min., 50 sec.
DIRECTOR: Alanis Obomsawin
PRODUCER: Douglas MacDonald, Alanis Obomsawin, Don Hopkins
SCRIPT AND TEXT: Alanis Obomsawin
IMAGES: Don Virgo, Simon Leblanc, Laval Fortier, Jacques Avoine, Bob Riddell
EDITOR: John Laing

SOUND: Richard Besse, Raymond Marcoux, Bev Davidson, Louis Echaquan, Bob Charlie, Christopher Tate, J. G. Normandin, Bill Graziadei, Claude Hazanavicius

VOICE AND NARRATION: Alanis Obomsawin

PRODUCERS: National Film Board of Canada

Amisk

1977, 40 min., 10 sec.

DIRECTOR: Alanis Obomsawin

PRODUCER: Alanis Obomsawin, Dorothy Courtois, Wolf Koenig

IMAGES: Buckley Petawabano, Bob Charlie

EDITOR: Judith Merritt, Buckley Petawabano, Daniel Wapachee, Jeanette Lerman

SOUND: Albert Canadian, Bill Graziadei

PRODUCERS: National Film Board of Canada

Canada Vignettes: Wild Rice Harvest Kenora

1979, 1 min., 0 sec.

DIRECTOR: Alanis Obomsawin

PRODUCER: Robert Verrall

SCRIPT AND TEXT: Alanis Obomsawin

PRODUCERS: National Film Board of Canada

Canada Vignettes: June in Povungnituk—Quebec Arctic

1980, 1 min., 0 sec.

DIRECTOR: Alanis Obomsawin

PRODUCER: Robert Verrall

SCRIPT AND TEXT: Alanis Obomsawin

VOICE AND NARRATION: Alanis Obomsawin

PRODUCERS: National Film Board of Canada

Incident at Restigouche

1984, 45 min., 57 sec.

DIRECTOR: Alanis Obomsawin

PRODUCER: Alanis Obomsawin, Adam Symansky, Andy Thomson, Robert Verrall

SCRIPT AND TEXT: Alanis Obomsawin

IMAGES: Roger Rochat, Savas Kalogeras

EDITOR: Alan Collins, Wolf Koenig

ANIMATION: Raymond Dumas

SOUND: Bev Davidson, Yves Gendron, Bill Graziadei

VOICE AND NARRATION: Alanis Obomsawin

PRODUCERS: National Film Board of Canada

Richard Cardinal: Cry from a Diary of a Métis Child

1986, 29 min., 10 sec.

ALSO AVAILABLE IN FRENCH: *Richard Cardinal: Le cri d'un enfant métis*

DIRECTOR: Alanis Obomsawin

PRODUCER: Alanis Obomsawin, Andy Thomson, Robert Verrall, Marrin Canell

CAST: Leslie Miller, Betty Smith, Cory Swan, Pauline Kerik

SCRIPT AND TEXT: Alanis Obomsawin

IMAGES: Roger Rochat

EDITOR: Rita Roy

MUSIC: Dario Domingues

SOUND: Bernard Bordeleau, Raymond Marcoux, Hans Peter Strobl, Jackie Newell

VOICE AND NARRATION: David Mitchell

PRODUCERS: National Film Board of Canada

Poundmaker's Lodge: A Healing Place

1987, 29 min., 27 sec.

ALSO AVAILABLE IN FRENCH: *La Maison Poundmaker—La voie de la guérison*

DIRECTOR: Alanis Obomsawin

PRODUCER: Alanis Obomsawin, Andy Thomson, Robert Verrall, Marrin Canell

SCRIPT AND TEXT: Alanis Obomsawin

IMAGES: Roger Rochat, Pierre Landry

EDITOR: Rita Roy

MUSIC: Shannon Two Feathers, Dario Domingues

SOUND: Jean-Pierre Joutel, Raymond Marcoux, Paul Demers

PRODUCERS: National Film Board of Canada

No Address

1988, 55 min., 58 sec.

ALSO AVAILABLE IN FRENCH: *Sans adresse*

DIRECTOR: Alanis Obomsawin

PRODUCER: Colin Neale, Alanis Obomsawin, Marrin Canell

SCRIPT AND TEXT: Alanis Obomsawin

IMAGES: Roger Rochat

EDITOR: Marrin Canell

MUSIC: Dominique Tremblay

SOUND: Jacques Drouin, Hans Peter Strobl, Yves Gendron, Wojtek Klis

PRODUCERS: National Film Board of Canada

Le Patro Le Prévost 80 Years Later

1991, 29 min., 9 sec.

DIRECTOR: Alanis Obomsawin

PRODUCER: Colin Neale, Alanis Obomsawin

SCRIPT AND TEXT: Alanis Obomsawin

IMAGES: Roger Rochat, Jacques Avoine, Lynda Pelley,
   Jean-Pierre Lachapelle

EDITOR: Marrin Canell

MUSIC: Pierre Potvin

SOUND: Marie-France Delagrave, Jean-Pierre Joutel, Hans Oomes,
   Yves Gendron, Claude Chevalier, Jackie Newell

PRODUCERS: National Film Board of Canada

Walker

1991, 13 min., 53 sec.

DIRECTOR: Alanis Obomsawin

PRODUCER: Colin Neale, Penny Ritco, Wolf Koenig

CAST: Kelly Ricard, Luis Brascoupe, Jamieson Boulanger, Chris Palin,
   Eric Tadros, Ruby Marie Dennis, Serge Simon

SCRIPT AND TEXT: Beatrice Mosionier

IMAGES: Susan Trow

EDITOR: Meiyen Chan

MUSIC: Mack MacKenzie

SOUND: Ismaël Cordeiro, Robert Labrosse

PRODUCERS: National Film Board of Canada

Kanehsatake: 270 Years of Resistance

1993, 119 min., 15 sec.

DIRECTOR: Alanis Obomsawin

PRODUCER: Colin Neale, Alanis Obomsawin, Wolf Koenig

SCRIPT AND TEXT: Alanis Obomsawin

IMAGES: Barry Perles, Roger Rochat, Jocelyn Simard, Susan Trow, François Brault, Zoe Dirse, Philippe Amiguet, André-Luc Dupont, Savas Kalogeras, Jean-Claude Labrecque

EDITOR: Yurij Luhovy

MUSIC: Claude Vendette, Francis Grandmont

SOUND: Marie-France Delagrave, Jean-Pierre Joutel, Raymond Marcoux, Catherine Van Der Donckt, Ismaël Cordeiro, Juan Gutierrez, Tony Reed, Don Ayer, Serge Fortin, Robert Verebely

VOICE AND NARRATION: Alanis Obomsawin

PRODUCERS: National Film Board of Canada

My Name Is Kahentiiosta

1995, 29 min., 50 sec.

ALSO AVAILABLE IN FRENCH: Je m'appelle Kahentiiosta

ALSO AVAILABLE UNDER: Oka: Behind the Barricade: The Kanehsatake Package

DIRECTOR: Alanis Obomsawin

PRODUCER: Alanis Obomsawin, Don Haig

SCRIPT AND TEXT: Alanis Obomsawin

IMAGES: Alanis Obomsawin, Roger Rochat, Susan Trow, Zoe Dirse, Raymond Dumas, André-Luc Dupont, Jacques Avoine, Lynda Pelley, Sylvain Julienne, Jean-Claude Labrecque, Pierre Landry

EDITOR: Ruby-Marie Dennis

MUSIC: Claude Vendette, Francis Grandmont

SOUND: Alanis Obomsawin, Jean-Pierre Joutel, Raymond Marcoux, Hans Oomes, Ismaël Cordeiro, Don Ayer

PRODUCERS: National Film Board of Canada

Spudwrench—Kahnawake Man

1997, 57 min., 50 sec.

ALSO AVAILABLE IN FRENCH: Spudwrench: L'homme de Kahnawake

ALSO AVAILABLE UNDER: Oka: Behind the Barricade

DIRECTOR: Alanis Obomsawin

PRODUCER: Alanis Obomsawin, Don Haig

SCRIPT AND TEXT: Alanis Obomsawin

IMAGES: Zoe Dirse, Savas Kalogeras, Michel Bissonnette, Yves Beaudoin, Lynda Pelley, Martin Duckworth, Pierre Landry

EDITOR: Donna Read

MUSIC: Claude Vendette, Francis Grandmont

SOUND: Alanis Obomsawin, Raymond Marcoux, Wojtek Klis, Ismaël Cordeiro, Serge Boivin, Geoffrey Mitchell, Richard Lavoie

PRODUCERS: National Film Board of Canada

Rocks at Whiskey Trench

2000, 105 min., 18 sec.

ALSO AVAILABLE IN FRENCH: Pluie de pierres à Whiskey Trench

DIRECTOR: Alanis Obomsawin

PRODUCER: Alanis Obomsawin, Sally Bochner

SCRIPT AND TEXT: Alanis Obomsawin

RESEARCH AND CONSULTANT: Denise Beaugrand-Champagne, Alanis Obomsawin

ART DIRECTION: Susan Phillips, Robert Verrall, Conway Jocks

IMAGES: Roger Rochat, Philippe Amiguet, René Siouï Labelle, Thea Pratt, Pierre Landry

EDITOR: Yurij Luhovy

MUSIC: Margaret Beauvais Jocks, Claude Vendette, Francis Grandmont

SOUND: Raymond Marcoux, Yves St-Jean, Ismaël Cordeiro, Tony Reed, Don Ayer, Jean Paul Vialard, Geoffrey Mitchell

VOICE AND NARRATION: Guy Nadon, Alanis Obomsawin

PRODUCERS: National Film Board of Canada

Is the Crown at War with Us?

2002, 96 min., 31 sec.

DIRECTOR: Alanis Obomsawin

PRODUCER: Alanis Obomsawin, Sally Bochner

SCRIPT AND TEXT: Alanis Obomsawin

RESEARCH AND CONSULTANT: Alanis Obomsawin

ART DIRECTION: Sgoagani

IMAGES: Yoan Cart, Philippe Amiguet, Michel La Veaux, Pierre Landry

MUSIC: Francis Grandmont

SOUND: Patrick Knup, Raymond Marcoux, Ismaël Cordeiro,

André Chaput, Serge Boivin, Jean Paul Vialard, Geoffrey Mitchell, Sylvain Cajelais

VOICE AND NARRATION: Alanis Obomsawin, Tony Robinow, Arthur Holden

PRODUCERS: National Film Board of Canada

Our Nationhood

2003, 96 min., 40 sec.

DIRECTOR: Alanis Obomsawin

PRODUCER: Alanis Obomsawin, Sally Bochner

SCRIPT AND TEXT: Alanis Obomsawin

RESEARCH AND CONSULTANT: Alanis Obomsawin, Meilan Lam

ART DIRECTION: Jean Dallaire

IMAGES: Yoan Cart, Alanis Obomsawin, Philippe Amiguet, Michel La Veaux, Pierre Landry

EDITOR: Alison Burns

MUSIC: Francis Grandmont

SOUND: Raymond Marcoux, Glenn Hodgins, Ismaël Cordeiro, André Chaput, Serge Boivin, Geoffrey Mitchell, Sylvain Cajelais

VOICE AND NARRATION: Alanis Obomsawin, Jean-René Ouellet

PRODUCERS: National Film Board of Canada

NATIVE DOCUMENTARIES

Because there is no comprehensive filmography of documentary films by Native Americans, readers might benefit from the brief list of titles included below. I tried to come up with a list of significant documentary titles, by which I mean projects of substantial length and/or creative significance, although this should be regarded as suggestive rather than comprehensive. Owing to the difficulty of obtaining some of the titles, I was not able to see all of them and sometimes relied on descriptions I came across in catalogs, Web sites, and scholarly books to make what is, admittedly, a highly subjective decision. That being said, in addition to Obomsawin's many films, interested readers might consider following:

Willie Dunn's *The Ballad of Crowfoot* (1968).[1] (A short film that I list here because of its historical importance as a Native first.)

Richard Whitman's *Red Reflections of Life: The Institute of American Indian Arts* (1973).

George Burdeau's *The Real People* (a six-part series, 1976), *Pueblo Peoples: First Contact* (1992), *Surviving Columbus: The Pueblo People* (1992; directed by Diane Reyna), *The Witness* (1997), *Backbone of the World: The Blackfeet* (1997).

Phil Lucas's *Images of Indian* (a five-part public television series, 1979–81, produced with Robert Hagopian), *The Honor of All* (1986), *Healing the Hurts* (1991), *Dances for the New Generation* (1993).

George Horse Capture, Larry Littlebird, and Larry Cesspooch's *I'd Rather Be Powwowing* (1983).

Chris Spotted Eagle's *The Great Spirit within the Hole* (1983) and *Our Sacred Land* (1984).

Rick Tailfeathers's *Powwow Fever* (1984).

Victor Masayesva's *Itam Hakim Hopiit* (1985), *Ritual Clowns* (1988), *Siskyavi: The Place of Chasms* (1991), *Imagining Indians* (1992).

Arlene Bowman's *Navajo Talking Picture* (1986) and *Song Journey* (1994).

Sandra Osawa's *In the Heart of Big Mountain* (1988), *Lighting the Seventh Fire* (1995), *Pepper's Powwow* (1995), *Usual and Accustomed Places* (1998), *On and Off the Res with Charlie Hill* (2000).

Mona Smith's *Her Giveaway: A Spiritual Journey with AIDS* (1988), *Honored by the Moon* (1990), *That Which I Between* (1991).

Zacharias Kunuk's *Qaqqiq/Gathering Place* (1989), one of *fifty* nonfiction videos he has produced about Inuit life since the 1980s.

Roy Bigcrane and Thompson Smith's *The Place of Falling Waters* (1990).

Dean Bearclaw's *Warrior Chiefs in a New Age* (1991).

Arvo Iho and Susan Stewart's *Crow Mapuche Connection* (1991).

Loretta Todd's *The Learning Path* (1991), *Hands of History* (1994), *Forgotten Warriors* (1997), *Today Is a Good Day: Remembering Chief Dan George* (1998), *Two Days Away/Akaitapiiwa* (2003).

Christine Lesiak and Matt Jones's *In the White Man's Image* (1992).

Allen Jamieson's *Indigenous Voices* (1992), *Do:ge Gagwego o'jagwada't: We Stood Together* (1993).

Ava Hamilton's *Everything Has a Spirit* (1992).

Ruby Sooktis's *Season of Children* (1992), *Trek North 95* (1995).

Derron Twohatchet's *Detour* (1993).

Beverly R. Singer's *He We Un Poh: Recovery in Native America* (1993), *A Video Book* (1994), *Hozho of Native Women* (1997).

Harriet Sky's *A Right to Be: The Story of an Indian Woman Who Took Back Control of Her Life* (1994).

Christine Welsh's *Keepers of the Fire* (1995), *The Story of the Coast Salish Knitters* (2000).

Barb Cranmer's *Laxwesa Wa: Strength of the River* (1995), *Qatuawas: People Gathering Together* (1996), *T'Lina: The Rendering of Wealth* (1999), *Gwishalaayt: The Spirit Wraps around You* (2001).

Daniel Prouty's *First Nation Blue* (1996), *Band-Aid* (2000).

Paul Rickard's *Ayouwin: A Way of Life* (1996), *Finding My Talk: A Journey into Aboriginal Languages* (2000).

Lena and Aaron Carr's *War Code: Navajo Code Talkers* (1996), *Kinaalda: Navajo Rite of Passage* (2000).

Carol Geddes's *Doctor, Lawyer, Indian Chief* (1994), *Picturing a People: George Johnston, Tlingit Photographer* (1997).

Puhipau's *Stolen Waters* (1996).

David H. Kalama Jr.'s *Kaho'olawe* (1997).

Gary Farmer's *The Gift* (1998), *Buffalo Tracks* (2000).

G. Peter Jemison's *House of Peace* (1999).

Jason Corwin and Janet Cavallo's *The Flickering Flame: The Life and Legacy of Chief Turkey Tayac* (1999).

James Fortier's *Alcatraz Is Not an Island* (2000).

Annie Frazier-Henry's *Singing Our Stories* (1998), *To Return: The John Walkus Story* (2000), *Spirit of the Game* (2003).

NOTES

Preface

1. Pick, "Storytelling and Resistance," 90.

2. White, "Alanis Obomsawin," 364.

3. Pick, "Storytelling and Resistance," 78.

4. Loft, "Sovereignty, Subjectivity, and Social Action."

5. Bird Runningwater quoted in Harewood, "Alanis Obomsawin."

6. Zimmermann, *States of Emergency*, 197.

7. George Pevere quoted on the back cover of Beard and White, eds., *North of Everything*.

8. Fiske, "Act Globally, Think Locally," 277.

9. Singer, *Wiping the War Paint off the Lens*, 9.

10. Olson, *Silences*, ix.

11. Kalafatic, "Knots," 68.

12. Jaimes-Guerrero, "Savage Erotica Exotica," 209.

1. Abenaki Beginnings

Epigraph from Alanis Obomsawin: Comment made in a public talk after a film screening, Norman, Oklahoma, spring 2002.

1. Alioff and Levine, "The Long Walk," 10.

2. Alioff and Levine, "The Long Walk," 10.

3. The Abenaki language is divided into Eastern and Western, which are distinct languages. By the 1970s, there were only twenty-one fluent speakers of Western Abenaki, all elderly (Day, "Western Abenaki" [1998], 221).

4. Background on Abenaki history and land comes from Day, "Western Abenaki" (1998), 205.

5. Obomsawin, *Bush Lady*, liner notes.

6. Day, "Western Abenaki" (1978), 153.

7. Alioff and Levine, "The Long Walk," 10.

8. Alanis Obomsawin, interview with author, Montreal, August 2002.

9. Wiseman, *The Voice of the Dawn*, 144.

10. Alioff and Levine, "The Long Walk," 10.

11. See Gallagher, *Breeding Better Vermonters*; and Perkins, "Review of Eugenics in Vermont."

12. Fisher, quoted in Wiseman, *The Voice of the Dawn*, 146 (for more on Fisher, see 146–47).

13. Wiseman, *The Voice of the Dawn*, 148 (on the Eugenics Survey, see generally 146–49). According to Wiseman: "The German scholars interested in eugenics found Vermont's Eugenics Survey useful for crafting the Final Solution that was later pursued by the Nazis" (227).

14. Alanis Obomsawin, interview with author, Montreal, August 2002.

15. Vermont's Sterilization Law of 1931, *Laws of Vermont*, 31st biennial sess. (March 31, 1931), no. 174, pp. 194–96.

16. Wiseman, *The Voice of the Dawn*, 149.

17. Greer, "Alanis Obomsawin," 27. Put into law in 1876, the Indian Act remains one of the most important pieces of legislation affecting Native peoples in Canada. In addition to bringing together existing legislation, the original act set controversial new standards for claiming Indian identity. Over the last 130 years, the act has been subjected to a number of important modifications. See Roy with Alfred, "Legislation Affecting Canada's Native People," 550.

18. Alioff and Levine, "The Long Walk," 10.

19. Information from Gordon M. Day cited in Foster and Cowan, eds., *New England's Native Past*, 73, 231.

20. Obomsawin, *Bush Lady*, liner notes.

21. Obomsawin, *Bush Lady*, liner notes.

22. The "dossier" (the 1940 *Positio of the Historical Section of the Sacred Congregation* . . .) is quoted in Dauria, "Kateri Tekakwitha," 67–68. Dauria's is the best article that I have found on Tekakwitha.

23. Dauria, "Kateri Tekakwitha," 68.

24. For more on *Drums along the Mohawk*, see Wilson, "Celluloid Sovereignty," 204–7.

25. Anderson, *Crucible of War*, 188.

26. Rogers, *Journals*, 107–9, quoted in Foster and Cowan, eds., *New England's Native Past*, 129.

27. *Atlantic Monthly*, August 1937, excerpted in James and Brown, eds., *Book Review Digest*, 837; *New Republic*, July 14, 1937, 287.

28. The film seems to have elicited equally little concern for the Abenaki. One present-day reviewer, not atypical among the comments I found online, wrote the following: " 'Noble savages' they ain't in *Northwest Passage*. Critic Pauline Kael didn't seem to like this bad attitude toward our Native American brethren but then again, Kael probably never had a hostile indian [*sic*] coming at her skull with a raised tomahawk" (Candidus, review of *Northwest Passage*).

29. Kilpatrick, *Celluloid Indians*, 48–49.

30. Bruchac, *Bowman's Store*, 43–44 (quotations), 8.

31. Chief Leonard George quoted in Wilson, "Confronting the 'Indian Problem,' " 55.

32. Information from Gordon M. Day cited in Foster and Cowan, eds., *New England's Native Past*, 133. According to a recent article: "[Panadis] was also a husband and a father, an artist and an active member of his community who wanted people to remember the old ways. . . . Panadis left behind a detailed documentary trail of Abenaki language, history, and culture" (Nash and Obomsawin, "Theophile Panadis," 76). In particular, Panadis was an important informant in the late 1950s for Gordon M. Day, one of the first academics to work on Abenaki culture and history (and to do so in a respectful manner that resulted in a body of work that remains useful and interesting today). See Day's writing in Foster and Cowan, eds., *New England's Native Past*.

33. Obomsawin, *Bush Lady*, liner notes.

34. Harewood, "Alanis Obomsawin."

35. Alanis Obomsawin, interview with author, Montreal, August 2002.

36. Alanis Obomsawin, interview with author, Montreal, August 2002.

37. Nadel, *Leonard Cohen*, jacket flap.

38. Information about Cohen's sources comes from Nadel, *Leonard Cohen*, 71.

39. Alioff and Levine, "The Long Walk," 10.

40. Cohen, *Beautiful Losers* (hereafter *BL*, 16. Page numbers for subsequent citations will be given parenthetically in the text.

41. At one point in the novel, when several white men violently confront the young girl, she urinates in terror, just like the schoolgirl Obomsawin attacked in her elementary school classroom, and creates a sound, "a monolithic tumult in eight ears," that causes the four men to pause in their violence. "It was the pure sound of impregnable nature and it ate like acid at their plot," Cohen writes. "It was a sound so majestic and simple, a holy symbol of frailty which nothing could violate" (*BL*, 61). After the novelist's (problematic) association of a Native girl with nature and simplicity, he goes on to describe how the four men "could not bear to learn that Edith was no longer Other, that she was indeed, Sister," because of this raw human act of urination. Yet, after a brief pause, their violence continues unabated.

42. Alioff and Levine, "The Long Walk," 11.

43. Alioff and Levine, "The Long Walk," 13.

44. Alioff and Levine, "The Long Walk," 10.

45. Alioff, "Dream Magic," 7.

46. Alanis Obomsawin, interview with author, Montreal, August 2002.

47. Dickinson and Young, *A Short History of Quebec*, 270, 313. Dickson and Young have two excellent chapters on the Quiet Revolution and its origins.

48. Alioff and Levine, "The Long Walk," 10.

49. Quoted in Alioff, "Dream Magic," 8.

50. Alanis Obomsawin, interview with author, Montreal, August 2002.

51. Obomsawin, *Bush Lady*, liner notes.

52. Chamberlain, "She's Informal but Captivating."

53. Alanis Obomsawin, interview with author, Montreal, August 2002.

54. Alioff, "Dream Magic," 8.

55. Robert Verrall and Obomsawin quoted in Cizek, "Alanis Obomsawin."

56. Mandate quoted on the NFB Web site: http://www.nfb.ca/atonf/organ isation.php?idcat=72&v=h&lg=en.

57. de Rosa, "Studio One," 331.

58. Evans, *In the National Interest*, 325.

59. This catalog description was posted on the Nativenet archive: http://na tivenet.uthscsa.edu/archive/nl/9610/0007.html.

60. See http://www.nfb.ca and search the film title under "Collections."

61. Barsam, *Nonfiction Film*, 328.

62. William Sloan of the Museum of Modern Art made this statement

about Greaves, which appears on the filmmaker's home page: http://www.will iamgreaves.com/biography.htm.

63. Information about Greaves's career comes from Arthur, "Springing Tired Chains," 290.

64. John Grierson quoted in Cizek, "Alanis Obomsawin."

65. Jones, *The Best Butler*, 191–93.

66. Obomsawin quoted in Cizek, "Alanis Obomsawin."

2. Early Films

1. The issue of children as political symbols that can be wielded in the mass media has been explored in Low, *NFB KIDS*.

2. Scott, *Weapons of the Weak*, 326. In this passage, Scott is summarizing, but not endorsing, a more limited construction of Gramsci's notion of hegemony.

3. Alanis Obomsawin, interview with author, Montreal, August 2002.

4. Alioff and Levine, "The Long Walk," 14.

5. The multiplicity of female voices in *Mother of Many Children* is one element of the film that evokes what Julia Lesage has called the *political aesthetics of feminist documentary* (see her classic "The Feminist Documentary Film"). Although in chapter 3 I suggest where Obomsawin diverged from feminist cinematic conventions of the 1970s, it is worth noting this aural similarity.

6. The film uses *Ojibway*, the older name of the Anishinabe, which is why I am using it in discussing the film.

7. The backwoods aspect must have appealed to the filmmaker on a personal level.

8. Bill C-31, sec. 15, chap. 1, was a landmark modification of the Indian Act. Passed in April 1985, C-31 ended discrimination against women with regard to tribal citizenship. For more in this bill (R.S.C. 1985, c. 32 [1st supp.]), see Roy with Alfred, "Legislation Affecting Canada's Native People," 577.

9. Dickason, *Canada's First Nations*, 313.

10. Treaty Six was signed in 1876 with Plains Indians of central Saskatchewan and Alberta. It was one of the key treaties numbered one through eleven that were signed between 1871 and 1921, setting the terms of the relationship between the Canadian government and its indigenous peoples (Dickason, *Canada's First Nations*, 252–57).

11. Dickason, *Canada's First Nations*, 397.

12. Alanis Obomsawin, interview with author, Montreal, August 2002.

13. Wendell Berry quoted in "Speaker Offers Some Good Ideas."

14. Alioff and Levine, "The Long Walk," 14.

15. Alioff and Levine, "The Long Walk," 14.

16. Alioff and Levine, "The Long Walk," 15.

17. Pick, "Storytelling and Resistance," 81.

18. Alioff and Levine, "The Long Walk," 15.

19. Alioff and Levine, "The Long Walk," 15.

20. Alioff and Levine, "The Long Walk," 15.

21. Alioff and Levine, "The Long Walk," 16.

22. Métis Population Betterment Act, *Statutes of Canada* 1938, c. 6, s. 2; Métis Settlement Act, *Statutes of Alberta* 1990, c. M-14.3, ss. 1, 111–29, sched. 3.

23. Sawchuk, "Negotiating an Identity," 75. See also the Web sites of the Metis Settlements General Council (http://www.msgc.ca) and the Métis National Council (http://www.metisnation.ca), the latter of which includes a helpful overview entitled "Who Are the Métis?" I am grateful to Jerry White for suggesting these Web sites.

24. Pick, "Storytelling and Resistance," 86. The exception for the 1990s, if not for Obomsawin's entire career, is a strange little documentary called *Le Patro Le Prévost: 80 Years Later* (1991). As her only film that does not deal with Native issues, *Le Patro* was a bit of a departure. In a well-meaning but blandly informative style that has made the NFB easy to lampoon, it profiles a Christian community center in Montreal that for the filmmaker seems to represent another "healing place" for children of all backgrounds. Perhaps *Le Patro*'s limited appeal is a result of the filmmaker's motivations: it is a film with more local aspirations. "I live in Montreal, and I love Montreal," Obomsawin has said. "I felt that the film was something I could do for my own city" (Greer, "Alanis Obomsawin," 27).

25. Waugh, ed., *"Show Us Life,"* xxii.

26. Obomsawin quoted in Steven, *Brink of Reality*, 185. One addendum: Waugh's notion of the committed documentary might be interpreted as a requirement for filmmakers to collaborate with their subjects in the making of the film, à la the ethnographic films of David and Judith MacDougall, in which camera work, editing, and other tasks are often shared between filmmaker and subject. Obomsawin has a deep commitment to and sense of solidarity with her subjects, but, like most filmmakers, even those within the "committed" ranks, she is not willing to give over the reigns in this manner. When asked if she would let a community member dictate what would be shot or how, Obomsawin replied, "No, I can't have that," before adding that she

remains open to suggestions during the research phase of a project (Steven, *Brink of Reality*, 39, 181).

27. Bailey, "What the Story Is," 38, quoted in Woods, "Srinivas Krishna," 206.

28. Obomsawin quoted in Cizek, "Alanis Obomsawin."

29. Jones, "Brave New Film Board," 29.

30. White, "Alanis Obomsawin," 366, 371.

31. Merata Mita quoted in "Indigenising the Screen—Film-Maker Merata Mita."

32. Obomsawin quoted in Steven, *Brink of Reality*, 179.

33. White, "Alanis Obomsawin," 370.

34. Panadis worked in the 1920s with A. Irving Hallowell from the University of Pennsylvania and in the 1950s and 1960s with Gordon M. Day from Dartmouth College (see Nash and Obomsawin, "Theophile Panadis").

35. Foster and Cowan, eds., *New England's Native Past*, 131–32.

36. Obomsawin, *Bush Lady*, liner notes.

37. Dorris, "Native American Literature," 156–57, quoted in Cruikshank, "Oral History, Narrative Strategies and Native American Historiography," 163.

38. Foster and Cowan, eds., *New England's Native Past*, 219.

39. Steven, *Brink of Reality*, 180.

40. Leslie Marmon Silko quoted in Arnold, ed., *Conversations with Leslie Marmon Silko*, 47.

41. Jerry White too eschews the "simple" reading of Obomsawin's work. For instance, he makes the fascinating observation that Obomsawin has more in common with the avant-garde than is commonly realized: the poetic, rather than pedantic, mode of address that characterizes her one-minute *Canadian Vignettes* (1980) and her willingness in *No Address* to blur the line between "actuality footage" and "re-creation" in a way that is reminiscent of the "performative documentaries" that Bill Nichols (*Introduction to Documentary*, 137) describes (a category that includes films such as Marlon Riggs's *Tongues Untied* [1989], which one might not otherwise associate with Obomsawin's work) ("Alanis Obomsawin," 370).

42. Harewood, "Alanis Obomsawin."

43. White, "Alanis Obomsawin," 366.

44. Baudrillard, *Simulations*, 119.

45. Poster, *The Mode of Information*, 6, cited in Keefer, "Postmodern Anxieties over Hypermedia."

46. Carol Geddes quoted in de Rosa, "Studio One," 331.

47. Loretta Todd quoted in Silverman, "Uncommon Visions," 389. Silverman's essay is a useful introduction to Todd's work.

48. Obomsawin quoted in Alioff, "Dream Magic," 9. "Animals have histories just like us," she has said. "They know their friends, and they know their enemies" (Alioff and Levine, "The Long Walk," 10).

49. Bruchac, *Bowman's Store*, 46.

50. Obomsawin quoted in Cizek, "Alanis Obomsawin."

51. Obomsawin quoted in Cizek, "Alanis Obomsawin."

52. Nichols, *Introduction to Documentary*, 50.

3. A Gendered Gaze?

Epigraph from Obomsawin, "Bush Lady," on *Bush Lady*, side 2.

1. See Giguére, "Women Filmmakers in Quebec."

2. Alanis Obomsawin, interview with author, Montreal, August 2002.

3. Merata Mita quoted in "Indigenising the Screen—Film-Maker Merata Mita."

4. Liz Garbus interviewed in "Liz Garbus," 123.

5. I am drawing here on the fascinating work of Bird, "Savage Desires." As she writes about westerns: "Indian women disappear or surface as minor plot devices" (82).

6. Klein and Ackerman, eds., *Women and Power*, 3.

7. The stereotypes run the gamut from "the erotic 'pagan nymphomaniac' to the picturesque erotic 'Cherokee princess' to the objectified 'Indian squaw,'" as Jaimes-Guerrero ("Savage Erotica Exotica," 187) has claimed.

8. Bird, "Savage Desires," 79.

9. Kaplan, *Looking for the Other*, xix.

10. Mihesuah, *American Indians*, 61.

11. Jeannette Armstrong quoted in Miller and Chuchryk, eds., *Women of the First Nations*, ix, xi.

12. Information about traditional Abenaki life comes from Calloway, *The Abenaki*, 30–33.

13. Giguére, "Women Filmmakers in Quebec," 378, 380, 383–84. One filmmaker who is something of an exception here is Anne Claire Poirier, who was the best-known woman working in French Canadian cinema in the

1970s. Born in 1932, the same year as Obomsawin, Poirier joined the NFB in 1960; she and Monique Fortier were the only women making films at the NFB during the 1960s. Her turn toward more personal, activist projects began in 1967 with the documentary *De mère en fille* and continued with consciousness-raising films such as *Les filles du Roy* (1974), an examination of Quebecois women that seemed to prefigure Obomsawin's *Mother of Many Children*. According to André Louselle, *Les filles du Roy* looks at the traditional roles afforded women in Quebecois society though an "effective mixture of historical reconstruction and personal commentary [that paints] a vibrant picture of a subject systematically ignored by male cinéastes" (*A Scream from Silence*, 6). However, Poirier's best-known work, the 1979 *Moirir à tue-tête* (also known as *A Scream from Silence*), shares little with Obomsawin's oeuvre aside from a desire to liberate and illuminate the lives of women in Canada. Unlike Obomsawin's more quiet documentaries of the 1970s, Poirier's rape docudrama pushed formal experimentation to great extremes to unsettle the audience, even to the point of visceral horror as the viewer endures a fifteen-minute rape sequence from the victim's point of view. Louselle (*A Scream from Silence*, 6) points out that, as if to acknowledge the pain inflicted on the audience in this sequence, the filmmaker and her editor next appear on-screen to discuss the challenges of such graphic filmmaking, before cutting to a sequence built around documentary footage of women maimed in war in Vietnam and elsewhere—a powerful, if hardly subtle, critique of the price of patriarchy that connects the personal to the global. If Obomsawin shared the engagé sensibility, the extrapolation from the personal to the social, and the desire to respect a multitude of female voices, she never took the aesthetic risks that marked—and perhaps marred—Poirier's most influential film.

14. If I have just suggested that issues of race and gender are enmeshed throughout Obomsawin's creative life, I think that we sometimes need to separate them for a moment to underscore a simple point: what Obomsawin is doing has a broader application than the *Native woman* categorization might suggest to some readers and viewers. At times that designation can marginalize her cultural production, as if Native film were important only to Native people—perhaps this is why a book called *Feminism and Documentary* would fail to mention her and other female Native filmmakers such as Sandra Day Osawa, Loretta Todd, Carol Geddes, Lena Carr, or Arlene Bowman, none of whom appear in the index to this otherwise excellent book (see Waldman

and Walker, eds., *Feminism and Documentary*). Somehow their gender has been subsumed into their race, even for academics who should know better.

15. French, ed., *Womenvision*, 44, 55.

16. One generalization about aboriginal filmmakers that fits Obomsawin without qualification comes from the visual anthropologist Faye Ginsburg: "Indigenous media producers acknowledge the traumas of contact history and the contradictions of life in the present and, most importantly, take these stories as a means to envision a cultural future for Indigenous people both locally and as part of larger social formations" (Ginsburg, "Mediating Culture," 5, quoted in Langston, "Grounded and Gendered," 47). Also, it is interesting to note that, unlike some successful documentarians, Obomsawin has expressed no interest in the idea of an autobiographical project.

17. Merata Mita is discussed in, and both quotations taken from, "Indigenising the Screen—Film-Maker Merata Mita."

18. MacDonald, "An Ugly Side of New Zealand," 10. Regarding indigenous children, Mita started a media training program for Maori youths (Billens, "Merata Mita").

19. Other than Billens's "Merata Mita," from which I take most of my information, and Lamche's "Interview with Merata Mita," I have been able to find little that has been written about Mita outside New Zealand. When I asked Obomsawin about Mita, she told me: "Mita is equal to me in terms of fighting to make films and make documentaries—she is a very strong woman" (Alanis Obomsawin, interview with author, Montreal, August 2002).

20. Loretta Todd quoted in Silverman, "Uncommon Visions," 385.

21. Barb Cranmer quoted in "Barb Cranmer—Messenger of Stories."

22. Gittings, *Canadian National Cinema*, 267.

23. "My initial goal was to make a portrait of my grandmother," Bowman has said to those who might find *Navajo Talking Picture* more solipsistic than biographical (Smith, "Filmmaker Makes the Most of a Disappointing Visit," J-20).

24. The credits indicate that Obomsawin provided "original research" for *The Learning Path*.

25. Singer, *Wiping the War Paint off the Lens*, 87.

26. *National Film Board Film and Video Catalog*, 54.

27. Trinh, *Woman Native Other*, 141, 72 (quoting Bronislaw Malinowski's *Argonauts of the Western Pacific* [1922]).

28. Trinh, *Woman Native Other*, 141.

29. For an analogous discussion of the controversial "ethic of care," see McLaughlin, *Feminist Social and Political Theory*, 77–89.

4. Documentary on the Middle Ground

1. York and Pindera, *People of the Pines*, 78, 45 (see also 84).

2. York and Pindera, *People of the Pines*, 78 (on calling in the sq), 21, 27.

3. David, preface, 11.

4. McFarlane, "Stolen Land," quoted in Alioff, "Dream Magic," 5.

5. York and Pindera, *People of the Pines*, 37.

6. York and Pindera, *People of the Pines*, 41.

7. York and Pindera, *People of the Pines*, 68.

8. Saxberg, "Kanehsatake," 34.

9. David, preface, 12.

10. Quoted in Alioff, "Dream Magic," 5.

11. Alanis Obomsawin, interview with author, Montreal, August 2002.

12. Grant, "Kanehsatake," 18.

13. Alanis Obomsawin, interview with author, Montreal, August 2002.

14. Alanis Obomsawin, interview with author, Montreal, August 2002.

15. Grant, "Kanehsatake," 20 (Obomsawin quote), 20 (review).

16. Yurij Luhovy quoted in Lysak, "Luhovy Named Best Editor," 10.

17. Pick, "Storytelling and Resistance," 80.

18. Marks, *The Skin of the Film*, 34.

19. See Restoule, "How Indians Are Read," 72.

20. Béla Bálazs, *Theory of Film*, excerpted in MacDonald and Cousins, eds., *Imagining Reality*, 31.

21. Saxberg, "Kanehsatake," 34.

22. Came, "Behind the Barricades," 58.

23. Obomsawin quoted in Loft, "Sovereignty, Subjectivity, and Social Action."

24. "Standoff on Kanehsatake," 12.

25. "Standoff on Kanehsatake," 12.

26. Saxberg, "Kanehsatake," 34.

27. Ellen Gabriel quoted in Cizek, "Alanis Obomsawin."

28. See "Assigning the Blame."

29. Jones, "Brave New Film Board," 36.

30. Quoted in White, "Alanis Obomsawin," 370. The progressive history

textbook to which I allude is Lichtenstein, Strasser, Rosenzweig, Brier, and Brown, eds., *Who Built America?*

31. Obomsawin quoted in Stangel, "Filmmaker Alanis Obomsawin," 10.

32. Obomsawin quoted in Hays, "Alanis Obomsawin."

33. Chase, "Thugs of the World Unite," 35. The right-wing analyst was John Thompson, then assistant director of the Mackenzie Institute, which Chase describes as "an independent Toronto think tank that examines conflicts" (35). Jerry White, who teaches at the University of Alberta, has encouraged me to note the reactionary nature of the *Alberta Report/Newsmagazine* as well as its distance from mainstream public opinion in Canada.

34. I am aware of but one real exception, a negative, defensive response to *Kanehsatake*: Marsolais, *L'aventure du cinéma direct revisitée*, 292–93. I am grateful to Jerry White for finding and translating Marsolais's comments. See White, "Alanis Obomsawin," 368 (White's translation), 374n12 (Marsolais's original French).

35. White, *The Middle Ground*, x, 52. To describe films on what I consider the middle ground of mass media, Laura Marks has coined the term *intercultural cinema* to describe what she sees as a place to "challenge the separateness of cultures and make visible the colonial and racist power relations that seek to maintain this separation." In this way such texts can pollute ideas of pure cultural distinction and "effect a transformation in the audience" (*The Skin of the Film*, xii).

36. Szasz, ed., *Between Indian and White Worlds*, 21.

37. Alanis Obomsawin, interview with author, Montreal, August 2002.

38. Hyer, "Pablita Velarde," 273.

39. Alanis Obomsawin, interview with author, Montreal, August 2002.

40. Hyer, "Pablita Velarde," 292.

41. Alioff and Levine, "The Long Walk," 11.

42. Data from Curry, "Half of Canadians Disbelieve Land Claims," citing the annual survey Portraits of Canada. (It should be noted that the *National Post*, for which Curry writes, is more conservative than mainstream Canadian public opinion and may have highlighted aspects of the survey that would undermine the land claims as part of a radical agenda without meaningful public support.) Quotation from Nancy Pine, a spokesperson for the Assembly of First Nations chief, Phil Fontaine.

43. Obomsawin quoted in Cizek, "Alanis Obomsawin."

44. Berry, "Two Minds," 22.

45. Pick, "Storytelling and Resistance," 77.

5. Why Documentary?

Epigraph from Solanas and Getino, "Toward a Third Cinema," 22, quoted in Armes, *Third World Film Making*, 83.

1. Obomsawin quoted in Greer, "Alanis Obomsawin," 27.

2. Beaver, "Producers' Forum I," quoted in Leuthold, "Historical Representation," 728.

3. Singer, *Wiping the War Paint off the Lens*, 33. The number is mentioned in passing, with no indication of how it was derived.

4. I have not included specific tribal affiliations for the filmmakers because this information is not always available. I am categorizing them as *Native productions* in some *substantial* sense on the basis of descriptions of the films in the scholarly literature, e.g., Leuthold, *Indigenous Aesthetics*, 211–13. Weatherford, ed., *Native Americans on Film and Video*, has also been a useful resource, certainly one that warrants updating in the way that the National Museum of the American Indian (NMAI) is now doing online. A listing of Native productions broken down by tribe, region, and director is available from Native Networks, the NMAI's Web site: http://www.nativenetworks.si.edu/eng/orange/index.htm. The NMAI list is somewhat confusing in that the vast majority, but not all, of its titles are the work of Native producers or directors. Much to its credit, however, it includes some Latin American and Pacific Islander contributions that are generally ignored in discussions of Native filmmaking.

5. Unless a director chose to keep his or her Native ancestry out of public view. Certainly, such maneuvers occurred at a time when visual artists did not want the racist stigma of primitivism attached to their work. For an exploration of the intersection of private Native identity and public creative expression, see my "The Native Roots of Modern Art."

6. Presently, it is available only from the filmmaker's Web site: http://www.naturallynative.com.

7. The Chirac and *New York Times* quotations, as well as others, are reprinted on the film's official Web site: http://www.atanarjuat.com/media_centre/index.html.

8. White, "Alanis Obomsawin," 364, 366. I take issue with White's characterization of Obomsawin as Griersonian but otherwise admire his "Alanis

Obomsawin," which is part of an outstanding collection that deserves greater currency in the United States.

9. John Grierson excerpted in MacDonald and Cousins, eds., *Imagining Reality*, 96.

10. John Grierson excerpted in MacDonald and Cousins, eds., *Imagining Reality*, 96, 101.

11. Obomsawin quoted in Harewood, "Alanis Obomsawin."

12. Evans, *In the National Interest*, 230. Among Obomsawin's films, *Kahentioosta* is closest to a biopic, but, like her other films with an individual's name in the title, it is less a standard profile than a springboard to a larger issue. As such, it is more thematic than biographical in nature.

13. Brian Winston calls the tradition of the victim Grierson's "most potent legacy" (*Claiming the Real*, 40).

14. Winston, *Claiming the Real*, 33.

15. Evans, *In the National Interest*, 104.

16. Alanis Obomsawin, interview with author, Montreal, August 2002. Challenge for Change (and its Francophone equivalent, Société nouvelle) is often mentioned as an early attempt to use film as an engine of social change, but few writers have gone beyond this obvious abstraction to describe the deeper motivations at work behind the program, which existed at the NFB from 1969 to 1980. As Ron Burnett has suggested, Challenge for Change grew out of a desire on the part of "politically committed cultural workers . . . [t]o connect with, and better understand, the audiences and communities they were addressing" ("The Politics of Culture and Community," 295). Although Obomsawin was passionate about connecting with disenfranchised communities as a filmmaker, she did not quite share the decentralized vision of media production that the program also espoused, one in which, according to Burnett, "'directors' were no longer directors, but 'media counselors' in charge of helping the local citizens use the media most effectively" (295)—she was never willing to relinquish her personal vision in the idealized manner of Challenge for Change rhetoric and (at times) practice. It is important to note that much more research is needed on the subject of Challenge for Change and its influence. Burnett claims that the only sustained analysis is Moore, "Canada's Challenge for Change." For more on Challenge for Change, see Burnett, "The Politics of Culture and Community," 295. For a useful, but brief, bibliography on the subject, see Mackenzie, "Société nouvelle," 82.

17. Ginsburg, "The After-Life of Documentary," 63.

18. Stoney, "You Are on Indian Land," 346, quoted in Ginsburg, "The After-Life of Documentary," 66. Not only does George Stoney's long career as a producer and teacher of nonfiction film warrant greater attention from scholars, but *You Are on Indian Land* in particular deserves an in-depth look.

19. Evans, *In the National Interest,* 172–73.

20. Fulford, column on Grierson and the documentary.

21. Winston, *Claiming the Real,* 46.

22. Fulford, column on Grierson and the documentary.

23. NFB producer quoted in and biographical information from Cizek, "Alanis Obomsawin."

24. John Grierson quoted in Macdonald, "Chairperson's Message."

25. The assertion that Obomsawin has made all the projects she has envisioned is true with one exception: a documentary mixture of live action and animation about children was postponed in the very early stages because of technical challenges and rapidly mounting expenses; she hints that someday she might return to it (Alanis Obomsawin, interview with author, Montreal, August 2002).

26. C$1 million is a sizable budget, although still less than half what it cost to make *Smoke Signals, The Doe Boy,* or *Atanarjuat.*

27. Hogarth, *Documentary Television in Canada,* 3, 4, 10.

28. Nichols, *Representing Reality,* 4, 263.

29. See Nichols, *Blurred Boundaries.*

30. Hogarth, *Documentary Television in Canada,* 139.

31. The indistinct line between fiction and nonfiction in everyday speech is always evident to me when my students insist on referring to biographies, memoirs, or works of journalism as *novels.*

32. Leuthold, "Historical Representation," 728.

33. Solanas and Getino, "Toward a Third Cinema," 22, quoted in Armes, *Third World Film Making,* 83.

34. Obomsawin quoted in Cizek, "Alanis Obomsawin."

35. Obomsawin quoted in Steven, *Brink of Reality,* 179.

36. Leuthold, "Historical Representation," 730, 733.

37. Leuthold, "Historical Representation," 730.

38. Georges E. Sioui quoted in Pick, "Storytelling and Resistance," 83.

39. Stewart, *A Space on the Side of the Road,* 3.

40. Wiseman, "Editing as a Four-Way Conversation," excerpted in MacDonald and Cousins, *Imagining Reality,* 282.

41. Nichols, *Representing Reality*, 178

42. Obomsawin quoted in Steven, *Brink of Reality*, 185.

43. Obomsawin quoted in Steven, *Brink of Reality*, 182.

44. For example, in a public presentation on the University of Oklahoma campus following a spring 2002 screening of her films.

45. Alioff and Levine, "The Long Walk," 14.

46. In "Up the Anthropologist," Laura Nader talked about "studying down" in her classic exhortation for anthropologists to "study up" and look at people more powerful than they themselves are.

47. Obomsawin quoted in Steven, *Brink of Reality*, 184.

48. Appleford, "Coming Out from Behind the Rocks," 116.

49. Obomsawin quoted in Steven, *Brink of Reality*, 180.

50. Loach, "Death of a Nation," excerpted in MacDonald and Cousins, eds., *Imagining Reality*, 303.

51. Vargas Llosa, "Why Literature?" 32.

52. Vargas Llosa, "Why Literature?" 32.

53. See Stephens, *The Rise of the Image*.

54. Vargas Llosa, "Why Literature?" 32.

55. Vargas Llosa, "Why Literature?" 33.

56. Vargas Llosa, "Why Literature?" 34.

57. Cohen, *Beautiful Losers*, 95; Nadel, *Leonard Cohen*, 73.

58. Pick, "Storytelling and Resistance," 78.

59. Agee and Evans, *Let Us Now Praise Famous Men*, 14.

60. Hugh Kenner quoted in White, *The Middle Mind*, 1.

61. Zimmermann, *States of Emergency*, 124, xxiii.

62. Marcorelles, *Living Cinema*, 37.

63. Tiziana Terranova quoted in Holmes, ed., *Virtual Globalization*, 104.

64. See Bruzzi, *New Documentary*, 5–7.

65. Gitlin, *Media Unlimited*, 7, 20.

6. Cinema of Sovereignty

The epigraph to the section "Is the Crown at War with Us?" is taken from Prins, *The Mi'kmaq*, 29. The epigraph to the section "The Politics of Indigenous Representation" is taken from Kundera, *Immortality*, 127.

1. Alanis Obomsawin, interview with author, Montreal, August 2002.

2. Mi'kmaq people live in both the United States and Canada, but, because

Obomsawin is dealing with towns in the latter, I am focusing on Canadian-Mi'kmaq relations in this chapter.

3. Runningwolf and Smith, *On the Trail of Elder Brother*, 57–63.

4. Prins, *The Mi'kmaq*, 44.

5. Miller, "The Mi'kmaq," 326.

6. Prins, *The Mi'kmaq*, 55–56.

7. Miller, "The Mi'kmaq," 343, 346. See also chapter 1 above.

8. Prins, *The Mi'kmaq*, 167.

9. Joe, *Song of Rita Joe*, 30.

10. Joe, *Song of Rita Joe*, 30, 64, 97, 101.

11. Prins, *The Mi'kmaq*, 11, 17.

12. J. S. Erskine quoted in Prins, *The Mi'kmaq*, 9.

13. Harald E. L. Prins, an anthropologist and documentary filmmaker who has worked on Mi'kmaq subjects in both capacities, has compiled a list of the few films on the tribe (see *The Mi'kmaq*, 237–38).

14. Fitzgerald, "Fishing for Stories."

15. Bunner, "Back on the Warpath."

16. Fitzgerald, "Fishing for Stories," 29.

17. Donham, "Lobster Wars and the Media," 7.

18. Unemployment rates from Fitzgerald, "Fishing for Stories," 32. Number of traps from DeMont, "Beyond Burnt Church," 35.

19. *R. v. Donald John Marshall Jr.*, [1999] 3 S.C.R. 456, 1999 CanLII 665 (S.C.C.), was issued by the Supreme Court of Canada on September 17, 1999. Two months later, on November 17, 1999, because of intense public controversy, the Court offered a clarification of its decision, *R. v. Donald John Marshall Jr.*, [1999] 3 S.C.R. 533, 1999 CanLII 666 (S.C.C.).

20. Entire books have been written on the Marshall case, including Wicken's excellent *Mi'kmaq Treaties on Trial*.

21. Harewood, "Alanis Obomsawin."

22. Eisner, "Our Nationhood."

23. Vancouver International Film Festival blurb quoted on http://www.cinematheque.bc.ca/JanFeb04/obomsawin.html.

24. Sidney Pobihushchy, a retired political science professor from the University of New Brunswick in Fredericton, quoted in DeMont, "Beyond Burnt Church," 35.

25. Sandweiss, *Print the Legend*, 215.

26. Sandweiss, *Print the Legend*, 217. For a fascinating in-depth look at the

relationship between a nineteenth-century Native American and the white photographers for whom he sat, see Goodyear, *Red Cloud*.

27. Prins, "Paradox," 248.

28. Obviously, I am coming to Native American studies as an outsider who hopes that he can add something new to the conversation, although, unlike some filmmakers, I am not claiming to represent an entire people. Nonetheless, there are certain parallels of which I am awkwardly aware.

29. Blood may shape experience, but it cannot substitute for it, as the work of the dislocated Navajo filmmaker Arlene Bowman makes clear. Her *Navajo Talking Picture* (1986) is a film that painfully demonstrates how much being a cultural insider depends on lived experience, not simply blood relation.

30. Jocks, "Combing Out Snakes," quoted in Garroutte, *Real Indians*, 105.

31. See Indian Arts and Crafts Act of 1990, Public Law 101-644, *U.S. Statutes at Large* 104 (1990): 4664.

32. Wilson, "Celluloid Sovereignty," 222.

33. Alfred, *Peace, Power, Righteousness*, 54.

34. Pico, "Sovereignty Is Absolute," A5.

35. Ivey, "Sovereignty," 3.

36. Alfred, *Peace, Power, Righteousness*, 54.

37. Audra Simpson and Atsenhaienton quoted in Alfred, *Peace, Power, Righteousness*, 65 and 109, respectively.

38. Even if political sovereignty is limited in its real-world application, as a term it still has value if we understand it as an aspect of indigenous nations that was their inherent right before (and after) contact, not a result of postcontact negotiations with a settler-state (see Mohawk, "On Sovereignty," 8).

39. Atsenhaienton quoted in Alfred, *Peace, Power, Righteousness*, 111.

40. Beaucage, "Films about Indigenous People," 29.

41. I say *generally unwritten* for this reason: despite the research of Leuthold, Kilpatrick, Singer, and other scholars, the subject of indigenous media in North America has many aspects that still warrant investigation.

42. The new spirit of collaboration even reached the Mi'kmaq, never the most studied or photographed tribe. When the anthropologist/filmmaker Harald E. L. Prins approached them in the early 1980s, he was careful to ask them how they wanted to be depicted in his film. The tribal leader Donald Sanipass told him that they wanted a film "in which our voices can be heard and in which we show how we live, how we work, and where we have chosen

to continue the life of our forefathers and mothers" ("Paradox," 55). According to Prins, the result, *Our Lives in Our Hands* (1985), made considerable strides toward showing the Mi'kmaq as they hoped to be represented to the world, and he argued that it provided a valuable means for attracting media attention to Mi'kmaq concerns ("Paradox," 67).

43. Mokuka quoted in Turner, "Indigenous Video," 75.

44. Michaels, *Bad Aboriginal Art*, 120.

45. Sam Yazzie quoted in Worth, Adair, and Chalfen, *Through Navajo Eyes*, 290.

46. For more on indigenous media as a problematic response to hegemonic media forces, see Weiner, "Televisualist Anthropology." One of the scholars who comes under fire in this highly charged polemic is Faye D. Ginsburg, who has responded: "We argue that far from being subsumed by contact with mass cultural forms, as these critics have argued, indigenous media-makers have taken on Western media technologies to defend themselves against what they see as the culturally destructive effects of mass media, producing work about their own lives, a strategy that some have called 'innovative traditionalism.' A more poetic phrasing, 'Starting Fire with Gunpowder,' used for the title of a film about the [Inuit Broadcasting Corporation] . . . , captures the sense of turning a potentially destructive Western form into something useful to the lives of indigenous people" (Ginsburg, "Screen Memories," 54).

47. Sturken and Cartwright, *Practices of Looking*, 327.

48. See Pick, "Storytelling and Resistance," 76–93.

49. Gittings, *Canadian National Cinema*, 198.

50. Buruma and Margalit (*Occidentalism*, 5, 11) describe Occidentalism as a "cluster of prejudices" and a "venomous brew" that results in a "dehumanizing picture of the West."

51. That is, she merely wants recognition of the notion of *indigenous nationhood*, on which see Alfred, *Peace, Power, Righteousness*, 47.

52. On Obomsawin's notion of film as a learning place, see the section "Documentary Film on Middle Ground" in chapter 4 above.

53. Smith, *Decolonizing Methodologies*, 2.

54. Churchill, *Fantasies of the Master Race*, 246, quoted in Wilson, "Celluloid Sovereignty," 222.

55. Harewood, "Alanis Obomsawin."

56. Sturken and Cartwright, *Practices of Looking*, 330–31.

57. Niezen, *The Origins of Indigenism*. The term *national imaginary* comes

from, among others, Annette Hamilton ("Fear and Desire"), who uses it to describe the formation of imagined communities (à la Benedict Anderson) via the visual mass media.

58. Garroutte, *Real Indians*, 101, 105, 102. See also Jocks, "Combing Out Snakes."

59. Alanis Obomsawin, interview with author, Montreal, August 2002.

60. Vizenor defines what he means by *"indian"* in, among other places, Vizenor and Lee, *Postindian Conversations*, 84.

61. Vizenor and Lee, *Postindian Conversations*, 165, 160.

62. Prins, "Paradox," 256, 263.

63. Carpenter, *Oh, What a Blow*, 99–100, quoted in Prins, "Paradox," 263.

64. See Hebdige, foreword, xix.

65. See Moore, "Marketing Alterity," 127.

66. Singer (*Wiping the War Paint off the Lens*, 92–99) has written on the pragmatic side of indigenous media production. She notes: "Native Americans have begun to take over the business end of film and media production, thus lessening our reliance on grants and other institutional support from outside our companies" (92). However, some of the examples that she cites were unsuccessful, including Valerie Red Horse's *Naturally Native* (1997), a project funded by the Mashantucket Pequot Tribal Nation that never made it past very limited release. Perhaps more promising has been the development of the Aboriginal Peoples Television Network in Canada, a nationwide network that premiered in 1999 with Obomsawin on its board of directors.

67. An almost ideal situation in this regard would be the local video production and distribution of the Inuit Broadcast Corporation, although even this has been the beneficiary of federal funding, as have indigenous media efforts among aboriginal people in Australia.

68. Miigam'agan and Obomsawin quoted in Cizek, "Alanis Obomsawin."

69. Michaels, *Bad Aboriginal Art*, 16.

70. Michaels, *Bad Aboriginal Art*, 17.

71. Daniel Lyman's "Remarks on the Province of New Brunswick" (1792) quoted in Reid, *Myth, Symbol, and Colonial Encounter*, 108.

72. Reid, *Myth, Symbol, and Colonial Encounter*, 98.

73. What I said in the previous chapter should offer some solace to those, like me, who hope to make strategic use of the "truth effects" that shroud documentary artifice—although much of what I call a *cinema of sovereignty* should function just as well in fiction or experimental realms.

74. Vizenor and Lee, *Postindian Conversations*, 180.

Conclusion

1. Nash, "Odanak durant les années 1920s," 31. I would like to thank Professor Nash for kindly sending me an English version of her article, in which the quotation in question appears on p. 34.

2. Wiseman, *The Voice of the Dawn*, 193.

3. Excerpts from the textbook *Vermont Our Own State* quoted in Wiseman, *The Voice of the Dawn*, 151.

4. Obomsawin quoted in Monastyrski, "Aboriginal Peoples Network," B6.

5. Loretta Todd quoted in Silverman, "Uncommon Visions," 382.

6. Cizek, "Alanis Obomsawin."

7. For more on this, see chapter 5.

8. See Mitchell, *Picture Theory*.

9. Mitchell, *Picture Theory*, 15.

10. Obomsawin quoted in Augustine, "Filming Aboriginal Voices."

11. Latour, "The Last Critique," 20.

12. Obomsawin quoted in Greer, "Alanis Obomsawin," 25.

13. Alanis Obomsawin, interview with author, Montreal, August 2002.

14. Beverley Singer does mention Obomsawin but devotes only two pages to her (see *Wiping the War Paint off the Lens*, 58–59). In noting Obomsawin's absence from the standard histories—Ellis, *The Documentary Idea*; Barnouw, *Documentary*; Barsam, *Nonfiction Film*; Kilpatrick, *Celluloid Indians*; Singer, *Wiping the War Paint off the Lens*—I should point out that I am not endorsing the notion of canon formation, only suggesting that, if we must have canons of great films, as the exigencies of higher education seem to require on some level, then Obomsawin's absence is unacceptable. Also, it is worth noting that Obomsawin fares much better in the latest books on Canadian cinema such Beard and White's *North of Everything*, where she is the subject of Jerry White's "Alanis Obomsawin," and Christopher Gittings's *Canadian National Cinema*, which includes an interesting subchapter on her work.

15. Nicholas Frasier excerpted in MacDonald and Cousins, eds., *Imagining Reality*, 367.

16. Lanzmann excerpted in MacDonald and Cousins, eds., *Imagining Reality*, 374. Lanzmann made his remarks on appearing at a joint retrospective of his work and that of the Japanese documentarian Noriaki Tsuchimoto in Tokyo, May 1996.

17. See Zimmermann, *States of Emergency*.

18. Chris Marker excerpted in MacDonald and Cousins, eds., *Imagining Reality*, 381.

19. Obomsawin quoted in Loft, "Sovereignty, Subjectivity, and Social Action."

20. Bourdieu, *Firing Back*, 64–65.

Appendix B. Native Documentaries

1. Although important in symbolic terms, the Native input in other NFB projects during the late 1960s seems too limited to warrant inclusion here.

BIBLIOGRAPHY

Agee, James, and Walker Evans. *Let Us Now Praise Famous Men*. Boston: Houghton Mifflin, 1941.

Alfred, Taiaiake. *Peace, Power, Righteousness: An Indigenous Manifesto*. Don Mills ON: Oxford University Press, 1999.

Alioff, Maurie. "Dream Magic: Alanis Obomsawin after Oka." *Matrix* (Quebec) 33 (spring 1991): 5–9.

Alioff, Maurie, and Susan Schouten Levine. "The Long Walk of Alanis Obomsawin." *Cinema Canada*, June 1987, 10–15.

Anderson, Fred. *Crucible of War: The Seven Year's War and the Fate of Empire in British North America*. New York: Vintage, 2001.

Appleford, Robert. "Coming Out from Behind the Rocks: Constructs of the Indian in Recent U.S. and Canadian Cinema." *American Indian Culture and Research Journal* 19, no. 1 (1995): 97–118.

Armes, Roy. *Third World Film Making and the West*. Berkeley and Los Angeles: University of California Press, 1987.

Arnold, Ellen L., ed. *Conversations with Leslie Marmon Silko*. Jackson: University Press of Mississippi, 2000.

Arthur, Paul. "Springing Tired Chains: Experimental Film and Video." In *Struggles for Representation: African American Documentary Film and Video*, ed. Phyllis R. Klotman and Janet K. Cutler, 268–97. Bloomington: Indiana University Press, 1999.

"Assigning the Blame." *Maclean's* 108, no. 35 (August 28, 1995): 23–32.

Augustine, Christine. "Filming Aboriginal Voices: An Interview with Alanis Obomsawin." *Fred: The Capital's Independent Voice* (Fredericton NB), [September] 2003.

Bailey, Cameron. "What the Story Is: An Interview with Srinivas Krishna." *CineAction!* 28 (spring 1992): 38–43.

Bálazs, Béla. *Theory of Film: Character and Growth of a New Art.* 1945. Translated by Edith Bond. London: D. Dobson, 1952. Excerpted in *Imagining Reality: The Faber Book of Documentary*, ed. Kevin MacDonald and Mark Cousins. London: Faber & Faber, 1996.

"Barb Cranmer—Messenger of Stories." *First Nations Drum*, winter 2000. http://www.firstnationsdrum.com/biography/winto0_cranmer.htm.

Barnouw, Erik. *Documentary: A History of the Non-Fiction Film.* New York: Oxford University Press, 1974.

Barsam, Richard. *Nonfiction Film: A Critical History.* 1973. Rev. ed. Bloomington: Indiana University Press, 1992.

Baudrillard, Jean. *Simulations.* New York: Semiotext(e), 1983.

Beard, William, and Jerry White, eds. *North of Everything: English-Canadian Cinema since 1980.* Alberta: University of Alberta Press, 2002.

Beaucage, Marjorie. "Films about Indigenous People." *Fuse*, winter 1992, 27–29.

Beaver, Tom. "Producers' Forum I: Uncovering the Lies." Paper presented at a symposium at the Two Rivers Native Film and Video Festival, Minneapolis, October 10, 1991.

Berry, Wendell. "Two Minds." *The Progressive*, November 2002, 21–29.

Billens, Sarah. "Merata Mita." Bonza, 1988. http://bonza.rmit.edu.au/ floyd/ essays/1998/merata_mita/index.php.

Bird, S. Elizabeth. "Savage Desires: The Gendered Construction of the American Indian in Popular Media." In *Selling the Indian: Commercializing and Appropriating American Indian Cultures*, ed. Carter Jones Meyer and Diana Royer, 62–98. Tucson: University of Arizona Press, 2001.

Bourdieu, Pierre. *Firing Back: Against the Tyranny of the Market 2.* New York: New Press, 2001.

Bruchac, Joseph. *Bowman's Store: A Journey to Myself.* New York: Lee & Low, 1997.

Bruzzi, Stella. *New Documentary: An Introduction.* New York: Routledge, 2000.

Bunner, Paul. "Back on the Warpath: Polite Canada Sits on Its Hands as Native

Militants Flout the Law and Demand the Moon." *Report Newsmagazine* (Alberta ed.) vol. 27, no. 10 (2000): 12–13.

Burnett, Ron. "The Politics of Culture and Community." In *Resolutions: Contemporary Video Practices*, ed. Michael Renov and Erika Suderburg, 283–303. Minneapolis: University of Minnesota Press, 1996.

Buruma, Ian, and Avishai Margalit. *Occidentalism: The West in the Eyes of Its Enemies*. New York: Penguin, 2004.

Calloway, Colin G. *The Abenaki*. New York: Chelsea House, 1989.

Came, Barry. "Behind the Barricades: A Native Film Director Puts Oka in Context." *Maclean's* 107, no. 5 (January 31, 1994): 58.

Candidus. Review of *Northwest Passage* (1940). The Colonial Movie Critic. http://www.rottentomatoes.com/click/movie-1015268/reviews.php?critic=all&sortby=default&page=1&rid=13754.

Carpenter, Edmund. *Oh, What a Blow That Phantom Gave Me!* New York: Holt, Rinehart & Winston, 1973.

Chamberlain, Bob. "She's Informal but Captivating." *Guelph Mercury*, [1960].

Chanan, Michael, ed. *Twenty-five Years of the New Latin American Cinema*. London: British Film Institute, 1983.

Chase, Steven. "Thugs of the World Unite." *Alberta Report/Newsmagazine* 20, no. 33 (August 2, 1993): 34–35.

Churchill, Ward. *Fantasies of the Master Race: Literature, Cinema, and the Colonization of American Indians*. Monroe ME: Common Courage, 1992.

Cizek, Katerina. "Alanis Obomsawin: Dream Magic." *Horizon Zero*, no. 9 (2003). http://www.horizonzero.ca. An interactive Web tribute with video and text by Cizek.

Cohen, Leonard. *Beautiful Losers*. 1966. Reprint, New York: Vintage, 1993.

Cruikshank, Julie. "Oral History, Narrative Strategies and Native American Historiography: Perspectives from the Yukon Territory, Canada." In *Clearing a Path: Theorizing the Past in Native American Studies*, ed. Nancy Shoemaker, 2–28. New York: Routledge, 2002.

Curry, Bill. "Half of Canadians Disbelieve Land Claims." *National Post*, November 27, 2003. Available at http://www.orwelltoday.com/indians disbelieved.shtml.

Dauria, Susan R. "Kateri Tekakwitha: Gender and Ethnic Symbolism in the Process of Making an American Saint." *New York Folklore* 20, nos. 3–4 (1994): 55–73.

David, Dan. Preface to *People of the Pines: The Warriors and the Legacy of Oka*, by Geoffrey York and Loreen Pindera, 9–14. Toronto: Little, Brown, 1991.

Day, Gordon M. "Western Abenaki." In *Handbook of North American Indians*, vol. 15, ed. Bruce G. Trigger, 148–59. Washington DC: Smithsonian Institution, 1978.

———. "Western Abenaki." In *In Search of New England's Native Past: Selected Essays by Gordon M. Day*, ed. Michael K. Foster and William Cowan, 202–22. Amherst: University of Massachusetts Press, 1998.

DeMont, John. "Beyond Burnt Church." *Maclean's* 112, no. 42 (October 18, 1999): 34–35.

Denvir, John, ed. *Legal Reelism: Movies as Legal Texts*. Urbana: University of Illinois Press, 1996.

De Rosa, Maria. "Studio One: Of Storytellers and Stories." In *North of Everything: English-Canadian Cinema since 1980*, ed. William Beard and Jerry White, 328–41. Alberta: University of Alberta Press, 2002.

Dickason, Olive Patricia. *Canada's First Nations: A History of Founding Peoples from Earliest Times*. 1992. 3rd ed. New York: Oxford University Press, 2002.

Dickinson, John, and Brian Young. *A Short History of Quebec*. 1993. 3rd ed. Montreal: McGill-Queen's University Press, 2003.

Donham, Parker Barss. "Lobster Wars and the Media." *Canadian Dimension* 34, no. 5 (September/October 2000): 7.

Dorris, Michael. "Native American Literature in an Ethnohistorical Context." *College English* 41, no. 2 (1979): 147–62.

Eisner, Ken. "Our Nationhood." *Variety*, December 22, 2003.

Ellis, Jack C. *The Documentary Idea: A Critical History of English-Language Documentary Film and Video*. Englewood Cliffs NJ: Prentice-Hall, 1989.

Evans, Gary. *In the National Interest: A Chronicle of the National Film Board from 1949 to 1989*. Toronto: University of Toronto Press, 1991.

Fiske, John. "Act Globally, Think Locally." In *Planet TV: A Global Television Reader*, ed. Lisa Parks and Shanti Kumar, 277–85. New York: New York University Press, 2002.

Fitzgerald, Paul. "Fishing for Stories at Burnt Church: The Media, the Marshall Decision, and Aboriginal Representation." *Canadian Dimension* 36, no. 4 (July/August 2002): 29–33.

Foster, Michael K., and William Cowan, eds. *In Search of New England's*

Native Past: Selected Essays by Gordon M. Day. Amherst: University of Massachusetts Press, 1998.

French, Lisa, ed. *Womenvision: Women and the Moving Image in Australia.* Victoria: Australian Catalogue Co., 2003.

Fulford, Robert. Column on Grierson and the documentary. *National Post,* October 3, 2000. Available online at http://www.robertfulford.com/John Grierson.html.

Gallagher, Nancy L. *Breeding Better Vermonters: The Eugenics Project in the Green Mountain State.* Hanover NH: University Press of New England, 1999.

Garroutte, Eva Marie. *Real Indians: Identity and the Survival of Native America.* Berkeley and Los Angeles: University of California Press, 2003.

Giguére, Nicole. "Women Filmmakers in Quebec: Documentaries and Feature Films." In *Women Filmmakers: Refocusing,* ed. Jacqueline Levitin, Valerie Raoul, and Judith Plessis, 373–85. Vancouver: University of British Columbia Press, 2002.

Ginsburg, Faye D. "Mediating Culture: Aboriginal Media and Social Transformations of Identity." 1996. http://www.usc.edu/dept/ancntr/pdcomm/ginsburg.html.

———. "The After-Life of Documentary: The Impact of *You Are on Indian Land.*" *Wide Angle* 21, no. 2 (March 1999): 60–67.

———. "Screen Memories: Resignifying the Traditional in Indigenous Media." In *Media Worlds: Anthropology on New Terrain,* ed. Faye D. Ginsburg, Lila Abu-Lughod, and Brian Larkin, 39–57. Berkeley and Los Angeles: University of California Press, 2002.

Ginsburg, Faye D., Lila Abu-Lughod, and Brian Larkin, eds. *Media Worlds: Anthropology on New Terrain.* Berkeley and Los Angeles: University of California Press, 2002.

Gitlin, Todd. *Media Unlimited: How the Torrent of Images and Sounds Overwhelms Our Lives.* New York: Holt, 2002.

Gittings, Christopher E. *Canadian National Cinema.* New York: Routledge, 2002.

Goodyear, Frank H., III. *Red Cloud: Photographs of a Lakota Chief.* Lincoln: University of Nebraska Press, 2003.

Grant, Agnes. "Kanehsatake." *Canadian Dimension* 28, no. 2 (March/April 1994): 18–21.

Greer, Sandy. "Alanis Obomsawin." *Turtle Quarterly*, spring/summer 1991, 22–27.

Hamilton, Annette. "Fear and Desire: Aborigines, Asians, and the National Imaginary." *Australian Cultural History* 9 (1990): 14-35.

Harewood, Adrian. "Alanis Obomsawin: A Portrait of a First Nation's Filmmaker." TAKE ONE, June–September 2003. An interview with Alanis Obomsawin. http://www.findarticles.com/cf_dls/moJSF/42_12/1047321 73/p1/article.jhtml.

Hays, Matthew. "Alanis Obomsawin Returns to Oka with *Rocks at Whiskey Trench*." *Montreal Mirror*, September 28, 2000. Available online at http://www.montrealmirror.com/ARCHIVES/2000/092800/film5.html.

Hebdige, Dick. Foreword to *Bad Aboriginal Art: Tradition, Media, and Technological Horizons*, by Eric Michaels, ix–xxv. Minneapolis: University of Minnesota Press, 1994.

Hogarth, David. *Documentary Television in Canada: From National Public Service to Global Marketplace*. Montreal: McGill-Queens University Press, 2002.

Holmes, David, ed. *Virtual Globalization: Virtual Spaces/Tourist Spaces*. New York: Routledge, 2001.

Hulan, Renée, ed. *Native North America: Critical and Cultural Perspectives*. Toronto: ECW, 1999.

Hyer, Sally. "Pablita Velarde: The Pueblo Artist as Cultural Broker." In *Between Indian and White Worlds: The Cultural Broker*, ed. Margaret Connell Szasz, 273–93. Norman: University of Oklahoma Press, 1994.

"Indigenising the Screen—Film-Maker Merata Mita." Media Resources/ Tourism New Zealand, n.d. Available at http://media.newzealand.com/ index.cfm/purenz_page/5E4AC01C-5DAB-46DB-B8D1-BCCDFEE907 F0.html.

Ivey, Roy. "Sovereignty—the Real Issue." *Sho-Ban News* 21, no. 18 (May 3, 1996): 3.

Jaimes-Guerrero, Marianette. "Savage Erotica Exotica: Media Imagery of Native Women in North America." In *Native North America: Critical and Cultural Perspectives*, ed. Rénee Hulan, 187–210. Toronto: ECW, 1999.

James, Mertice M., and Dorothy Brown, eds. *Book Review Digest*, 1937. Vol. 33. New York: H. W. Wilson, 1938.

Jocks, Christopher. "Combing Out Snakes: Violence and the Construction of Knowledge in Longhouse Traditions." Paper presented at the annual meeting of the American Academy of Religion, Native Traditions in the Americas Group, session "Knowing the World: Native American Epistemologies," Chicago, November 21, 1994.

Joe, Rita. *Song of Rita Joe: Autobiography of a Mi'kmaq Poet.* Lincoln: University of Nebraska Press, 1996.

Jones, D. B. *Movies and Memoranda: An Interpretative History of the National Film Board of Canada.* Ottawa: Canadian Film Institute/Deneau, 1981.

———. *The Best Butler in the Business: Tom Daly of the National Film Board of Canada.* Toronto: University of Toronto Press, 1996.

———. "Brave New Film Board." In *North of Everything: English-Canadian Cinema since 1980,* ed. William Beard and Jerry White, 19–45. Alberta: University of Alberta Press, 2002.

Kalafatic, Carol. "Knots." In *As We Are Now: Mixed Blood Essays on Race and Identity,* ed. William S. Penn, 67–81. Berkeley and Los Angeles: University of California Press, 1997.

Kalant, Amelia. *National Identity and the Conflict at Oka: Native Belonging and Myths of Postcolonial Nationhood in Canada.* New York: Routledge, 2004.

Kaplan, E. Ann. *Looking for the Other: Feminism, Film, and the Imperial Gaze.* New York: Routledge, 1997.

Keefer, Don. "Postmodern Anxieties over Hypermedia." Paper presented at the conference "Computing and Philosophy," New Haven CT, 1990. Available at http://faculty.risd.edu/faculty/dkeefer/web/anx.htm.

Kilpatrick, Jacquelyn. *Celluloid Indians: Native Americans and Film.* Lincoln: University of Nebraska Press, 1999.

Klein, Laura F., and Lillian A. Ackerman, eds. *Women and Power in Native North America.* Norman: University of Oklahoma Press, 1995.

Kundera, Milan. *Immortality.* 1988. Translated by Peter Kussi. New York: Harper Perennial Modern Classics, 1999.

Lamche, Pascale. "Interview with Merata Mita." *Framework,* no. 25 (1984): 2–11.

Langston, Marcia. "Grounded and Gendered: Aboriginal Women in Australian Cinema." In *Womenvision: Women and the Moving Image in Australia,* ed. Lisa French, 43–56. Victoria: Australian Catalogue Co., 2003.

Latour, Bruno. "The Last Critique." *Harper's,* April 2004, 20–24.

Lesage, Julia. "The Political Aesthetics of the Feminist Documentary Film." *Quarterly Review of Film Studies* 3, no. 4 (fall 1978): 507–23.

Leuthold, Steven. "Historical Representation in Native Documentary." *Ethnohistory* 44, no. 4 (fall 1997): 727–41.

———. *Indigenous Aesthetics: Native Art, Media, and Identity*. Austin: University of Texas Press, 1998.

Levitin, Jacqueline, Valerie Raoul, and Judith Plessis, eds. *Women Filmmakers: Refocusing*. Vancouver: University of British Columbia Press, 2002.

Lewis, Randolph. *Emile de Antonio: Radical Filmmaker in Cold War America*. Madison: University of Wisconsin Press, 2000.

———. "The Native Roots of Modern Art: Rereading the Paintings of Leon Polk Smith." *American Indian Quarterly* 25 (winter 2001): 93–113.

Lichtenstein, Nelson, Susan Strasser, Roy Rosenzweig, Stephen Brier, and Joshua Brown, eds. *Who Built America? Working People and the Nation's Economy, Politics, Culture, and Society*. New York: Pantheon, 1992.

"Liz Garbus—Confronting Humanity." In *Documentary Filmmakers Speak*, ed. Liz Stubbs, 109–26. New York: Allsworth, 2002.

Loach, Ken. "Death of a Nation." Excerpted in *Imagining Reality: The Faber Book of Documentary*, ed. Kevin MacDonald and Mark Cousins, 302–3. London: Faber & Faber, 1996.

Loft, Steve. "Sovereignty, Subjectivity, and Social Action: The Films of Alanis Obomsawin." Available at http://conseildesarts.ca/prizes/ggavma/xh127 240204281875000.htm?subsiteurl=%2fcanadacouncil%2farchives%2f prizes%2fggvma%2f2001%2f2001-06-e.asp.

Louselle, André. *Moirir à tue-tête/A Scream from Silence*. Wiltshire: Flicks Books, 2000.

Low, Brian L. NFB *Kids: Portrayals of Children by the National Film Board of Canada, 1939–1989*. Waterloo ON: Wilfred Laurier Press, 2002.

Lysak, A. "Luhovy Named Best Editor." *Ukrainian Weekly* 62, no. 5 (January 30, 1994): 10.

MacDonald, Kevin, and Mark Cousins, eds. *Imagining Reality: The Faber Book of Documentary*. London: Faber & Faber, 1996.

MacDonald, Robert. "Film Shows an Ugly Side of New Zealand." *Sydney Morning Herald*, July 17, 1984, 10.

Macdonald, Sandra. "Chairperson's Message." Available at http://www.nfb.ca/publications/en/annualreports/rep1999–2000/04presidente00.html.

Mackenzie, Scott. "Société nouvelle: The Challenge for Change in the Alternative Public Sphere." *Canadian Journal of Film Studies* 5, no. 2 (fall 1996): 67–84.

MacLaine, Craig, and Michael Baxandale. *This Land Is Our Land: The Mohawk Revolt at Oka*. Montreal: Optimum, 1990.

Marcorelles, Louis. *Living Cinema: New Directions in Contemporary Film-Making*. Translated by I. Quigly. New York: Praeger, 1973.

Marks, Laura. *The Skin of the Film: Intercultural Cinema, Embodiment, and the Senses*. Durham NC: Duke University Press, 2000.

Marsolais, Gilles. *L'aventure du cinéma direct revisitée*. Laval: Les 400 Coups, 1997.

Mayne, Judith. *The Woman at the Keyhole: Feminism and Women's Cinema*. Bloomington: Indiana University Press, 1990.

McFarlane, Peter. "Stolen Land." *Canadian Forum*, November 1990, 18–21.

McLaughlin, Janice. *Feminist Social and Political Theory*. New York: Palgrave, 2003.

Meyer, Carter Jones, and Diana Royer, eds. *Selling the Indian: Commercializing and Appropriating American Indian Cultures*. Tucson: University of Arizona Press, 2001.

Michaels, Eric. *Bad Aboriginal Art: Tradition, Media, and Technological Horizons*. Minneapolis: University of Minnesota Press, 1994.

Mihesuah, Devon A. *American Indians: Stereotypes and Realities*. Atlanta: Clarity, 1997.

Miller, Christine, and Patricia Chuchryk, eds. *Women of the First Nations: Power, Wisdom, and Strength*. Winnipeg: University of Manitoba Press, 1996.

Miller, Virginia P. "The Mi'kmaq: A Maritime Woodland Group." In *Native Peoples: The Canadian Experience*, ed. R. Bruce Morrison and C. Roderick Wilson, 324–52. Toronto: McClelland & Stewart, 1986.

Mitchell, W. J. T. *Picture Theory: Essays on Verbal and Visual Representation*. Chicago: University of Chicago Press, 1994.

Mohawk, John. "On Sovereignty." *Akwesasne Notes* 1, nos. 3–4 (December 31, 1995): 8.

Monastyrski, Jamie. "Aboriginal Peoples Network Adds Some Color to Tube." *Indian Country Today (Lakota Times)* 19, n. 29 (January 12, 2000): B6.

Moore, Rachel. "Marketing Alterity." In *Visualizing Theory: Selected Essays from V.A.R., 1990–1994*, ed. Lucien Taylor, 127–39. New York: Routledge, 1994.

Moore, Rick. "Canada's Challenge for Change: Documentary Film and Video as an Exercise of Power through the Production of Cultural Reality." PhD diss., University of Oregon, 1987.

Morrison, Andrea P., ed. *Justice for Natives: Searching for Common Ground.* Montreal: McGill-Queen's University Press, 1997.

Morrison, Kenneth M. *The Embattled Northeast: The Illusive Ideal of Alliance in Abenaki-Euramerican Relations.* Berkeley and Los Angeles: University of California Press, 1984.

Nadel, Ira. *Leonard Cohen: A Life in Art.* London: Robson, 1994.

Nader, Laura. "Up the Anthropologist: Perspectives Gained from Studying Up." In *Reinventing Anthropology*, ed. Dell H. Hymes, 284–311. New York: Random House, 1972.

Nash, Alice. "Odanak durant les années 1920s: Un prisme reflétant d'histoire abénaquise" (Odanak in the 1920s: A prism of Abenaki history). Translated by Claude Gélinas. *Recherches amérindiennes au Québec* 31, no. 1 (2002): 17–33.

Nash, Alice, and Réjean Obomsawin. "Theophile Panadis (1889–1966): An Abenaki Guide." *Recherches amérindiennes au Québec* 33, no. 2 (2003): 75–91.

National Film Board Film and Video Catalog, 1999–2000. Montreal: National Film Board of Canada, 1999.

Nichols, Bill. *Representing Reality: Issues and Concepts in Documentary.* Bloomington: Indiana University Press, 1992.

———. *Blurred Boundaries: Questions of Meaning in Contemporary Culture.* Bloomington: Indiana University Press, 1994.

———. *Introduction to Documentary.* Bloomington: Indiana University Press, 2001.

Niezen, Ronald. *The Origins of Indigenism: Human Rights and the Politics of Identity.* Berkeley and Los Angeles: University of California Press, 2003.

Obomsawin, Alanis. *Bush Lady.* Wawa Productions, 1988. LP.

Olson, Tillie. *Silences.* New York: Delacorte, 1978.

Parks, Lisa, and Shanti Kumar, eds. *Planet TV: A Global Television Reader.* New York: New York University Press, 2002.

Perkins, H. F. "Review of Eugenics in Vermont." *Vermont Review*, September/October 1926, 56–59.

Pertusati, Linda. *In Defense of Mohawk Land: Ethnopolitical Conflict in Native North America.* Albany: State University of New York Press, 1997.

Pick, Zuzana. "Storytelling and Resistance: The Documentary Practice of Alanis Obomsawin." In *Gendering the Nation: Canadian Women's Cinema*, ed. Kay Armatage, Kass Banning, Brenda Longfellow, and Janine Marchessault, 76–93. Toronto: University of Toronto Press, 1999.

Pico, Anthony R. "Sovereignty Is Absolute for Native Nations." *Indian Country Today* 17, no. 1 (July 7, 1998): A5.

The Positio of the Historical Section of the Sacred Congregation of Rites on the Introduction of the Cause for Beatification and Canonization and on the Virtues of the Servant of God Katharine Tekakwitha the Lily of the Mohawks—Being the Original Documents First Published at the Vatican Polyglot Press Now Done into English and Presented for the Edification of the Faithful. New York: Fordham University Press, 1940.

Poster, Mark. *The Mode of Information: Poststructuralism and Social Context.* Chicago: University of Chicago Press, 1990.

Prins, Harald E. L. *The Mi'kmaq: Resistance, Accommodation, and Cultural Survival.* New York: Harcourt Brace, 1996.

———. "The Paradox of Primitivism: Native Rights and the Problem of Imagery in Cultural Survival Films." *Visual Anthropology* 9 (1997): 243–66.

Reid, Jennifer. *Myth, Symbol, and Colonial Encounter: British and Mi'kmaq in Acadia, 1700–1867.* Ottawa: University of Ottawa Press, 1995.

Restoule, Jean-Paul. "How Indians Are Read: The Representation of Aboriginality in Films by Native and Non-Native Directors." MA thesis, Department of Communication Studies, University of Windsor, 1997.

Roberts, Kenneth. *Northwest Passage.* Garden City NY: Doubleday, Doran, 1936.

Rogers, Robert. *Journals of Major Robert Rogers.* London: J. Millan, 1765.

Rosenthal, Alan, ed. *The Documentary Conscience: A Casebook in Film Making.* Berkeley and Los Angeles: University of California Press, 1980.

Roy, Audrey Jane, with Taiaiake Alfred. "Legislation Affecting Canada's Native People." In *The Native North American Almanac*, ed. Duane Champagne, 548–60. Farmington Hills, MI: Gale, 2001.

Runningwolf, Michael B., and Patricia Clark Smith. *On the Trail of Elder Brother: Glous'gap Stories of the Mi'kmaq Indians.* New York: Persea, 2000.

Sandweiss, Martha A. *Print the Legend: Photography and the American West.* New Haven CT: Yale University Press, 2002.

Sawchuk, Joe. "Negotiating an Identity: Métis Political Organization, the Canadian Government, and Competing Concepts of Aboriginality." *American Indian Quarterly* 24, no. 3 (summer 2000): 73–92.

Saxberg, Kelly. "Kanehsatake: 270 Years of Resistance." *Canadian Dimension* 27, no. 5 (September/October 1993): 34.

Scott, James C. *Weapons of the Weak: Everyday Forms of Resistance.* New Haven CT: Yale University Press, 1985.

Silverman, Jason. "Uncommon Visions: The Films of Loretta Todd." In *North of Everything: English-Canadian Cinema since 1980*, ed. William Beard and Jerry White, 376–89. Alberta: University of Alberta Press, 2002.

Singer, Beverly. *Wiping the War Paint off the Lens.* Minneapolis: University of Minnesota Press, 2001.

Smith, Leo. "Filmmaker Makes the Most of a Disappointing Visit with Her Navajo Grandmother." *Los Angeles Times*, April 25, 1991, J-20.

Smith, Linda Tuhiwai. *Decolonizing Methodologies: Research and Indigenous People.* London: Zed, 1999.

Solanas, Fernando, and Octavio Getino. "Toward a Third Cinema." In *Twenty-five Years of the New Latin American Cinema*, ed. Michael Chanan, 17–29. London: British Film Institute, 1983.

"Speaker Offers Some Good Ideas." *Goshen IN News*, September 20, 2002. Available online at http://www.goshennews.com/news/files/2002/9/9–20-2002/edit.html.

Spivak, Gayatri Chakravorty. *A Critique of Postcolonial Reason: Toward a History of the Vanishing Present.* Cambridge MA: Harvard University Press, 1999.

"Standoff on Kanehsatake." *Maclean's* 106, no. 40 (October 4, 1993): 12–14.

Stangel, Foster. "Filmmaker Alanis Obomsawin Brings New Documentary to Minnesota." *The Circle* 22, no. 2 (February 28, 2001): 10.

Stephens, Mitchell. *The Rise of the Image and the Fall of the Word.* New York: Oxford University Press, 1998.

Steven, Peter. *Brink of Reality: New Canadian Documentary Film and Video.* Toronto: Between the Lines, 1993.

Stewart, Kathleen. *A Space on the Side of the Road: Cultural Poetics in an "Other" America.* Princeton NJ: Princeton University Press, 1996.

Stoney, George. "You Are on Indian Land." In *The Documentary Conscience: A Casebook in Film Making*, ed. Alan Rosenthal, 346–58. Berkeley and Los Angeles: University of California Press, 1980.

Sturken, Marita, and Lisa Cartwright. *Practices of Looking: An Introduction to Visual Culture.* New York: Oxford University Press, 2001.

Szasz, Margaret Connell, ed. *Between Indian and White Worlds: The Cultural Broker.* Norman: University of Oklahoma Press, 1994.

Torres, Sasha, ed. *Living Color: Race and Television in the United States.* Durham NC: Duke University Press, 1998.

Trinh T. Minh-ha. *Woman Native Other: Writing Postcoloniality and Feminism.* Bloomington: Indiana University Press, 1989.

Turner, Terence. "Representation, Politics, and Cultural Imagination in Indigenous Video: General Points and Kayapo Examples." In *Media Worlds: Anthropology on New Terrain,* ed. Faye D. Ginsburg, Lila Abu-Lughod, and Brian Larkin, 75–89. Berkeley and Los Angeles: University of California Press, 2002.

Vargas Llosa, Mario. "Why Literature?" *New Republic,* May 14, 2001, 31–36.

Vetromile, Eugene. *The Abenaki and Their History; or, Historical Notices on the Aborigines of Acadia.* New York: James B. Kirker, 1866.

Vizenor, Gerald, and A. Robert Lee. *Postindian Conversations.* Lincoln: University of Nebraska Press, 1999.

Waldman, Diane, and Janet Walker, eds. *Feminism and Documentary.* Minneapolis: University of Minnesota Press, 1999.

Waugh, Thomas, ed. *"Show Us Life": Toward a History and Aesthetics of the Committed Documentary.* Metuchen NJ: Scarecrow, 1984.

Weatherford, Elizabeth, ed. *Native Americans on Film and Video.* New York: Museum of the American Indian, 1981.

Weiner, James. "Televisualist Anthropology: Representation, Aesthetics, Politics." *Current Anthropology* 38, no. 2 (1997): 197–236.

White, Curtis. *The Middle Mind: Why Americans Don't Think for Themselves.* New York: HarperCollins, 2003.

White, Jerry. "Alanis Obomsawin, Documentary Form, and the Canadian Nation(s)." In *North of Everything: English-Canadian Cinema since 1980,* ed. William Beard and Jerry White, 364–75. Alberta: University of Alberta Press, 2002.

White, Richard. *The Middle Ground: Indians, Empires, and Republics in the Great Lakes Region, 1650–1815.* New York: Cambridge University Press, 1991.

Wicken, William C. *Mi'kmaq Treaties on Trial: History, Land, and Donald Marshall Junior.* Toronto: University of Toronto Press, 2002.

Wilson, Pamela. "Confronting the 'Indian Problem': Media Discourses of Race, Ethnicity, Nation, and Empire in 1950s America." In *Living Color: Race and Television in the United States*, ed. Sasha Torres, 35–61. Durham NC: Duke University Press, 1998.

Wilson, Terry. "Celluloid Sovereignty: Hollywood's 'History' of Native Americans." In *Legal Reelism: Movies as Legal Texts*, ed. John Denvir, 199–224. Urbana: University of Illinois Press, 1996.

Winston, Brian. *Claiming the Real: The Griersonian Documentary and Its Legitimations*. London: BFI, 1995.

Wiseman, Frederick. "Editing as a Four-Way Conversation." In *Imagining Reality: The Faber Book of Documentary*, ed. Kevin MacDonald and Mark Cousins, 278–82. London: Faber & Faber, 1996. Originally published in *Documentary Film Quarterly*, no. 1 (spring 1994): 4–6.

Wiseman, Frederick Matthew. *The Voice of the Dawn: An Autohistory of the Abenaki Nation*. Hanover NH: University Press of New England, 2001.

Woods, Lysandra. "Srinivas Krishna and the New Canadian Cinema." In *North of Everything: English-Canadian Cinema since 1980*, ed. William Beard and Jerry White, 206–15. Alberta: University of Alberta Press, 2002.

Worth, Sol, John Adair, and Richard Chalfen, eds. *Through Navajo Eyes: An Exploration in Film Communication and Anthropology*. Albuquerque: University of New Mexico Press, 1997.

York, Geoffrey, and Loreen Pindera. *People of the Pines: The Warriors and the Legacy of Oka*. Toronto: Little, Brown, 1991.

Zimmermann, Patricia. *States of Emergency: Documentaries, Wars, Democracy*. Minneapolis: University of Minnesota Press, 1999.

INDEX

*Song of Rita Joe: Autobiography
of a Mi'kmaq Poet*
By Rita Joe

*Viet Cong at Wounded Knee:
The Trail of a Blackfeet Activist*
By Woody Kipp

Catch Colt
By Sidner J. Larson

*Alanis Obomsawin: The
Vision of a Native Filmmaker*
By Randolph Lewis

*Alex Posey: Creek Poet,
Journalist, and Humorist*
By Daniel F. Littlefield Jr.

First to Fight
By Henry Mihesuah
Edited by Devon Abbott
Mihesuah

*Mourning Dove:
A Salishan Autobiography*
Edited by Jay Miller

*I'll Go and Do More: Annie
Dodge Wauneka, Navajo
Leader and Activist*
By Carolyn Niethammer

*Elias Cornelius Boudinot:
A Life on the Cherokee Border*
By James W. Parins

*John Rollin Ridge:
His Life and Works*
By James W. Parins

*Singing an Indian Song: A
Biography of D'Arcy McNickle*
By Dorothy R. Parker

*Crashing Thunder:
The Autobiography of an
American Indian*
Edited by Paul Radin

*Turtle Lung Woman's
Granddaughter*
By Delphine Red Shirt and
Lone Woman

*Telling a Good One: The
Process of a Native American
Collaborative Biography*
By Theodore Rios and Kathleen
Mullen Sands

*William W. Warren: The
Life, Letters, and Times of
an Ojibwe Leader*
By Theresa M. Schenck

*Sacred Feathers: The Reverend
Peter Jones (Kahkewaquonaby)
and the Mississauga Indians*
By Donald B. Smith

Grandmother's Grandchild:
My Crow Indian Life
By Alma Hogan Snell
Edited by Becky Matthews
Foreword by Peter Nabokov

No One Ever Asked Me: The
World War II Memoirs of an
Omaha Indian Soldier
By Hollis D. Stabler
Edited by Victoria Smith

Blue Jacket:
Warrior of the Shawnees
By John Sugden

Muscogee Daughter: My Sojourn
to the Miss America Pageant
By Susan Supernaw
Foreword by Geary Hobson

I Tell You Now:
Autobiographical Essays by
Native American Writers
Edited by Brian Swann and
Arnold Krupat

Postindian Conversations
By Gerald Vizenor and
A. Robert Lee

Chainbreaker:
The Revolutionary War Memoirs
of Governor Blacksnake
As told to Benjamin Williams
Edited by Thomas S. Abler

Standing in the Light:
A Lakota Way of Seeing
By Severt Young Bear and R. D.
Theisz

Sarah Winnemucca
By Sally Zanjani

To order or obtain more
information on these or
other University of
Nebraska Press titles, visit
www.nebraskapress.unl.edu.

CPSIA information can be obtained
at www.ICGtesting.com
Printed in the USA
LVOW01s0152041116
511539LV00014BA/173/P